Moodle 3.x Developer'

Customize your Moodle apps by creating custom plugins, extensions, and modules

Ian Wild

BIRMINGHAM - MUMBAI

Moodle 3.x Developer's Guide

First published: June 2017

Production reference: 1270617

Published by Packt Publishing Ltd.
Livery Place
35 Livery Street
Birmingham
B3 2PB, UK.
ISBN 978-1-78646-711-9

www.packtpub.com

Credits

Author
Ian Wild

Copy Editor
Safis Editing

Reviewer
Susan Smith Nash

Project Coordinator
Ritika Manoj

Commissioning Editor
Amarabha Banerjee

Proofreader
Safis Editing

Acquisition Editor
Reshma Raman

Indexer
Tejal Daruwale Soni

Content Development Editor
Aditi Gour

Graphics
Jason Monteiro

Technical Editor
Shweta Jadhav

Production Coordinator
Melwyn Dsa

About the Author

Ian Wild is an experienced software developer, solutions architect, author, and educator with over 20 years' experience in the field of software design and implementation.

Fifteen years working in private industry saw Ian specializing in the design and development of access and learning aids for blind, visually impaired, dyslexic, and dyscalculic computer users, while also working part-time as a tutor and lecturer. Teaching only part-time meant not spending as much time with his students as he would have wished and this, coupled with his background in the development of communication technologies, and seeded his long-time interest in e-learning.

Ian is also, author of *Moodle Course Conversion: Beginner's Guide* and *Moodle Math*. He was also technical reviewer of *Science Teaching with Moodle*, *Moodle Multimedia* and *Practical XMPP*.

About the Reviewer

Susan Smith Nash is involved in the design, development, and administration of e-learning and m-learning programs for learners pursuing degrees, certification, credentialing, and professional development. Her current research interests include the effective design of competency-based education, knowledge management, knowledge transfer, and leadership. Her articles and columns have appeared in magazines and refereed journals. She received her PhD from the University of Oklahoma, and in addition to e-learning, Nash has also been involved in international economic development training, interdisciplinary studies, interdisciplinary petroleum geosciences programs, and sustainable business and career training. Her book, *Leadership and the E-Learning Organization*, was co-authored with George Henderson, and published by Charles Thomas and Sons. Her most recent books include *E-Learning Success: From Courses to Careers*, and *E-Learner Survival Guide*, Texture Press. Her edublog, *E-Learning Queen* has received numerous awards and recognition's.

www.PacktPub.com

For support files and downloads related to your book, please visit www.PacktPub.com.

Did you know that Packt offers eBook versions of every book published, with PDF and ePub files available? You can upgrade to the eBook version at www.PacktPub.com and as a print book customer, you are entitled to a discount on the eBook copy. Get in touch with us at service@packtpub.com for more details.

At www.PacktPub.com, you can also read a collection of free technical articles, sign up for a range of free newsletters and receive exclusive discounts and offers on Packt books and eBooks.

https://www.packtpub.com/mapt

Get the most in-demand software skills with Mapt. Mapt gives you full access to all Packt books and video courses, as well as industry-leading tools to help you plan your personal development and advance your career.

Why subscribe?

- Fully searchable across every book published by Packt
- Copy and paste, print, and bookmark content
- On demand and accessible via a web browser

Table of Contents

Preface

For any organization that's considering implementing an online learning environment, Moodle is often the number one choice. Key to its success is the free, open source ethos that underpins it. Not only is the Moodle source code fully available to developers, but Moodle itself has been developed to allow the inclusion of third-party plugins. Everything from how users access the platform and the kinds of teaching interactions that are available through to how attendance and success can be reported--in fact, all the key Moodle functionalities--can be adapted and enhanced through plugins.

Using real-world examples, this book will show you how to enhance a default Moodle installation with novel plugins to authenticate and enroll users on to courses, new and interesting teaching interactions, new custom skins, and enhanced course layouts.

Obviously, a book of this length won't be able to cover every single plugin type, but by the end of Chapter 9, *Moodle Analytics*, you will have a thorough grounding in Moodle plugin structure, a detailed understanding of how plugins should interact with Moodle's internal **Application Programming Interfaces (APIs)**, and plenty of great ideas to help you enhance your Moodle installation with new, custom plugins. If you have developed a plugin you feel would be useful to the Moodle community, you should certainly consider submitting it to the Moodle Plugins Directory at https://moodle.org/plugins/.

What this book covers

Chapter 1, *Getting to Grips with the Moodle 3 Architecture*, introduces the ethos of the Moodle project and how it has influenced the internal architecture. We prepare ourselves for plugin development by installing the tools we need.

Chapter 2, *Moodle plugins – What Can I Plug In?*, investigates the main plugin types, such as those dealing with users and how they access the platform. Also, it covers plugins that provide the learning interactions that users experience when they take a course. We also looks at the less obvious plugins, such as filters.

Chapter 3, *Internal Interfaces*, shows the different types of application programming interfaces (APIs) Moodle provides to support plugin development.

Chapter 4, *Course Management*, demonstrates how courses can be enhanced through the development of novel course formats. We see how plugins can be used to modify course structure and, by so doing, enhance teaching.

Chapter 5, *Creative Teaching – Developing Custom Resources and Activities*, shows that there are two types of teaching interaction: resources and activities. Both of these are types of course module plugin. In this chapter, you will learn how Moodle course plugins work, which scripts need to be present in order for your plugin to behave correctly, and how to modify course plugins to fit your needs.

Chapter 6, *Managing Users – Letting in the Crowds*, explores how plugins can manage users in a variety of different contexts. We develop two novel plugins, one to authenticate users against an external WordPress site using OAuth, and another to automatically enroll users onto courses when they connect to Moodle via WordPress.

Chapter 7, *Creating a Dashboard – Developing a Learner Homepage*, teaches us how plugins can be used to create an enhanced learner homepage. Gamification is all about using the same tricks and techniques employed by game developers to entice learners into progressing with courses. In this chapter, we learn how plugins can be developed to promote similar techniques.

Chapter 8, *Creating a New Skin*, focuses on aesthetics after we have concerned ourselves with functionality. We investigate how Moodle can be rebranded through theme plugins, with a particular focus on support for mobile and tablet devices.

Chapter 9, *Moodle Analytics*, showcases how to develop plugins to monitor and analyze learner behavior. We learn how to extract data efficiently, how to judge the effectiveness of that extraction, and the various means by which data can be reported, including via a secure external interface.

What you need for this book

You will need a computer suitable for software development, one that can run a web server and a separate development environment (Chapter 1, *Getting to Grips with the Moodle 3 Architecture*, guides the reader through the necessary configuration steps). This book is aimed at developers, so it is assumed that you will be able to install Moodle with minimum fuss. If you need more information on Moodle administration, check out *Moodle Administration*, also available from Packt (visit https://www.packtpub.com/hardware-and-creative/moodle-3-administration-third-edition for details).

Who this book is for

This book is for Moodle developers who are familiar with the basic Moodle functionalities and have an understanding of the types of scenarios in which the Moodle platform can be usefully employed. You must have medium-level PHP programming knowledge and should be familiar with the HTML and XML protocols. You do not need to have prior knowledge of Moodle-specific terminology.

Conventions

In this book, you will find a number of text styles that distinguish between different kinds of information. Here are some examples of these styles and an explanation of their meaning.

Code words in text, database table names, folder names, filenames, file extensions, pathnames, dummy URLs, user input, and Twitter handles are shown as follows: "For example, an administration setting named `local_duallang/primarylanguage` is accessed by calling `get_config('local_duallang', 'primarylanguage')`."

A block of code is set as follows:

```
var col_complete = completion_data.colors.completed_colour;
var col_incomplete = completion_data.colors.notCompleted_colour;
var col_submitted = completion_data.colors.submittednotcomplete_colour;
var col_failed = completion_data.colors.futureNotCompleted_colour;
```

Any command-line input or output is written as follows:

```
$repeatarray[] = $mform->createElement('text', 'option',
get_string('optionno', 'choice'));
with
$repeatarray[] = $mform->createElement('editor', 'option',
get_string('option','enhancedchoice'), null,
array('maxfiles'=>EDITOR_UNLIMITED_FILES, 'noclean'=>true,
'context'=>$this->context));
```

New terms and **important words** are shown in bold. Words that you see on the screen, for example, in menus or dialog boxes, appear in the text like this: "When the learner clicks on the **Description** button, the client wants a **Course information** page to be displayed."

 Warnings or important notes appear in a box like this.

Tips and tricks appear like this.

Reader feedback

Feedback from our readers is always welcome. Let us know what you think about this book--what you liked or disliked. Reader feedback is important for us as it helps us develop titles that you will really get the most out of.

To send us general feedback, simply e-mail feedback@packtpub.com, and mention the book's title in the subject of your message.

If there is a topic that you have expertise in and you are interested in either writing or contributing to a book, see our author guide at www.packtpub.com/authors.

Customer support

Now that you are the proud owner of a Packt book, we have a number of things to help you to get the most from your purchase.

Downloading the example code

You can download the example code files for this book from your account at http://www.packtpub.com. If you purchased this book elsewhere, you can visit http://www.packtpub.com/support and register to have the files e-mailed directly to you.

You can download the code files by following these steps:

1. Log in or register to our website using your e-mail address and password.
2. Hover the mouse pointer on the **SUPPORT** tab at the top.
3. Click on **Code Downloads & Errata**.
4. Enter the name of the book in the **Search** box.
5. Select the book for which you're looking to download the code files.
6. Choose from the drop-down menu where you purchased this book from.
7. Click on **Code Download**.

Once the file is downloaded, please make sure that you unzip or extract the folder using the latest version of:

- WinRAR / 7-Zip for Windows
- Zipeg / iZip / UnRarX for Mac
- 7-Zip / PeaZip for Linux

The code bundle for the book is also hosted on GitHub at `https://github.com/PacktPubl ishing/Moodle-3-Developer's-Guide`. We also have other code bundles from our rich catalog of books and videos available at `https://github.com/PacktPublishing/`. Check them out!

Downloading the color images of this book

We also provide you with a PDF file that has color images of the screenshots/diagrams used in this book. The color images will help you better understand the changes in the output. You can download this file from `https://www.packtpub.com/sites/default/files/down loads/Moodle3Developer'sGuide_ColorImages.pdf`.

Errata

Although we have taken every care to ensure the accuracy of our content, mistakes do happen. If you find a mistake in one of our books-maybe a mistake in the text or the code-we would be grateful if you could report this to us. By doing so, you can save other readers from frustration and help us improve subsequent versions of this book. If you find any errata, please report them by visiting `http://www.packtpub.com/submit-errata`, selecting your book, clicking on the **Errata Submission Form** link, and entering the details of your errata. Once your errata are verified, your submission will be accepted and the errata will be uploaded to our website or added to any list of existing errata under the Errata section of that title.

To view the previously submitted errata, go to `https://www.packtpub.com/books/conten t/support` and enter the name of the book in the search field. The required information will appear under the **Errata** section.

Piracy

Piracy of copyrighted material on the Internet is an ongoing problem across all media. At Packt, we take the protection of our copyright and licenses very seriously. If you come across any illegal copies of our works in any form on the Internet, please provide us with the location address or website name immediately so that we can pursue a remedy.

Please contact us at copyright@packtpub.com with a link to the suspected pirated material.

We appreciate your help in protecting our authors and our ability to bring you valuable content.

Questions

If you have a problem with any aspect of this book, you can contact us at questions@packtpub.com, and we will do our best to address the problem.

1
Getting to Grips with the Moodle 3 Architecture

Have you ever experienced the frustration of being held back by technology? Perhaps you or your colleagues have wanted to teach something in a particular way and have found that your **Virtual Learning Environment (VLE)** doesn't support the feature you really needed. Maybe you are a learning manager, and you need to report on the numbers of learners from a particular postcode who have completed specific courses because this data is critical to ensuring continued funding. How many times have you held conversations about your VLE that began with "Wouldn't it be great if our learning platform could allow a learner/a manager to... ?".

The purpose of this book is to show you, through real-world examples, the details of plugin design and development. However, the key to plugin wisdom is understanding the Moodle architecture and, for that, you will need to understand Moodle itself. This chapter forms a general introduction to the Moodle philosophy, Moodle history, and the Moodle community.

In this chapter, we will also learn what a Moodle plugin is, what can be achieved with plugins, and cover not only how your plugins will actually plug in to Moodle but also what functionality Moodle can provide to your plugin (through dedicated application programming interfaces that your plugin can call upon).

This chapter will also help you set up your development environment ready to start developing. We will show you how to install and configure a local web server, the Eclipse IDE, and the Chrome Xdebug plugin for remote script debugging.

By the end of this chapter, you will be able to do the following:

- Understand the importance of **Application Programming Interfaces (APIs)**, both generally and in the context of Moodle plugin development
- Be able to configure Moodle on a local development computer (for example, your personal laptop)
- Be able to configure an integrated development environment, ready to start creating your first Moodle plugin

The final part of this chapter sees us walking through the process of creating our very first Moodle plugin--a language-switching plugin to support a UK/China joint venture. We won't go into the details of how plugins operate at this stage (that will be covered in the rest of the book), but you will get an appreciation of just a few of the decisions that must be made before and during the development process.

Let's begin our journey by exploring the background of the Moodle project a little.

Understanding Moodle

There are three reasons Moodle has become so important and much talked about in the world of online learning (refer to The Campus Computing Project at `http://www.campusco mputing.net/` new.html): one technical, one philosophical, and the third educational.

From a technical standpoint, Moodle--an acronym for **Modular Object-Oriented Dynamic Learning Environment (Moodle)**--is highly customizable. As a Moodle developer, always remember that the "M" in Moodle stands for modular. If you are faced with a client feature request that demands a feature Moodle doesn't support, don't panic. The answer is simple-- we create a new custom plugin to implement it. Check out the Moodle plugins directory (`https://moodle.org/plugins/`) for a comprehensive library of supported third-party plugins that Moodle developers have created and given back to the community. This leads to the philosophical reason why Moodle dominates.

Moodle is, from a philosophical perspective, grounded firmly in a community-based, open source ethos (check out `https://en.wikipedia.org/wiki/Open-source_model`). However, what does this mean for us as developers? Fundamentally, it means that we have complete access to the source code, and within reason, unfettered access to the people who develop it. Access to the application itself is free--you don't need to pay to download it, and you don't need to pay to run it. However, be aware of what free means. Hosting and administration, for example, take time and resources are very unlikely to be free.

You will very often hear beer talked about in the context of **free** software (and I have purposefully stressed the word free): free software means free as in freedom, not free as in beer. Possibly, a better way of stating the case is to say that the Moodle developers in general--and *Martin Dougiamas*, the creator of Moodle, in particular--have given us freedom to do what we must. What we have not been granted is license to do what we want. Note that, again and like the beer example, this isn't quite the same as *gratis* (free of price) and *libre* (free of restriction--refer to `https://en.wikipedia.org/wiki/Gratis_versus_libre`). As Moodle developers, we are bound by the duties specified in the free Software Foundation's GPLv3 license (check out `http://www.gnu.org/licenses/gpl-3.0.txt`), and it is worth having an appreciation of these duties before you start developing.

Finally, as an educational tool, Moodle was developed to support social constructionism (refer to `https://docs.moodle.org/31/en/Pedagogy`); if you are not familiar with this concept, it is essentially suggesting that building an understanding of a concept or idea can be best achieved by interacting with a broad community. The impact on us as Moodle plugin developers is that there is a highly active group of users and developers. Before you begin developing any Moodle plugins, come and join us at `https://moodle.org/mod/foru m/?id=5`.

More on Moodle plugins

As briefly described earlier, if we are faced with a need to enhance or alter the functionality of Moodle in some way, then the prescribed approach is to create a plugin. Refer to `https://docs.moodle.org/dev/Moodle_architecture#Moodle_as_a_modular_system` for a further description of Moodle's modular architecture. The `https://docs.moodle.org/dev/Moodle_architecture` page is also a good reference for learning about the basic plugin types and where these plugin types are to be found in the application folder structure.

In the following sections, we will set ourselves up ready to start developing our own plugins. First, we need to learn how to run a Moodle on our development computers.

Running a local Moodle

Moodle is a web application; so, you will need a web server in order to run it. In this section, we will be configuring a local development server that can run on your local machine.

Moodle architecture - the LAMP/WAMP stack

Moodle is a web application running typically (but not exclusively) in a web browser. A Moodle user interacts with a user interface on a client computer. The client requests resources from the application server (generally known as **middleware**) that provides the requested resources. It can do so by calling on another server, known as the **data server**. The data server provides the application server with the data it requires:

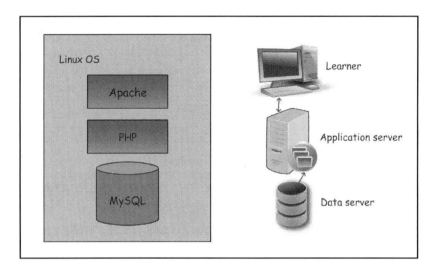

Check out `https://en.wikipedia.org/wiki/LAMP_(software_bundle)` for more information on the stack.

Generally, this architecture is referred to either as a WAMP stack or LAMP stack, the W or L referring to Windows or Linux, depending on the operating system you are running. A is for the web server Apache, M for the database server MySQL, and P for PHP, the scripting language Moodle is authored in. It should be noted that other web servers and databases are available and Moodle will run quite happily on them; refer to the online Moodle documentation.

Setting up an Internet ready Moodle server is beyond the scope of this book--see Moodle 3.0 Administration, also from Packt, for details. Instead, we will install a local web server running on Windows, using WampServer.

Installing WampServer

The WampServer development stack can be downloaded from
`http://www.wampserver.com/en/`. Ensure that you download either the 32-bit or 64-bit
version to suit your computer. Also, ensure that you run the install with Administrator
privileges as both Apache and MySQL run as Windows services and the installer will
require elevated privileges to install these. Once installed and running, the WampServer
icon will be visible in the taskbar--green means everything is operating as it should and
your local web server is up and running:

WampServer and Skype

Do you use Skype on your development machine? If so, you will likely experience a
configuration conflict between the Apache instance in WampServer and Skype as Apache
attempts to use ports 80 (for HTTP) and 443 (for HTTPS) to display web pages. By default,
Skype is configured to use both these ports as alternatives for data transfer, so you will need
to reconfigure Skype accordingly:

1. Open Skype and click on the **Tools** menu option and slide down to **Options...**.
2. Select **Advanced** and then click on **Connection**.
3. Uncheck the **Use port 80 and 443 as alternatives for incoming connections**
   option and press **Save**.
4. Restart Skype.

Setting up an Integrated Development Environment (IDE)

As discussed earlier, the Moodle application consists of a great number of text scripts that
can, in practice as well as theory, be edited with any simple text editor. However, you will
be far better off using an *integrated development environment* for your development. An IDE
will contain tools for code completion and code insight; for example, if you have forgotten
the name of a class method, or if you need quick access to a function declaration, or the
instances where a variable is used.

Perhaps more importantly, IDEs contain integrated debugging tools that allow you to step through the code as it runs (more on this later). The examples in this book use a special PHP version of the Eclipse IDE called Eclipse PDT, which can be downloaded from `http://www.eclipse.org/pdt/`.

Configuring the Eclipse IDE

Once installed, there are a number of recommended configuration preferences to change, and these are outlined in the Moodle developer documentation at `https://docs.moodle.org/dev/Setting_up_Eclipse#Setting_the_preferences_for_Moodle_development`.

Once the development environment is configured, we need to consider how we will debug any code we write. For that, we need to set up and configure remote debugging, which we discuss next.

Configuring remote debugging

We will use the Chrome browser for development using the integrated JavaScript, CSS, and HTML debugging tools. To debug PHP scripts, we will need to install and configure a PHP remote debugger. The debugger we will use is called Xdebug--`https://xdebug.org/index.php`. Xdebug needs to be installed and configured in three places:

- The web server (Apache running our local development server)
- The development environment (Eclipse)
- The browser (Chrome)

The first step is to configure Xdebug in Apache. In order to determine which version of Xdebug is required, you will need to obtain a copy of the full output from `phpinfo()`--refer to `http://php.net/manual/en/function.phpinfo.php`--and paste that into `https://xdebug.org/wizard.php`, as follows:

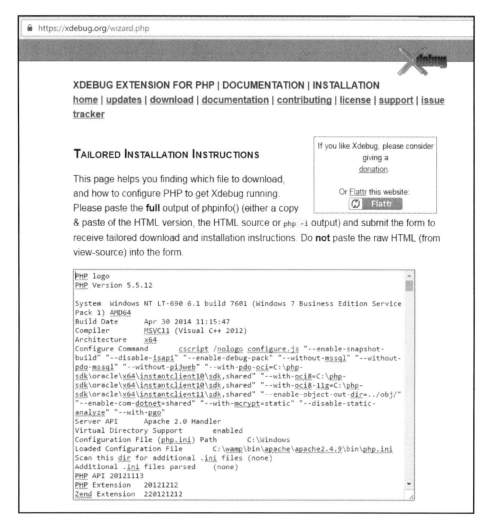

Press the **Analyse my phpinfo() output** button at the bottom of the page for instructions on how to download and configure Xdebug.

Next, we need to configure Xdebug in the IDE. Instructions are available in the Eclipse documentation at `https://wiki.eclipse.org/Debugging_using_XDebug`.

Finally, we need to install an Xdebug plugin into the browser. For Chrome, we will be using *Xdebug helper*. Check out `https://github.com/mac-cain13/xdebug-helper-for-chrome` for details, but the helper itself is easily installed through the Chrome Web Store (you can find relevant links on the GitHub page).

Installing and configuring Moodle

Where should we install our development Moodle? It is always easier to debug an application that is running on the same (local) machine as your integrated development environment, although the PHP debugging tools described in this book also support remote debugging. If it's a separate development server (and not your local machine) you are working with, be sure to check out the guidance on how to configure remote debugging online as this can be tricky to set up. Each remote setup is different, so there is no definitive guide. The Eclipse forums are a great place to look for help, for example, http://www.eclipse.org/forums/index.php/mv/msg/365474/890896/#msg_890896.

The latest version of Moodle can be downloaded from https://download.moodle.org/. Download the latest version and unpack in the www directory created by WampServer. Before running the installation, you will need to follow the setting up instructions at https://docs.moodle.org/31/en/Windows_installation_using_XAMPP. Note that these instructions are for XAMPP, an alternative web server based on LAMP (https://www.apachefriends.org/download.html), but the principles of configuring Moodle running on WampServer are exactly the same. Before you install Moodle, ensure that the required PHP modules are installed and enabled (refer to https://docs.moodle.org/31/en/PHP for details) as failure to do so can result in you experiencing almost impossible to debug blank pages during the installation process.

Introducing the project

Now is the time to introduce the project we will be developing as we work through this book. The project brief is to develop a learning platform to promote research into societal and economic resilience. The Moodle instance we will be working on forms part of a much larger product landscape; so, it is vital that the Moodle we will be helping to develop integrates seamlessly into this landscape. Not only that, but there are features required of the e-learning platform itself that a vanilla Moodle doesn't support. For that, we will need to develop features to support learner management (one requirement is that authentication is via WordPress), course management (for example, access to materials based on your location), and novel teaching interactions (specifically, a three-dimensional model viewer). However, rather than presenting the details of the entire project at this early stage, we will be introducing features as they are required.

As a developer, don't be concerned purely with creating code. All the world's best designers, architects, builders, and planners have an appreciation and understanding of where they are coming from and where they are going; the art is knowing where to start and the science is in the planning and execution. In the rest of this section, we discuss the importance of planning.

Planning is everything

Creating a new Moodle installation doesn't just involve configuring servers and installing software. That's just a very small part of the process. The most important part of the process is *planning*. Before you can plan, you have to understand the environment (that is, the people and the organization) that you are planning for. It is best to design your new server architecture in baby steps:

1. Audit the current environment, that is, your whole organization: How is your network configured? How will the new Moodle be accessed? How will the new Moodle interface with legacy systems? Will Moodle work at all?

2. Produce an options analysis: Designing a new architecture is a problem, not a puzzle (puzzles only have certain solutions whereas problems can have many solutions, some more effective than others). Each potential solution will have benefits and risks; these need to be understood.

3. Recommend a solution: The preceding two steps will make it clear why you have reached your particular recommendation.

Only when you reach an informed decision on which architecture you will implement, should you go ahead and implement it.

Obviously, how rigorous you need to be during the planning stage will depend on the organization you are planning for, still preparation is everything.

Agile software development

In this book, we will follow an Agile software development methodology. There is plenty of information available on the internet on Agile and the principles themselves are fairly straightforward to follow. The only aspect of Agile that you really need to be aware of is that client requirements will be described in terms of user stories, which are very different to the typical use cases you may be familiar with. At the requirements stage, we can treat Moodle plugins like little black boxes.

Essentially, the difference between use cases and user stories is this:

- A use case explains what a black box is meant to do
- A user story explains what a black box is meant to achieve

You will be encountering far more user stories as you read this book as our focus is on what can be achieved with new Moodle plugins rather than what they do and, of course, with what goes on inside the little black box--the software development.

Version control

Maintaining source code is impossible without some measure of version control. There are many version control systems available, but one of the most popular--and the one used by the Moodle community--is Git. Git is a **Distributed Version Control System (DVCS)**, and it makes sense that the Moodle source code should be managed using some form of distributed system as Moodle's development community is scattered worldwide. The Moodle community uses GitHub--`https://github.com`. Delving into the details of how you use Git and GitHub are beyond the scope of this book. You are encouraged to read `https://docs.moodle.org/dev/Git_for_developers` before you start developing plugins properly. For more information on GitHub, check out GitHub Essentials, also from Packt (`https://www.packtpub.com/application-development/github-essentials`).

Moodle Internals - Application Programming Interfaces (APIs)

Essential to the creation of any new feature in Moodle is an understanding of Moodle's internal application programming interfaces. The *oo* in Moodle stands for object-oriented and at the outset, it is worth unpacking what this means to us as plugin developers.

An object-oriented philosophy

Object orientation is all about treating features of a system as little interconnecting black boxes. We have no idea what goes on inside a black box, but each black box can be described in three ways:

- Each box behaves in a particular way and by making a box act out predefined, built-in behaviors, you can make it do different things
- At any moment, a box is in a particular state
- Every box has its own identity

Also, in fact, our little black boxes are *objects* and each object has a *state*, exhibits certain *behaviors*, and every object is uniquely identifiable as each has its own *identity*.

Objects themselves are of a particular type, called a class. Your pet cat shares some of the features of a mountain lion because they are both feline, and felines are types of mammals, so all mammals share similar characteristics, and so on. It is the same way with objects in Moodle:

If there is a specific programming task you need to perform in Moodle, you need to look for the correct API with which to carry out that task. Visit `https://docs.moodle.org/dev/Core_APIs` for a list of all of Moodle's internal APIs. For example, do you need to display a string on the screen? If so, use the String API. Why? It is because the String API automatically handles issues such as formatting and internationalization.

Each one of these APIs is accessed via an object. For example, use the global $DB object to access Moodle's database. This is an instance of the **Data Manipulation Language (DML)** API. Again and as with using the String API to display text on the screen, don't try to access the database other than through the interface Moodle provides. Why? It is because issues such as SQL injection hacks and verifying data integrity are already handled in the $DB object interface, so you don't have to worry about it.

However, what if there is a behavior that a particular interface doesn't support? This is solved by the notion of inheritance--see
https://en.wikipedia.org/wiki/Inheritance_(object-oriented_programming). If, for example, the String API is missing a behavior our project requires, or we need to modify a behavior in order for it to fit our needs, we can declare a new class and base it on the String API. The new class is called a *child* class and the class upon which we have based the child is called the *parent* class. Certainly, in the case of the String API, we can reconfigure Moodle to use our new API. We will be learning how to modify an API (using the String API specifically) later in this chapter.

This section is merely a brief overview of the object-oriented philosophy, intended to be just enough of an explanation before you start Moodle plugin development. For more details on the object-oriented philosophy in general, check out the Wikipedia page on object-oriented Programming at https://en.wikipedia.org/wiki/Object-oriented_programming.

Types of APIs

For a complete list of Moodle's core internal APIs, take a look at `https://docs.moodle.org/dev/Core_APIs`. The first set of APIs are listed as *General APIs*. They are the interfaces upon which most plugins are built, for example, the Data Manipulation API for reading and writing to the Moodle database or the Form API that displays web forms and handles their form data. In the next section, we will create a simple plugin that overrides (in the object-oriented sense) and calls on the String API to change the way language strings are displayed in Moodle's user interface.

The "Other General APIs", listed next, are the ones that are still fundamental and likely to be used in any type of plugin but, that said, are much less likely to be called upon, for example, the Calendar API or the Competency API.

Then, there are the APIs that are specific to certain plugin types, such as the Activity Completion and Plagiarism APIs, which will only be employed by a Moodle activity module.

Our first plugin - a custom string manager

As described earlier, we will be working together to develop plugins for a new global Moodle-based learning management system in this book. For the rest of this chapter, we will be working through the development of a simple plugin, one that modifies the way language strings are displayed on the user interface. Note that the intention isn't to demonstrate the finer details of how to write a Moodle plugin; that is the purpose of the rest of the book. The rest of this chapter is written to outline the kind of thought processes that one would engage in when being tasked with developing a new feature in Moodle. So, let's begin with finding out what the task that we have been set is.

The user story

In true agile fashion, the following user story has been assigned to us:

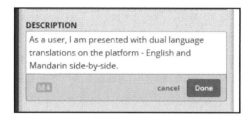

The client requires two languages to be displayed on the screen at the same time: English and Mandarin Chinese. Moodle supports language switching (refer to `https://docs.moodle.org/31/en/Language_settings` for details) but doesn't show two languages at the same time. Also, on the face of it, this seems a fairly straightforward problem. However, let's always ensure that we take a methodical approach to any request and avoid the temptation to simply start developing. By being disciplined, we can ensure that the plugin we develop is not only the most effective fit for this immediate requirement, but also that:

- It is future proof
- It is reusable
- It is ready, potentially, to be offered back to the development community (IPR issues not withstanding)

The development process

Let's spend the rest of this section learning about the development process. There are many well-defined development processes, and these will be explored in the rest of the book. The art, however, is knowing where to start, and we should always start by attempting to thoroughly understand the problem in every way.

Step 1: Understanding the problem

It is, perhaps, a statement of the obvious, but before you start developing, ensure that you fully understand the problem you have been asked to solve. The standard journalist's questions are a good framework to aid your understanding. Consider the following:

- **Who**: Will the two languages be displayed to all users or only to certain users? *In our case, all users.*
- **What**: Are we talking about US English or UK English? Does the client want "Mandarin", which means mainland Chinese displayed using the simplified character set? *Our client has specified UK English and simplified Chinese Mandarin.*
- **Why**: Is this because our users are bilingual, or is this being included as a teaching aid? *The client is wanting two languages on the screen simultaneously as they are expecting the platform to be used in group teaching.*

- **Where**: Moodle language switching toggles the language on the platform only; it doesn't toggle languages in any teaching materials. *This client wants both the platform and the courses to be bilingual.*
- **When**: Are two languages to be displayed everywhere or only in particular contexts? *Dual languages are to be displayed throughout the platform.*

Also, having gained an understanding of the problem, it's time to consider the **how**.

Step 2: Researching potential solutions

Moodle already supports a range of languages through installable language packs, and for version 3.1, these are listed at https://download.moodle.org/langpack/3.1/. The language pack we need is zn_ch.zip, which is simplified Chinese Mandarin. Follow the instructions at https://docs.moodle.org/31/en/Language_packs to install this pack into your local development Moodle:

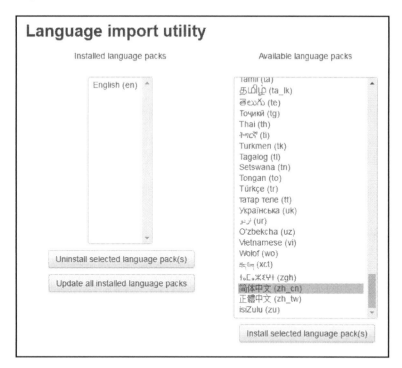

Having installed the relevant language pack, we can now experiment with creating a test Moodle user whose native language is simplified Chinese:

Having satisfied ourselves that we can switch to the Chinese language, we now need to assess options for displaying two languages on the screen at the same time. For that--and in the spirit of social constructivist learning in general--we need to go out into the world... Let's start with the main Moodle website at `https://www.moodle.org`.

Moodle plugin directory

Take a look at `https://moodle.org/plugins` and search for **language**:

Unfortunately, nothing is available to support dual language display in the plugins directory.

Moodle community forums

Martin Dougiamas created Moodle as a platform not only to support social constructivist teaching, but he also wanted to have development of the platform supported along social constructivist lines. So, the main Moodle website hosts a variety of forums where users and developers can openly discuss issues and address support-related and frequently asked questions. Visit `https://moodle.org/course/` for a full list of forums (you will need to create a user account if you want to post any messages). The language forum itself is at `https://moodle.org/mod/forum/view.php?id=43`.

If you don't find anything relevant in the user forums, we can take a look at the Moodle Tracker next.

Moodle Tracker

Detailed discussions on Moodle developments tend to take place in the Moodle Tracker at `https://tracker.moodle.org/secure/Dashboard.jspa`. A general search on string management has revealed a discussion on the ability to provide an alternate string manager; Tracker ticket ID MDL-49361 `https://tracker.moodle.org/browse/MDL-49361`:

 Moodle / MDL-49361

Ability to provide alternate strings manager

Description

Currently, the factory function get_string_manager() returns singleton instance of core_string_manager_install() in early stages of the site installation, or instance of core_string_manager_standard().

Proposal

This is a proposal to introduce a new config.php setting like $CFG->alternativestringmanager. If that setting is found and it contains a valid class name, and that class implements interface core_string_manager, then it is used as the string manager instead of the default one. The class would be typically provided by an additional plugin. The setting must be defined via config.php only. The value in mdl_config table will be ignored (so that malicious plugin can't inject it secretly).

Use-cases

- String usage accounting plugin - this will allow us to implement a plugin that collects and logs string usage (together with the context, user role etc). This can lead to a report on what strings are most important ones to be translated (for students, for teachers etc).
- Ability to override strings in one component via additional plugin - see ~~MDL-46582~~
- Ability to have a plugin that allows local language customization and/or language pack contribution directly at the page where the string appears (it would log all the get_string() calls in the current request and then somehow inject them into the page footer so that they could be used by a JS on the client, for example).
- Experimental implementations of advanced plural handling, Google translator integration and all other crazy stuff.

String API

For a detailed explanation of the String API, visit
`https://docs.moodle.org/dev/String_API`. The String API documentation reveals that the
most effective method of having Moodle display two language strings on the screen at the
same time is to author our own string manager, within which we have implemented a
custom `get_string()` function. Luckily, the reporter of ticket MDL-49361 has already
created an example, Moodle plugin **moodle-local_stringman,** and made it available
through GitHub (refer to the preceding section, **Source control discipline**):

You will see that the README notes for the **moodle-local_stringman** plugin stress that the code provided should be used for illustration purposes only. So, we will need to download a copy of the source and create our own GitHub repository to work on:

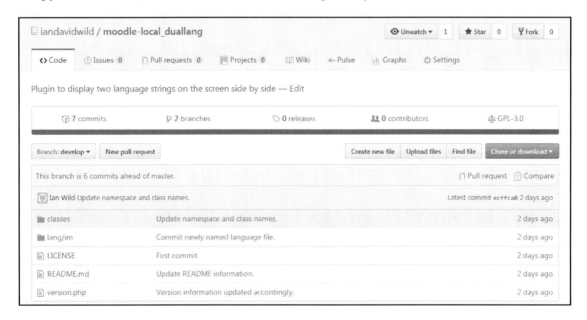

That done, it's time to work on our solution.

Step 3: Implementing the solution

We will create a new *local* plugin. Essentially, local plugins are the place to put enhancements to core Moodle that don't fit into any other obvious place (that is, an enhancement that isn't a new course activity or a new user authentication method). We will learn much more about local plugins in Chapter 2, *Moodle Plugins - What Can I plug In*? I have called this new plugin *duallang*. This is publicly available on GitHub at `https://github.com/iandavidwild/moodle-local_duallang`.

Standard plugin features

Download the plugin from GitHib. Now, let's take a look at the structure of the *duallang* plugin together. There are three files worth mentioning:

- `version.php`: This contains not only the version information of the plugin itself but also the minimum version of Moodle required to run it. It also, optionally, contains a list of dependencies. The following is a copy of the relevant code from our new plugin:

```php
$plugin->component = 'local_duallang';
$plugin->release = 'alpha1';
$plugin->version = 2016112300;
$plugin->requires = 2015030900;
$plugin->maturity = MATURITY_ALPHA;
$plugin->dependencies = array();
```

- `lang/en/local_duallang.php`: This contains the plugin's language strings. There is only one language string required for this basic plugin and that is the name of the plugin itself:

```php
$string['pluginname'] = 'Dual language string manager';
```

- `classes/duallang_string_manager.php`: This script contains the overridden implementation of the `core_string_manager` class, specifically, the `get_string()` function, which has been modified to construct a language string from both the UK English and the simplified Chinese Mandarin language packs:

```php
class duallang_string_manager extends
\core_string_manager_standard {

    /**
     * Implementation of the get_string() method to display both
     simplified
     * Chinese and UK English simultaneously.
     *
     * @param string $identifier the identifier of the string to
     search for
     * @param string $component the component the string is
     provided by
     * @paramstring|object|array $a optional data placeholder
     * @param string $langmoodle translation language, null means
     use
     * current
     * @return string
     */
```

```
public function get_string($identifier, $component = '', $a =
null,
$lang = null) {

    $string = parent::get_string($identifier, $component, $a,
    'en');

    $zh_cn = parent::get_string($identifier, $component, $a,
    'zh_cn');

    if(strlen($zh_cn) > 0) {
        $string .= ' | ' . $zh_cn;
    }

    return $string;
}
}
```

Note that in order to specifically load UK English and simplified Chinese, we simply call the method in the parent class (refer to the *An objected-oriented philosophy* section for some elaboration on the parent/child class relationship).

At the top of each PHP script, you will find a general comment header, important copyright, and optional version control information. You will also see the following line of code:

```
defined('MOODLE_INTERNAL') || die();
```

This prevents someone from outside of Moodle from accessing the PHP script. To install the plugin, we can either copy the files to Moodle's local folder or use Moodle's built-in plugin installer (for details, visit `https://docs.moodle.org/31/en/Installing_plugins#Instal ling_via_uploaded_ZIP_file`):

Once installed, we will also need to add a line to Moodle's `config.php` file (located in Moodle's root directory):

```
Window   Help

   duallang_string_manager.php        config.php

 1   <?php  // Moodle configuration file
 2
 3   unset($CFG);
 4   global $CFG;
 5   $CFG = new stdClass();
 6
 7   $CFG->dbtype     = 'mysqli';
 8   $CFG->dblibrary  = 'native';
 9   $CFG->dbhost     = 'localhost';
10   $CFG->dbname     = 'moodle313';
11   $CFG->dbuser     = 'moodle313';
12   $CFG->dbpass     = 'moodle313';
13   $CFG->prefix     = 'mdl_';
14   $CFG->dboptions = array (
15     'dbpersist' => 0,
16     'dbport' => '',
17     'dbsocket' => '',
18   );
19
20   $CFG->customstringmanager = '\local_duallang\duallang_string_manager';
21
22   $CFG->wwwroot    = 'http://moodle313.localhost';
23   $CFG->dataroot   = 'C:\\wamp\\www\\moodledata313';
24   $CFG->admin      = 'admin';
25
26   $CFG->directorypermissions = 0777;
27
28   require_once(dirname(__FILE__) . '/lib/setup.php');
29
30   // There is no php closing tag in this file,
31   // it is intentional because it prevents trailing whitespace problems!
32

     Problems    Console    Browser Output    Debug Output    Search    Debug    Progress

   No search results available. Start a search from the search dialog...
```

Return to Moodle's home page and you will now see the UK English and simplified Chinese Mandarin language strings displayed side by side:

Summary

In this chapter, we began our Moodle plugin development journey. We started with an investigation of the history of Moodle and the philosophy that underpins it. Having gained an understanding of Moodle, we then learned how to set ourselves up for plugin development. We set up a local development web server based on WampServer and then configured the Eclipse IDE and the Chrome Xdebug plugin for remote debugging.

We spent the second half of this chapter developing a simple dual-language plugin. We followed the plugin development process from user story to deployment in order to understand just a few of the thought processes and decisions that need to be made before plugin development begins.

In the next chapter, we will be delving deeper into the types of plugins that are available and learn how to change the layout of a Moodle course through the development of a custom course format plugin.

2
Moodle Plugins - What Can I Plug In?

Having readied our development environment and explored the thought processes that support building a Moodle plugin, in this chapter we will be investigating the types of plugin Moodle supports. Remember that the "M" in Moodle stands for modular; if there is a feature you need that Moodle doesn't support then we can build a plugin to implement it. Any aspect of the user experience can be enhanced and/or modified by a plugin. In this chapter, we will be mapping out the most common user journeys through the platform, from initial log on (authentication), through being assigned to courses (enrolment), and ultimately completion reporting.

As described in the previous chapter, we will be taking an Agile approach to plugin development, and that means we will be working with user stories (a description of what our work needs to achieve) rather than the more standard use cases (what our work needs to do) that you may be used to. This will require us to have an appreciation of how a user will interact with Moodle.

By the end of this chapter, you will:

- Have gained an appreciation of the more common user journeys, and will know how this understanding will inform the need for a new plugin
- Have a thorough understanding of the types of Moodle plugins available
- Have a complete understanding of the structure of a plugin (building on ideas introduced in `Chapter 2`, *Moodle Plugins - What Can I Plug In?*)
- Be able to select the best type of plugin to develop for the particular task in hand

Let us begin by considering plugins that manage getting users onto the platform.

Managing users

Getting users onto courses is a two-step process. Firstly, a user needs to have a user account created in Moodle--the *authentication* step. Next, they need to be given access to a course through course *enrolment*. Both of these steps are supported--and can be enhanced--by plugins. Let's start by looking at authentication.

Authentication

Log in to your development Moodle as an administrator and, from the **Site administration** menu, slide down to **Plugins**, then **Authentication**, and then click on **Manage authentication**:

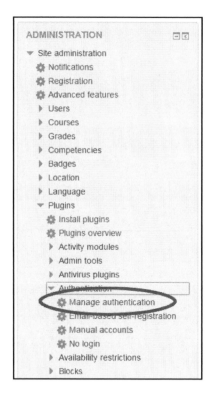

The **Manage authentication** page lists the available authentication plugins (together with general configuration settings further down the page):

Manage authentication

Available authentication plugins

Name	Users	Enable	Up/Down	Settings	Test settings	Uninstall
Manual accounts	3			Settings		
No login	0			Settings		
Email-based self-registration	0	👁		Settings		Uninstall
CAS server (SSO)	0	🚫		Settings		Uninstall
External database	0	🚫		Settings	Test settings	Uninstall
FirstClass server	0	🚫		Settings		Uninstall
IMAP server	0	🚫		Settings		Uninstall
LDAP server	0	🚫		Settings		
LTI	0	🚫		Settings		Uninstall

Check out the Moodle docs for details of the authentication process at `https://docs.moodle.org/dev/Authentication_plugins#Overview_of_Moodle_authentic ation_process`. What is important to realize about the authentication process is that it isn't simply a question of either creating a new user account in Moodle or verifying user credentials against a third-party system.

Let's spend a little time studying the authentication process in detail. Open Eclipse and navigate to `login/index.php`:

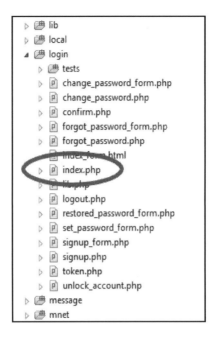

Authentication begins and the Moodle login page is displayed. It requests the user's credentials:

When the login form is submitted, `login/index.php` loops through the enabled authentication plugins, in order, to fire the login event to each plugin's login hook:

```
 ▷ 📁 lib                                  75  /// Check for timed out sessions
 ▷ 📁 local                                76  if (!empty($SESSION->has_timed_out)) {
 ▲ 📁 login                                77      $session_has_timed_out = true;
    ▷ 📁 tests                             78      unset($SESSION->has_timed_out);
    ▷ 📄 change_password_form.php          79  } else {
    ▷ 📄 change_password.php               80      $session_has_timed_out = false;
    ▷ 📄 confirm.php                       81  }
    ▷ 📄 forgot_password_form.php          82
    ▷ 📄 forgot_password.php               83  /// auth plugins may override these - SSO anyone?
       📄 index_form.html                 84  $frm  = false;
    ▷ 📄 index.php                         85  $user = false;
    ▷ 📄 lib.php                           86
    ▷ 📄 logout.php                        87  $authsequence = get_enabled_auth_plugins(true); // auths, in sequence
    ▷ 📄 restored_password_form.php        88  foreach($authsequence as $authname) {
    ▷ 📄 set_password_form.php             89      $authplugin = get_auth_plugin($authname);
    ▷ 📄 signup_form.php                   90      $authplugin->loginpage_hook();
    ▷ 📄 signup.php                        91  }
    ▷ 📄 token.php                         92
    ▷ 📄 unlock_account.php                93
 ▷ 📁 message                             94  /// Define variables used in page
 ▷ 📁 mnet                                95  $site = get_site();
                                         96
                                         97  // Ignore any active pages in the navigation/settings.
                                         98  // We do this because there won't be an active page there, and by ignoring
                                         99  // navigation and settings won't be initialised unless something else needs
                                        100  $PAGE->navbar->ignore_active();
```

An authentication plugin hook may return user details at this point--typically preventing the user logging in as part of a debugging process or because of a configuration error of some kind. The authentication plugins are called from the `authenticate_user_login()` function in `lib/moodlelib.php`. The `auth_login()` function is called on each authentication plugin:

```
foreach ($auths as $auth) {
    $authplugin = get_auth_plugin($auth);

    // On auth fail fall through to the next plugin.
    if (!$authplugin->user_login($username, $password)) {
        continue;
    }

    // Successful authentication.
    if ($user->id) {
        // User already exists in database.
        if (empty($user->auth)) {
            // For some reason auth isn't set yet.
            $DB->set_field('user', 'auth', $auth, array('id' => $user->id));
            $user->auth = $auth;
        }
```

The authentication plugins themselves are to be found in the `auth` folder; for example, the default authentication method is *manual accounts*:

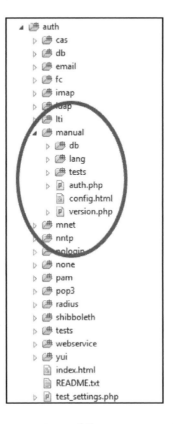

Feel free to take a look now at the structure of the `manual` authentication plugin. Authentication plugins have the same general structure:

The script that actually authenticates, and each plugin contains one, is `auth.php`. The `auth.php` file contains a declaration of a class based on `auth_plugin_base`, the authentication base class declared in `/lib/authlib.php`. We will be studying the structure and operation of authentication plugins in general (as well as developing our own) in `Chapter 6`, *Managing Users - Letting in the Crowds*.

Enrolment

Course enrolment can only take place if there is a user to enrol. The standard plugins are listed when, from the **Site administration** menu, you click on **Plugins**, then **Enrolments**, and finally select **Manage enrol plugins**. The available course enrolment plugins are displayed on the **Manage enrol plugins** page:

Manage enrol plugins

Available course enrolment plugins

Name	Instances / enrolments	Version	Enable	Up/Down	Settings	Test settings	Uninstall
Manual enrolments	1 / 0	2016052300	👁	↓	Settings		
Guest access	1 / 0	2016052300	👁	↑ ↓	Settings		Uninstall
Self enrolment	1 / 0	2016052301	👁	↑ ↓	Settings		Uninstall
Cohort sync	0 / 0	2016052300	👁	↑	Settings		Uninstall
Category enrolments	0 / 0	2016052300	👁		Settings		Uninstall
External database	0 / 0	2016052300	👁		Settings	Test settings	Uninstall
Flat file (CSV)	0 / 0	2016052300	👁		Settings		Uninstall

Check out the documentation on enrolment plugins at
`https://docs.moodle.org/dev/Enrolment_plugins`. The best way of understanding the
operation of enrolment plugins is by going back to the Moodle source in Eclipse in
`lib/enrollib.php`. Take a look in `enrollib.php` for the `enrol_plugin` class
declaration:

```
1068
1069  /**
1070   * All enrol plugins should be based on this class,
1071   * this is also the main source of documentation.
1072   */
1073  abstract class enrol_plugin {
1074      protected $config = null;
1075
1076      /**
1077       * Returns name of this enrol plugin
1078       * @return string
1079       */
1080      public function get_name() {
1081          // second word in class is always enrol name, sorry, no fancy plugin names with _
1082          $words = explode('_', get_class($this));
1083          return $words[1];
1084      }
1085
1086      /**
1087       * Returns localised name of enrol instance
1088       *
1089       * @param object $instance (null is accepted too)
1090       * @return string
1091       */
1092      public function get_instance_name($instance) {
```

The first thing to notice is that enrolment plugins belong to courses and not to the system as
a whole--this makes sense as this allows us to enroll users on a variety of courses by a
variety of means. Also note that we can enable more than one enrolment plugin per course.
For information on configuring course enrolment, see
`https://docs.moodle.org/31/en/Course_enrolment`.

Users are enrolled on courses and allocated different roles (as in real life, it is the role a user
is allocated that defines exactly what they are able to do--that is, users with the *editing
teacher* role can edit the course and users with the *student* role can't), but note that enrolling
and allocating roles are two separate processes in Moodle.

You will see from the documentation that enrolment plugins also need to handle the following:

- Suspended and expired users
- Self-enrolment (where a user enrolls themselves onto a course)
- Payment gateways

As with authentication, the enrolment process can be hooked: Events are fired at each stage of the enrolment process that our enrolment plugin can listen out for and, when it hears a specific type of event, it can perform some kind of event-specific task.

Now navigate through Eclipse PHP Explorer to the self-enrolment plugin located in `/enrol/self`:

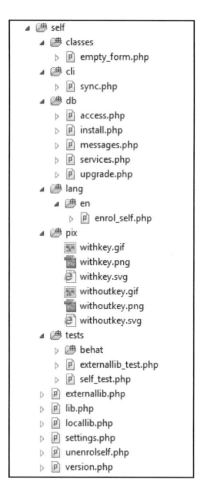

Clearly one of the more obvious differences between an authentication and an enrolment plugin is the amount of complexity: There are far more PHP scripts to an enrolment plugin compared to an authentication plugin. The `cli` folder contains a `cron` script that calls the `sync()` function that, depending on the type of enrolment plugin, will allow us to set up timed synchronization of enrolments to, say, an external database during some quiet period. You will also see that the `db` folder contains scripts not only for upgrading, but also for installing. It also contains a script to manage access to enrolment functionality based on the capabilities of a user's role (`access.php`). There will be a deeper exploration of enrolment plugins, as well as development of our own, in `Chapter 6`, *Managing Users - Letting in the Crowds*.

Learner competencies

It is fair to say that Moodle started life as a straightforward VLE--basically an online platform where learning takes place and not much beyond that. It is true that one could evidence learning through quizzes, workshops, assignments, and lessons, but that only goes so far; you are simply testing a learner's knowledge. Through the introduction of **competency-based education** (**CBE**), Moodle is now much more of a **learning management system** (**LMS**) than in previous versions (in spite of the earlier introduction of learning objectives). In other words, not only a platform where learning takes place, but also where learning is *managed*.

Learning isn't just about gaining knowledge. The instructional designers we are developing for won't want their students to simply regurgitate facts. They will also want them to be able to exhibit competency--or proficiency--when carrying out tasks. What influence will this approach have on the platform?

For example, most of us are aware that making a decent cup of coffee requires hot water, ground coffee beans, and perhaps milk and sugar to suit your taste. But there is a world of difference between knowing that a cup of coffee requires these ingredients and being proficient at making one. And, continuing from that, would students be capable of discerning decisions on, for example, choices of ingredients--from perhaps choosing to use Fairtrade Foundation coffee (`http://www.fairtrade.org.uk/`) or organic milk and sugar? You can very quickly see that even something as seemingly simple as assessing students on the ability to make coffee can require quite a complex framework of skills against which a student can be judged. This is what we might refer to as the Coffee Maker's Competency Framework.

Competency frameworks are very often found in work-based learning. For example, workers in the UK's **National Health Service** (**NHS**) are typically required to demonstrate a basic level of competency defined in the Core Skills Training Framework (`http://www.skillsforhealth.org.uk/services/item/146-core-skills-training-frame work`). Clearly having a competent (or otherwise) healthcare worker could potentially be a matter of life or death, and this does make the Coffee Maker's Competency Framework seem rather trivial, but the principle is the same.

More recent versions of Moodle allow us to create competency based frameworks--see `https://docs.moodle.org/31/en/Competencies` for details. If we need to import competency frameworks into Moodle from an external source (for example, the Core Skills Training Framework mentioned earlier) then this can be achieved through developing a plugin. Check out the Moodle plugins directory for third-party competency framework plugins (`https://moodle.org/plugins/index.php?q=competency%20framework`). Fortunately, there is an API that allows us to manage competencies and the evidence to support them--see `https://docs.moodle.org/dev/Competency_API` for details.

Plugins to support site configuration--that is, of the type that would be used by site administrators, such as a plugin to import learner competencies--are to be found under `admin/tool`:

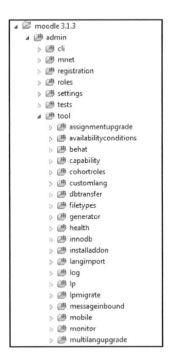

Having now got to grips with how we might develop custom plugins to manage users, let's take a look at how we can begin to manage the spaces in which learning takes place: courses. Managing courses is the subject of the next section.

Managing courses

Moodle courses are where learning takes place, and in order to ensure Moodle is as flexible a learning tool as possible, the Moodle platform has been designed to allow developers to provide as much course design flexibility as possible through the plugin system. We start this section by investigating how plugins might be used to alter the standard Moodle course layout.

Course layout

Moodle comes supplied with four standard course layouts:

- Weekly
- Topics
- Social
- Single activity

The course format is specified from the **Course format** page:

For example, setting a course to a `Topics` format containing five sections will configure a course to display three columns: a central column where teaching interactions can be added, with two columns to the left and right that contain blocks of supporting content.

The code for these four formats is to be found under `\course\format`, as in the following screenshot taken from Eclipse:

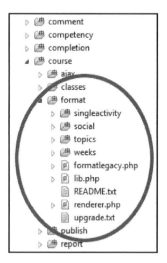

Any new `course` format we create will need to be included in this folder. Let's take a look at the structure of the `topics` format plugin in Eclipse:

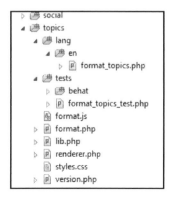

The folder structure of a course format plugin is rather more simple than an enrolment plugin. They both share a `lang` and a `tests` folder. We will be working together to develop a custom course layout in `Chapter 4`, *Course Management*.

Course content

In this section, we consider the types of interaction that an **instructional designer** (ID) might want the learner to engage in. Developing new learner interactions is described in much more detail in `Chapter 5`, *Creative Teaching - Developing Custom Resources and Activities*. In the meantime, let us look at the types of interaction Moodle supports out of the box and how to select the correct type of interaction based on the requirements presented to us by the ID.

Moodle supports two basic types of learner interaction: *resources* and *activities*. Let's start by looking at resources.

Resources

A Moodle resource plugin transmits information to the learner--it expects nothing in return. A resource plugin expects the learner to be passive. Obvious examples of resources are text to read, videos to watch, and audio to listen to. That is not to say that the resource won't form the basis of some form of interaction outside of Moodle, but we certainly don't expect any aspect of that interaction to be captured in Moodle.

Does the ID want to present information to their learners and not be concerned about capturing any learner interaction in Moodle? If so, then we should be considering developing a new resource plugin.

Activities

Compared to a resource, an activity expects some form of learner interaction - this is Moodle in receive mode. This could be an obvious example, such as a quiz where the learner will type in a response for Moodle to mark, or it could be a forum where social constructionist learning takes place.

Does the ID want to capture input from the student? If so, then it's a new activity plugin that we need to develop.

Note that there are subsets of plugins that apply to different interaction types. In the rest of this section, we consider just two of these plugin types: quiz plugins and assignment plugins. These are the two most common types of learner interaction to be queried by an instructional designer.

Quiz plugins

A Moodle quiz activity comes with a set of standard question types (see `https://docs.moodle.org/31/en/Question_types` for details). These question types are themselves plugins, and if our ID identifies a need for a different type of quiz question behavior, then there is the opportunity for this to be developed.

The code for the question plugins is found in the `question/type` folder:

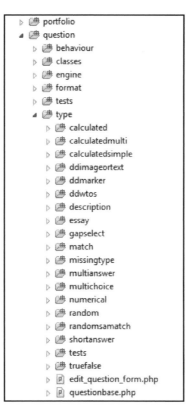

Again, it is worth taking a look at the Moodle plugins directory for third-party quiz question types at `https://moodle.org/plugins/browse.php?list=category&id=29`.

Assignment plugins

There are two types of assignment plugin:

- Assignment submissions
- Assignment feedback

See `https://moodle.org/plugins/browse.php?list=category&id=12` for details and for the lists of available plugins. Note that also listed on this page are assignment types. **Assignment types** plugins are for Moodle 2.2 and earlier.

If our IDs specify a non-standard way for learners to hand in/upload work to Moodle, then we would do well to check out the available third-party assignment submission types in the plugins directory at `https://moodle.org/plugins/browse.php?list=category&id=42`.

Where to find course interaction plugins

The plugins for both resources and activities are found in the `mod` folder, and any new course interaction plugins we create will be installed here:

Other important course plugin types

Moodle resource and activity plugins are an obvious type of teaching-related plugin. There are others that can have a big influence on teaching (again, it's worth taking a look at the Moodle plugins directory at `https://moodle.org/plugins/` and checking out the **Plugin type** dropdown menu). In this section, we will pick on one obvious and two less obvious plugin types--but still two that are well worth taking a look at. We start with course blocks.

Blocks

Course blocks appear on course pages, typically down the left and/or right of the main content, and provide a region where pretty much anything (that will fit) can be displayed to the learner. This could be the latest news items, or a list of the library books that you currently have on loan, or some suggested links, or the top five most recent posts from a particular Twitter feed. You will find the standard block plugins under `blocks`:

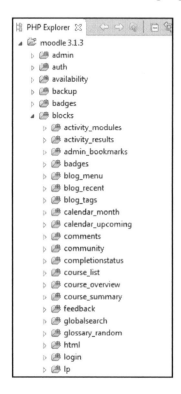

Given that blocks can be considered a key component of the layout of a course, we will revisit blocks--and go on to develop one--in `Chapter 4`, *Course Management*.

Editor plugins

Another important type of plugin to consider is text editor plugins. The text editor built into Moodle is called **Atto** (which replaced the earlier TinyMCE editor) and this is also extensible through installable plugins. Take a look in the Moodle plugin directory for supported Atto plugins, for example, `https://moodle.org/plugins/browse.php?list=category&id=53`.

For example, two very common requirements for secondary teaching are the ability to edit and copy chemical and mathematical symbols into the Moodle text editor. There are, by way of example, two editor plugins that can achieve this: check out `https://moodle.org/plugins/atto_chemistry` and `https://moodle.org/plugins/atto_mathslate`. Both of these plugins create text in a special format that requires filter plugins to convert the text into a form that's more meaningful. Let's look at filter plugins next.

Text filters

For more information on text filters, take a look at the Moodle documentation at `https://docs.moodle.org/dev/Filters`. The idea of a filter is that it can transform Moodle text before it is outputted to the screen. For example, text filters are used to transform the code generated by the chemistry and mathematical symbol editor plugins described in the previous section into the actual symbols displayed to the user, or replace a link to a video with an embedded video player.

It is worth noting that text filters are one of the easiest types of plugin to create. It is also worth noting that text filters can cause a big performance hit if we aren't careful with the way they are implemented. Text filters will process every bit of text displayed on the screen through the `format_text()` function (see `https://docs.moodle.org/dev/Output_functions#format_text.28.29`), so it makes sense to implement some form of caching if, for example, your filter is having to access the database or generate an image. We talk more about caching later in this chapter.

Reporting and analytics

Once students have been introduced onto the platform and have started to learn, we need to be able to report on, among other things, the activities students have been undertaking. Luckily, Moodle also takes a modular approach to report development. Both course and site administrator report scripts are to be found in the `report` folder:

Take a look in the documentation at `https://docs.moodle.org/dev/Reports` for details on the general structure of reports. Whenever you are querying the database, it is vital to remember the following:

- Use the data manipulation API (`https://docs.moodle.org/dev/Data_manipulation_API`), accessible through the global `$DB` object.
- Don't overload the database with complex queries.

We will be learning how to create custom reports in `Chapter 9`, *Moodle Analytics*.

Look and feel

Each plugin can be provided with its own /styles.css script to customise that plugin's look and feel. Over and above that, Moodle provides a flexible plugin-based theming framework--check out the Moodle directory at https://docs.moodle.org/dev/Themes. A new Moodle theme is possibly one of the more complicated plugin types you might need to develop. Go to Eclipse and navigate the PHP Explorer to the theme folder:

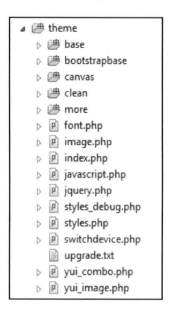

The trick to developing a new Moodle theme is to take a pre-existing theme and modify it to your requirements. Take a look in the Moodle plugins directory (https://moodle.org/plugins/browse.php?list=category&id=3) for third-party themes.

Let's take a look at the general structure of a Moodle theme plugin. In Eclipse, open the `theme/canvas` folder:

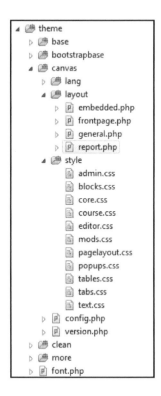

In the previous screenshot, you will see two folders that have been expanded: `layout` and `style`. Double-click on the `config.php` file to look at the structure. The code comments in `config.php` are self-explanatory. Particular attention needs to be paid to which style sheets and which layouts are loaded in which contexts. For example, let's take a look at the theme layouts:

```
/////////////////////////////////////////////////
// An array of stylesheets not to inherit from the
// themes parents
/////////////////////////////////////////////////

$THEME->layouts = array(
    'base' => array(
        'file' => 'general.php',
        'regions' => array('side-pre', 'side-post'),
        'defaultregion' => 'side-pre',
    ),
    'standard' => array(
        'file' => 'general.php',
        'regions' => array('side-pre', 'side-post'),
        'defaultregion' => 'side-pre',
    ),
    'course' => array(
        'file' => 'general.php',
        'regions' => array('side-pre', 'side-post'),
        'defaultregion' => 'side-pre'
    ),
```

The entry for "course" specifies that the structure of a course page will be created using the `general.php` file. Take a look at `https://docs.moodle.org/dev/Themes_overview#Layout_files` for more information.

Let's open the `general.php` file now and take a look inside. Essentially, you will see the page header, page content, and finally the footer being sent to the output as a mixture of HTML and echoed PHP. Change the page structure specified in this file and you change the page structure for the page types specified by the `$THEME->layouts` array.

We will be investigating the development of Moodle themes much more fully in `Chapter 8`, *Creating a New Skin*.

Other major plugin types

All major plugin types are described in the Moodle documentation at `https://docs.moodle.org/dev/Plugin_types`. For completeness, they are listed here:

Plugin type	Description
Activity modules	Activity modules are essential types of plugin in Moodle as they provide activities in courses. For example: Forum, Quiz, and Assignment.
Antivirus plugins	Antivirus scanner plugins provide functionality for scanning user uploaded files using third-party virus scanning tools in Moodle. For example: ClamAV.

Assignment submission plugins	Different forms of assignment submissions.
Assignment feedback plugins	Different forms of assignment feedback.
Book tools	Small information displays or tools that can be moved around pages.
Database fields	Different types of data that may be added to the database activity module.
Database pre-sets	Predefined templates for the database activity module.
LTI sources	LTI providers can be added to external tools easily through the external tools interface see the documentation on external tools. This type of plugin is specific to LTI providers that need a plugin that can register custom handlers to process LTI messages.
File converters	Allow conversion between different types of user-submitted file, such as from .doc to PDF.
LTI services	Allows the implementation of LTI services as described by the IMS LTI specification.
Quiz reports	Display and analyze the results of quizzes, or just plug miscellaneous behavior into the quiz module.
Quiz access rules	Add conditions to when or where quizzes can be attempted; for example, only from some IP addresses, or only when the student enters a password.
SCORM reports	Analysis of SCORM attempts.
Workshop grading strategies	Define the type of grading form and implement the calculation of the grade for submission in the workshop module.
Workshop allocation methods	Define how submissions are assigned for assessment in the workshop module.
Workshop evaluation methods	Implement the calculation of the grade for assessment (grading grade) in the workshop module.
Question types	Different types of question (such as multiple choice, drag-and-drop) that can be used in quizzes and other activities.

Question behaviors	Control how students interact with questions during an attempt.
Question import/export formats	Import and export question definitions to/from the question bank.
Text filters	Automatically convert, highlight, and transmogrify text posted into Moodle.
Editors	Alternative text editors for editing content.
Atto editor plugins	Extra functionality for the Atto text editor.
Enrolment plugins	Ways to control who is enrolled in courses.
Authentication plugins	Allows connection to external sources of authentication.
Admin tools	Provides utility scripts that are useful for various site administration and maintenance tasks.
Log stores	Event logs storage backends.
Availability conditions	Conditions to restrict user access to activities and sections.
Calendar types	Defines how dates are displayed throughout Moodle.
Messaging consumers	Represent various targets where messages and notifications can be sent to (such as email, SMS, Jabber/XMPP).
Course formats	Different ways of laying out the activities and blocks in a course.
Data formats	Formats for data exporting and downloading.
User profile fields	Add new types of data to user profiles.
Reports	Provides useful views of data in a Moodle site--typically for admins and teachers.
Gradebook export	Export grades in various formats.
Gradebook import	Import grades in various formats.
Gradebook reports	Display/edit grades in various layouts and reports.
Advanced grading methods	Interfaces for actually performing grading in activity modules (such as rubrics).
Webservice protocols	Define new protocols for web service communication (such as SOAP, XML-RPC, JSON, REST).

Repository plugins	Connect to external sources of files to use in Moodle.
Portfolio plugins	Connect external portfolio services as destinations for users to store Moodle content.
Search engines	Search engine backends to index Moodle's contents.
Media players	Pluggable media players.
Plagiarism plugins	Define external services to process submitted files and content.
Cache store	Cache storage backends.
Cache locks	Cache lock implementations.
Themes	Change the look of Moodle by changing the HTML and the CSS.
Local plugins	Generic plugins for local customizations.

This is clearly a long list, and this book isn't going to be able to delve into the details of every one. Again, if you are faced with a seemingly complex Moodle customization, then the first step is to determine which plugin type will best provide the change to Moodle you require.

What cannot be done with plugins?

Having explored what can be done with plugins, it is worth mentioning what can't be done. Moodle plugins have to fit into a general framework, namely one where users are associated with courses. Note that this means Moodle is course-centric and not user-centric. This can mean that some user-centric plugin types, such as user competencies, can seem an awkward fit (especially when attempting to collate user data from across a course-centric relational database--but that is discussed in more detail in Chapter 9, *Moodle Analytics*). Likewise, creating an individualised learner dashboard, which learners will see when they first log in, can be achieved (and is indeed the subject of Chapter 7, *Creating a Dashboard - Developing a Learner Homepage*), but it may seem as though you are jumping through hoops at first. If you are worried that a particular development cannot be achieved by anything other than a core code change then ask yourself this: is what I am being asked to develop against the grain of Moodle's core social constructivist principles? If so then it is likely that the wrong platform has been selected and a step back needs to be taken. If not, take a good look at plugin types listed at https://docs.moodle.org/dev/Plugin_types and choose which is the best to develop to achieve the desired feature.

Summary

In this chapter, we investigated the main plugin types: those dealing with users and how they access the platform and also plugins managing learning and the interactions learners experience in a course. We also looked at the less obvious plugin types, such as text filters and text editor plugins. Remember that the "M" in Moodle stands for *modular*: if there is an adaption or new feature you need then there is probably a plugin available--or one we can develop--to implement it.

In the next chapter, we study Moodle's internal APIs in more detail, experimenting with the main interfaces as we begin to develop our Resilience platform. We start with accessing data through the Data manipulation API.

3
Internal Interfaces

In the previous chapter, we investigated the types of plugin that we can develop to enhance the Moodle platform. But how does a plugin talk to Moodle? In Chapter 1, *Getting to Grips with the Moodle 3 Architecture*, we introduced a few of the Moodle **Application Programming Interfaces** (**APIs**), specifically discussing why as developers we should use the data manipulation API to talk to the Moodle database rather than manipulating the database directly.

We begin this chapter by taking up the local plugin we developed in Chapter 1, *Getting to Grips with the Moodle 3 Architecture* and begin to enhance it to do some more interesting things--for example, it would be more useful if we can configure the languages it displays and it might be useful if we can specify the order in which the languages are displayed.

By the end of this chapter, you will have:

- A good appreciation of the different types of APIs available
- Worked with the main presentation APIs--form, and output renderers
- Gained a deeper understanding of the architecture of a Moodle plugin

Let's get started by taking our dual language plugin and begin to consider adding some useful configuration options.

Adding configuration settings

As it currently stands, our dual language plugin displays UK English on the left and simplified Chinese Mandarin on the right:

Once our local plugin is installed, this behavior is both impossible to configure and impossible to turn off. The following user story has been submitted:

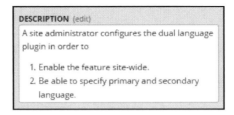

This, in itself, seems quite a straightforward story. However, we also need to remember that not all languages read from left to right, so we also need to include some means of configuring the reading order. So, with that understanding in mind and before we begin to cut any code, it will be best to agree with the client exactly what the configuration screen is going to look like. For that we will need to start wireframing.

Wireframing

Everyone has an opinion on software user interfaces. I am sure, like me, you have been sat in many long meetings with clients who seem very keen to discuss the color of a button without applying very much thought to what the button should actually do when you press it. Wireframing is the best means of agreeing with your client exactly what a Moodle web page is going to look like without suffering the pain of having to run through iterations of changes to code. There are many wireframing tools available (as a quick Internet search will reveal) but the wireframing tool I am going to use is an often-overlooked technology for sketching out initial designs, which I'm sure you will be familiar with: a pencil and a piece of paper.

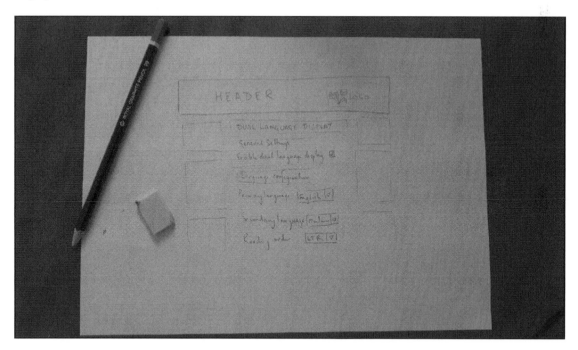

Once we are happy with this, we can then mock this up in a wireframing tool to share with the client:

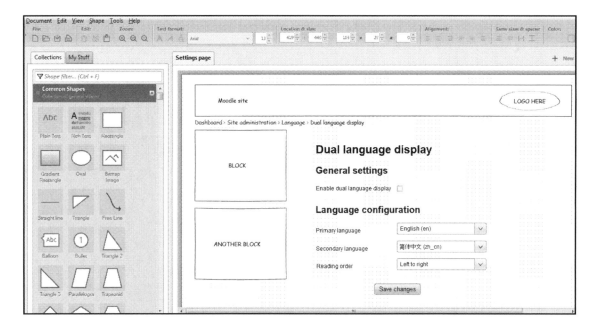

Note that if you are working remotely then being able to share screens to talk through ideas can be incredibly effective. One collaborative approach is to use an online whiteboard such as Scribblar (see `https://scribblar.com/` for details).

Moodle application layers

In terms of application architecture, Moodle can be thought of as having three layers--diagrammatically looking rather like a layer cake:

By shine Oa (originally posted to Flickr as wedding cake) [CC BY 2.0 (`http://creativecommons.org/licenses/by/2.0`)], via Wikimedia Commons

At the top is the *presentation layer*--this displays output to the user but also accepts data from users through HTML forms. Next is the business layer and, beneath that, the data layer. The *data layer* is relatively easy to understand: it is where user data is maintained, where quiz questions would be stored, where grades are recorded, and so on. The business layer is where the information from the data layer is processed ready to be passed up to the presentation layer--for example, quiz questions are formed into a quiz. The business layer is also responsible for taking data from the presentation layer and processing this ready for storage by the data layer--for example, the final grade from a quiz.

In the previous section, we have been considering what the user will see (the presentation layer). At the core of Moodle sits the application data--the contents of the Moodle database. Sat between these three layers (including between the presentation layer and the user)--and the means by which application layers talk to each other--are the APIs.

Storing configuration data

Having agreed with the client what the configuration screen is going to look like, we need to decide what information we need to store in the database to support these options. Our dual language plugin is a site administration plugin and so let's use the Admin settings API to store and retrieve the plugin's configuration data--see

`https://docs.moodle.org/dev/Admin_settings`.

Because they are meant for functionality that doesn't quite fit the typical categories of a plugin, local plugins are a good place to gain an understanding of the interaction between frontend and backend APIs, as we are allowed to be flexible with the APIs we can experiment with.

In Eclipse, under /local/duallang, create a new file called settings.php:

And now copy in the following code:

```php
<?php
// This file is part of Moodle - http://moodle.org/
//
// Moodle is free software: you can redistribute it and/or modify
// it under the terms of the GNU General Public License as published by
// the Free Software Foundation, either version 3 of the License, or
// (at your option) any later version.
//
// Moodle is distributed in the hope that it will be useful,
// but WITHOUT ANY WARRANTY; without even the implied warranty of
// MERCHANTABILITY or FITNESS FOR A PARTICULAR PURPOSE.  See the
// GNU General Public License for more details.
//
// You should have received a copy of the GNU General Public License
// along with Moodle.  If not, see <http://www.gnu.org/licenses/>.
/**
 * Local plugin "duallang" - Settings
 *
 * @package    local_duallang
 * @copyright  2016 Ian Wild
 * @license    http://www.gnu.org/copyleft/gpl.html GNU GPL v3 or later
 */
defined('MOODLE_INTERNAL') || die();

if ($hassiteconfig)
{
     // Configuration settings to go here
}
```

Before moving on, let's take a brief look at the structure of this script.

It starts with the standard Moodle copyright heading, which contains a shortened version of Moodle's terms and conditions. Then comes a second set of comments bracketed with /** ... **/, which are DocBlock standard comments--if you have not encountered these before, then see `https://en.wikipedia.org/wiki/PHPDoc#DocBlock` for more details.

Then you will see a `defined('MOODLE_INTERNAL')` or die statement that ensures this script cannot be run outside of Moodle.

Finally, we have a check to determine if the current user has the capability of changing site configuration settings--as only site administrators should have the ability to alter the language display settings. In Eclipse, try highlighting the variable name, then right clicking, and finally selecting **Open Declaration** from the pop-up context menu. The variable `$hassiteconfig` is declared in `index.php`.

Now we need to add in some code to actually set the configuration data and for that we will use a set of functions that provide the means to manage the **Site administration** settings tree in the **Administration** block. The finished configuration screen, accessed through a new menu option under **Language** in the administration tree, is shown in the following screenshot:

We will learn how to code this page in the next section.

Creating an admin settings page

Let us start by creating a new instance of the `admin_settingpage` class. We will call this new instance `$settings`. Add the following code to the `if ($hassiteconfig)` clause:

```
$settings = new admin_settingpage('local_duallang',
get_string('local_duallang', 'local_duallang'));
```

We should note at this stage that I am not intending to delve too deeply into function parameters as they are very well described in Moodle's source code. For example, in Eclipse highlight the text **admin_settingpage**, right-click with the mouse, and from the pop-up context menu, click on **Open Declaration**. Eclipse navigates you to the class constructor--which is preceded by a detailed DocBlock:

```
/**
 * see admin_settingpage for details of this function
 *
 * @param string $name The internal name for this external page.
Must
 *  be unique amongst ALL part_of_admin_tree objects.
 * @param string $visiblename The displayed name for this external
 * page. Usually obtained through get_string().
 * @param mixed $req_capability The role capability/permission a
user
 * must have to access this external page. Defaults to
 * 'moodle/site:config'.
 * @param boolean $hidden Is this external page hidden in admin
tree
 * block? Default false.
 * @param stdClass $context The context the page relates to. Not
sure
 * what happens if you specify something other than system or front
 * page. Defaults to system.
 */
public function __construct($name, $visiblename,
                           $req_capability='moodle/site:config',
                           $hidden=false, $context=NULL)
{
     $this->settings     = new stdClass();
     $this->name         = $name;
     $this->visiblename  = $visiblename;
       if (is_array($req_capability))
       {
           $this->req_capability = $req_capability;
       }
       else
       {
```

```
        $this->req_capability = array($req_capability);
    }
    $this->hidden        = $hidden;
    $this->context       = $context;
}
```

Having added code to create a settings page, we can use the `admin_settingpage add()` method to include specific settings. Add the following code into the `if` clause:

```
$settings->add(new
admin_setting_configcheckbox('local_duallang/enabled',
get_string('enableduallangs', 'local_duallang')));
$languages = get_string_manager()->get_list_of_translations();
$currentlang = current_language();
$settings->add(new
admin_setting_configselect('local_duallang/primarylanguage',
get_string('primarylang', 'local_duallang'),
get_string('primarylang_desc', 'local_duallang'), $currentlang,
$languages));
$settings->add(new
admin_setting_configselect('local_duallang/secondarylanguage',
get_string('secondarylang', 'local_duallang'),
get_string('secondarylang_desc', 'local_duallang'), $currentlang,
$languages));
$readingorder = array('LTR' => get_string('lefttoright', 'local_duallang'),
'RTL' => get_string('righttoleft', 'local_duallang'));
$settings->add(new
admin_setting_configselect('local_duallang/readingorder',
get_string('readingorder', 'local_duallang'),
get_string('readingorder_desc', 'local_duallang'), 'LTR', $readingorder));
```

Firstly, note that each admin setting type is declared using its own class. For example, checkboxes are constructed by declaring a new instance of the `admin_setting_configcheckbox` class and the drop-down combo boxes through declaring instances of the `admin_setting_configselect` class.

Secondly, take a look at the code that returns an array of installed language packs:

```
$languages = get_string_manager()->get_list_of_translations();
```

The array `$languages` is, in fact, returned by the String API, the interface we are overriding in order to display two languages on the screen.

The new admin settings page will be displayed when the language manager plugin is initially installed:

You can see in this code that there are also multiple calls to the `get_string()` function. These language strings will be loaded from the relevant language file in our plugin's `lang` folder. Let's include the necessary language strings using Eclipse:

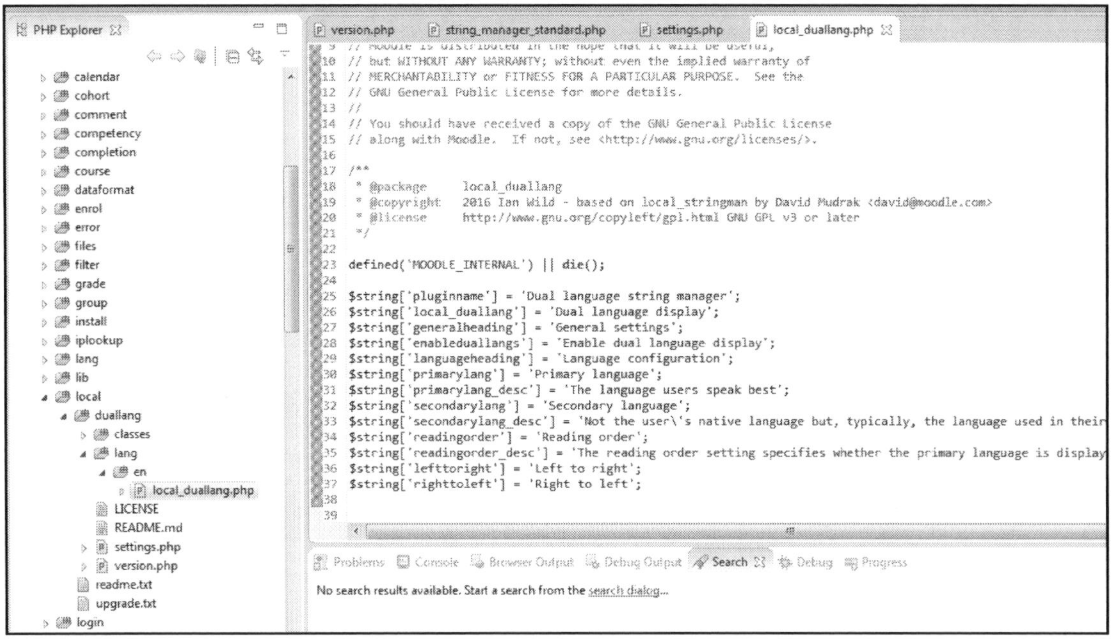

As previously, add the following lines to the relevant `local_duallang.php` file:

```
$string['local_duallang'] = 'Dual language display';
$string['generalheading'] = 'General settings';
$string['enableduallangs'] = 'Enable dual language display';
$string['languageheading'] = 'Language configuration';
$string['primarylang'] = 'Primary language';
$string['primarylang_desc'] = 'The language users speak best';
$string['secondarylang'] = 'Secondary language';
$string['secondarylang_desc'] = 'Not the user\'s native language but,
typically, the language used in their locale';
$string['readingorder'] = 'Reading order';
$string['readingorder_desc'] = 'The reading order setting specifies whether
the primary language is displayed to the left or the right of the secondary
language';
$string['lefttoright'] = 'Left to right';
$string['righttoleft'] = 'Right to left';
```

Finally, and in order to match the agreed wireframe, we need to include section headers (the language strings for these headers have already been specified). Headers are constructed using the `admin_setting_heading` class. For example:

```
$settings->add(new admin_setting_heading('local_duallang/generalheading',
get_string('generalheading', 'local_duallang'), ''));
```

After adding two extra section headers, and some general code tidying, the completed `if` clause now looks as follows:

```
if ($hassiteconfig)
{
    // New settings page
    $settings = new admin_settingpage('local_duallang',
                get_string('local_duallang', 'local_duallang'));
    $settings->add(new
                admin_setting_heading('local_duallang/generalheading',
                get_string('generalheading', 'local_duallang'), ''));
    $settings->add(new
                admin_setting_configcheckbox('local_duallang/enabled',
                get_string('enableduallangs', 'local_duallang')));
    $settings->add(new
                admin_setting_heading('local_duallang/languageheading',
                get_string('languageheading', 'local_duallang'), ''));

    // obtain list of available languages from the language manager
    $languages = get_string_manager()->get_list_of_translations();
    $currentlang = current_language();

    // Primary language
    $settings->add(new
                admin_setting_configselect('local_duallang/
                primarylanguage', get_string('primarylang',
                'local_duallang'), get_string('primarylang_desc',
                'local_duallang'), $currentlang, $languages));
    // Secondary language
    $settings->add(new
                admin_setting_configselect('local_duallang/
                secondarylanguage', get_string('secondarylang',
                'local_duallang'), get_string('secondarylang_desc',
                'local_duallang'), $currentlang, $languages));

    // Reading order
    $readingorder = array('LTR' => get_string('lefttoright',
                    'local_duallang'), 'RTL' =>
                    get_string('righttoleft', 'local_duallang'));
    $settings->add(new
            admin_setting_configselect('local_duallang/readingorder',
            get_string('readingorder', 'local_duallang'),
            get_string('readingorder_desc', 'local_duallang'), 'LTR',
            $readingorder));

    // Add settings page to administration tree
    $ADMIN->add('language', $settings);
}
```

Finally, the settings page is added to the administration tree through the global $ADMIN object:

```
$ADMIN->add('language', $settings);
```

Here is how it will look in the tree:

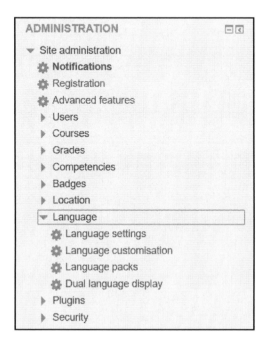

Again take a look at the Admin API documentation, specifically
`https://docs.moodle.org/dev/Admin_settings#How_the_tree_is_built`, for details on the $ADMIN object.

To force the loading of the updated dual language plugin--and by doing so enabling the new settings page--we can simply change the version number in `version.php`. Moodle will update the relevant administrator configuration settings.

Updating the get_string() function

We will now need to update our overridden get_string() function (contained in \local\duallang\classes\duallang_string_manager) to utilize these new settings. Here is the modified code:

```
public function get_string($identifier, $component = '', $a = null, $lang = null)
{
    $string = ''; // returns an empty string by default
    if(get_config('local_duallang', 'enabled'))
    {
        $order = get_config('local_duallang', 'readingorder');
        $primarylang = parent::get_string($identifier, $component,
        $a, get_config('local_duallang', 'primarylanguage'));
        $secondarylang = parent::get_string($identifier,
        $component, $a, get_config('local_duallang',
        'secondarylanguage'));
        // ordering is only left to right or right to left so just
        check the first letter of the string
        if($order[0] == 'L')
        {
            $string = $primarylang . ' (' . $secondarylang . ')';
        }
        else
        {
            $string = '(' . $secondarylang . ') ' . $primarylang;
        }
    }
    else
    {
        $string = parent::get_string($identifier, $component, $a,
        $lang);
    }
    return $string;
}
```

See how the relevant configuration setting is loaded using the get_config() function. For example, an administration setting named local_duallang/primarylanguage is accessed by calling get_config('local_duallang', 'primarylanguage').

Plugin language strings

Now we will need to translate the plugin's own language strings. For example, in order to support the Romanian language, we will need to add a new directory called `ro` to `\local\duallang\lang`:

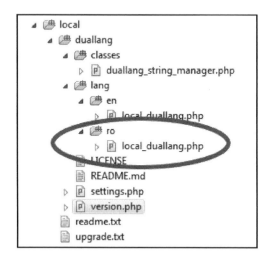

Note that you will need to increment the plugin's version number before the new language strings are loaded:

```
/**
 * @package     local_duallang
 * @copyright   2016 Ian Wild - based on local_stringman by David Mudrak <david@moodle.com>
 * @license     http://www.gnu.org/copyleft/gpl.html GNU GPL v3 or later
 */

defined('MOODLE_INTERNAL') || die();

$plugin->component = 'local_duallang';
$plugin->release = 'alpha1';
$plugin->version = 2016122101;
$plugin->requires = 2015030900;
$plugin->maturity = MATURITY_ALPHA;
$plugin->dependencies = array();
```

System APIs

Having built a basic administration plugin in the first half of this chapter, in the next we will be looking at a simple Moodle course plugin and, by doing so, investigate five more basic internal programming interfaces:

- Events API
- File Storage API
- Cache API
- Form API
- Output API

The plugin we will be investigating in this chapter (and will continue to develop in Chapter 5, *Creative Teaching - Developing Custom Resources and Activities*) is an enhanced multiple choice interaction, based on the choice activity (see https://docs.moodle.org/31/en/Choice_activity).

Our **instructional design (ID)** colleagues who have been developing the Organizational Resilience Training Program have been working on **multiple-choice questions (MCQs)** that contain images in the distractors and key. The following is an extract from the storyboard:

72	Outcome h			
73	be familiar with the different type of fire extinguishers, state their use and identify the safety precautions associated with their use			
74	Outcome 6	Questions	Feedback for correct answers	Feedback for incorrect answers
75	Question 1	Which types of fire extinguisher should you use on live electrical equipment?(Select TWO of the following options) 2#4 Water Dry chemical/powder Foam CO2	Correct answer. The types of fire extinguisher to be used on live electrical equipment are dry chemical/powder and CO2	Incorrect answer. The types of fire extinguisher to be used on live electrical equipment are dry chemical/powder and CO2. Water and foam are conductors of electricity and could result in the user being electrocuted.

This question is to be used as part of a face-to-face classroom teaching exercise. An image of each type of fire extinguisher is to be included in the question. However, Moodle's choice activity doesn't support including images in the choices:

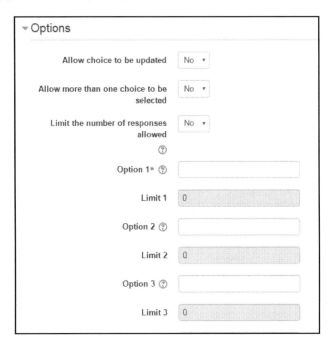

To enable the inclusion of images in the options, we will need to develop a new type of choice activity. We will be exploring the underlying operation of course plugins in the next chapter but, by way of introduction, let's begin the work now by starting to create a new `enhancedchoice` activity.

In Eclipse, make a copy of the choice plugin code and rename it `enhancedchoice`:

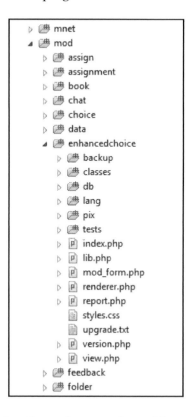

We then need to begin refactoring the code--meaning taking pre-existing code and modifying it for our purposes. We start with, where necessary, replacing any occurrence of `choice` with the word `enhancedchoice`. This is where the use of an integrated development environment comes into its own, especially given the number of scripts that make up this particular, relatively straightforward, plugin.

Let's start with the \classes folder (and the \event and \search folders contained therein). In each of the scripts, wherever you see choice in the code then replace this with enhancedchoice. The Eclipse **Find/Replace--Replace/Find** function makes this exercise straightforward:

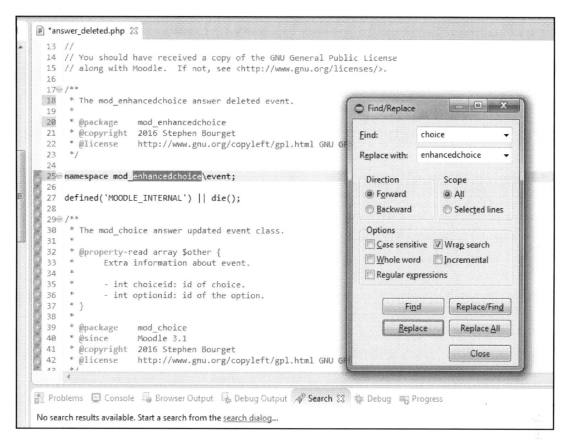

It is important that when users interact with our new enhanced choice activity, their interactions are logged. This might be for obvious auditing purposes, or for determining where an error might lie if something goes wrong with our code during testing or in a production environment. To this end, let's take a look at the *Events API*, which is the subject of the next section.

Events API

In the \events folder are scripts that will allow our new plugin to support for the Moodle events system: in this case, for recording user interactions to the Moodle log. Take a look at the Moodle documentation at https://docs.moodle.org/dev/Event_2. These scripts are the event dispatchers, with each dispatcher in a separate file (as they are auto loaded by Moodle on the fly). Event dispatchers are essentially classes that are all extensions of the \core\event\base class. For example, when a choice is submitted the answerupdated event is triggered. Here is the code in \lib.php that creates and triggers this event:

```php
    // Now record completed event.
  if (isset($answerupdated))
    {
        $eventdata = array();
        $eventdata['context'] = $context;
        $eventdata['objectid'] = $choice->id;
        $eventdata['userid'] = $userid;
        $eventdata['courseid'] = $course->id;
        $eventdata['other'] = array();
        $eventdata['other']['choiceid'] = $choice->id;

        if ($answerupdated)
        {
            $eventdata['other']['optionid'] = $formanswer;
            $event = \mod_choice\event\answer_updated
                    ::create($eventdata);
        }
        else
        {
            $eventdata['other']['optionid'] = $formanswers;
            $event = \mod_choice\event\answer_submitted
                    ::create($eventdata);
        }
        $event->add_record_snapshot('course', $course);
        $event->add_record_snapshot('course_modules', $cm);
        $event->add_record_snapshot('choice', $choice);
        foreach ($answersnapshots as $record)
        {
            $event->add_record_snapshot('choice_answers', $record);
        }
        $event->trigger();
    }
```

Events can be captured by an event sink and Moodle is told about event sink handler functions by the `events.php` script contained in the `\db` folder. Note that the enhanced choice activity doesn't need to capture events.

Let us next refactor the `\db` folder.

Plugin data and services

Roles and permissions are specified through the `access.php` script. These permissions are loaded when the plugin is installed or updated. Again, this file can be refactored easily using Eclipse.

Next to refactor is `log.php`. See `https://docs.moodle.org/dev/Logging_API#Mod.2F.2A.2Fdb.2Flog.php_Files` for details on the structure of this file. This file specifies how logging information should be displayed to the end user.

Then there is the file `services.php`. This script will expose web service functions from our plugin--which will be needed for the Moodle Mobile app.

 We will be developing our own Web Service API in `Chapter 9`, *Moodle Analytics*.

As this is essentially a brand new plugin, the code in `upgrade.php` can be replaced with the following:

```
function xmldb_enhancedchoice_upgrade($oldversion)
{
    // Moodle v2.9.0 release upgrade line.
    // Put any upgrade step following this.

    // Moodle v3.0.0 release upgrade line.
    // Put any upgrade step following this.

    // Moodle v3.1.0 release upgrade line.
    // Put any upgrade step following this.

    return true;
}
```

The final script to tackle is `install.xml`. This file requires careful manipulation as it defines the structure of the database table and is used to create it at installation time. Aside from changing instances of `choice` to `enhancedchoice`, we also need to modify the table used to store the actual choices. Replace the XML for this table with the following (noting the addition of the `textformat` column):

```xml
<TABLE NAME="enhancedchoice_options" COMMENT="available options to choice"
PREVIOUS="enhancedchoice" NEXT="enhancedchoice_answers">
<FIELDS>
        <FIELD NAME="id" TYPE="int" LENGTH="10" NOTNULL="true"
        SEQUENCE="true" NEXT="choiceid"/>
        <FIELD NAME="choiceid" TYPE="int" LENGTH="10" NOTNULL="true"
        DEFAULT="0" SEQUENCE="false" PREVIOUS="id" NEXT="text"/>
        <FIELD NAME="text" TYPE="text" NOTNULL="false" SEQUENCE="false"
        PREVIOUS="choiceid" NEXT="textformat"/>
        <FIELD NAME="textformat" TYPE="int" LENGTH="4" NOTNULL="true"
        SEQUENCE="false" PREVIOUS="text" NEXT="maxanswers"
DEFAULT="0"></FIELD>
        <FIELD NAME="maxanswers" TYPE="int" LENGTH="10" NOTNULL="false"
        DEFAULT="0" SEQUENCE="false" PREVIOUS="textformat"
        NEXT="timemodified"/>
        <FIELD NAME="timemodified" TYPE="int" LENGTH="10" NOTNULL="true"
        DEFAULT="0" SEQUENCE="false" PREVIOUS="maxanswers"/>
</FIELDS>
<KEYS>
        <KEY NAME="primary" TYPE="primary" FIELDS="id" NEXT="choiceid"/>
        <KEY NAME="choiceid" TYPE="foreign" FIELDS="choiceid"
        REFTABLE="choice" REFFIELDS="id" PREVIOUS="primary"/>
</KEYS>
</TABLE>
```

This code is used to create a new database table to store any "enhanced" choices. Here is the table, once created, viewed in phpMyAdmin:

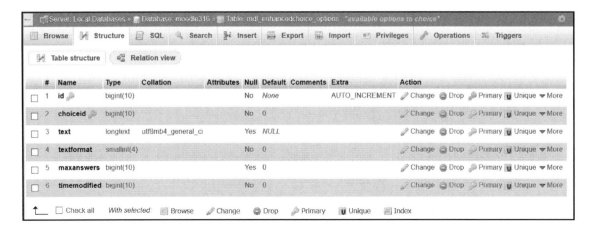

Form API

Having prepared the data layer, we now need to consider how to update the plugin configuration form. In Eclipse, open `\mod_form.php` and let's look at the declaration of `mod_choice_mod_form`. It extends `moodleform_mod`, the base class upon which all Moodle forms should be based (details are available at `https://docs.moodle.org/dev/Form_API`). Check out how Moodle creates repeated elements:

```
$repeatarray = array();
$repeatarray[] = $mform->createElement('header', '',
                   get_string('option','enhancedchoice').' {no}');
$repeatarray[] = $mform->createElement('editor', 'option',
                   get_string('option','enhancedchoice'), null,
                   array('maxfiles'=>EDITOR_UNLIMITED_FILES,
                   'noclean'=>true, 'context'=>$this->context));
$repeatarray[] = $mform->createElement('text', 'limit',
                   get_string('limit','enhancedchoice'));
$repeatarray[] = $mform->createElement('hidden', 'optionid', 0);

$menuoptions = array();
$menuoptions[0] = get_string('disable');
$menuoptions[1] = get_string('enable');
$mform->addElement('header', 'timerestricthdr', get_string('limit',
       'enhancedchoice'));
$mform->addElement('select', 'limitanswers', get_string('limitanswers',
       'enhancedchoice'), $menuoptions);
$mform->addHelpButton('limitanswers', 'limitanswers',
       'enhancedchoice');
    if ($this->_instance)
{
```

```
                $repeatno = $DB->count_records('enhancedchoice_options',
                array('choiceid'=>$this->_instance));
                $repeatno += 2;
        }
        else
        {
                $repeatno = 5;
        }

    $repeateloptions = array();
            $repeateloptions['limit']['default'] = 0;
            $repeateloptions['limit']['disabledif'] = array('limitanswers',
            'eq', 0);
            $repeateloptions['limit']['rule'] = 'numeric';
            $repeateloptions['option']['helpbutton'] =
            array('enhancedchoice_options', 'enhancedchoice');

            $mform->setType('optionid', PARAM_INT);

            $this->repeat_elements($repeatarray, $repeatno,
            $repeateloptions, 'option_repeats', 'option_add_fields', 3);
```

The change implemented here is to replace the line:

```
$repeatarray[] = $mform->createElement('text', 'option',
get_string('optionno', 'choice'));
with
$repeatarray[] = $mform->createElement('editor', 'option',
get_string('option','enhancedchoice'), null,
array('maxfiles'=>EDITOR_UNLIMITED_FILES, 'noclean'=>true,
'context'=>$this->context));
```

We are replacing a basic text input field with an HTML editor:

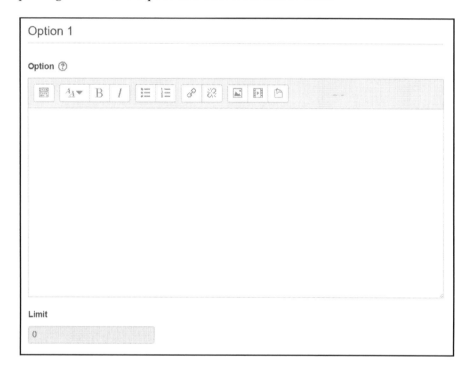

The type of HTML editor is itself a plugin--see
`https://moodle.org/plugins/browse.php?list=category&id=23` for available third-party
editor plugins. The reason for needing to change the input control from basic text to HTML
is to allow the inclusion of images. But where to store the images once a user has included
them in the text? The answer to this lies in the File Storage API.

File Storage API

A detailed guide on the use of the File Storage API in a Moodle form is provided in the
documentation at `https://docs.moodle.org/dev/Using_the_File_API_in_Moodle_forms`.
Essentially, any file (and in our case this will be an image) a user adds to the editor is given
a unique identifier and then stored as a draft file in the file storage area--which bit of the
storage area depends on the component type.

This process is handled in the call to `data_preprocessing()` as follows:

```
function data_preprocessing(&$default_values)
{
    global $DB;
    if (!empty($this->_instance) && ($options = $DB-
        >get_records_menu('choice_options',array('choiceid'=>$this-
        >_instance), 'id', 'id,text'))
        && ($options2 = $DB->get_records_menu('choice_options',
        array('choiceid'=>$this->_instance), 'id', 'id,maxanswers'))
        )
    {
    $choiceids=array_keys($options);
    $options=array_values($options);
    $options2=array_values($options2);

    $editoroptions = enhancedchoice_get_editor_options();

    $idx = 0;
        foreach (array_keys($options) as $key)
        {
            $draftid = file_get_submitted_draft_itemid
                        ('option['.$key.']');
            $defaulttext = file_prepare_draft_area($draftid,
            $this->context->id,
                        'mod_enhancedchoice',
                        'option',
                        !empty($choiceids[$key]) ? (int)
                        $choiceids[$key] : null, // Itemid.,
                        $editoroptions,
                        $options[$key]->text);
            $default_values['option['.$key.']']['text'] =
            $defaulttext;
            $default_values['option['.$key.']']['itemid'] =
            $draftid;
            $default_values['limit['.$key.']'] = $options2[$key];
            $default_values['optionid['.$key.']'] =
            $choiceids[$key];
            $idx++;
        }

    }
    if (empty($default_values['timeopen']))
    {
        $default_values['timerestrict'] = 0;
    }
    else
    {
```

```
                    $default_values['timerestrict'] = 1;
         }
    }
```

Check out the calls to `file_get_submitted_draft_itemid()` and
`file_prepare_draft_area()`, which handle loading files into the draft file area. Only
when a new instance of an enhanced choice is added to the course do we need to move the
files from the draft files area to the file storage area proper:

```
function enhancedchoice_add_instance($choice)
{
     global $DB;

     $choice->timemodified = time();

     if (empty($choice->timerestrict))
     {
          $choice->timeopen = 0;
          $choice->timeclose = 0;
     }

     //insert answers
     $choice->id = $DB->insert_record("enhancedchoice", $choice);
     $context = context_module::instance($choice->coursemodule);
     $editoroptions = enhancedchoice_get_editor_options();

     foreach ($choice->option as $key => $value)
     {
     if (isset($value) && $value['text'] <> '')
     {
          $value['text'] = trim($value['text']);
          $option = new stdClass();

          $option->text = $value['text'];
          $option->textformat = $value['format'];
          $option->choiceid = $choice->id;
          if (isset($choice->limit[$key]))
          {
              $option->maxanswers = $choice->limit[$key];
          }
          $option->timemodified = time();
          $option->id = $DB->insert_record("enhancedchoice_options",
          $option);
          $option->text = file_save_draft_area_files(
                          $value['itemid'],
                          $context->id,
                          'mod_enhancedchoice', 'option',
                          $option->id, $editoroptions,
```

```
                              $value['text']);
              $DB->set_field("enhancedchoice_options", "text", $option-
              >text, array('id' => $option->id));
              }
      }
      return $choice->id;
  }
```

Check out the `file_save_draft_area_files()` function, which actually restores the files in the correct area.

We will revisit the development of the enhanced choice plugin (covering much more detail) in `Chapter 5`, *Creative Teaching - Developing Custom Resources and Activities.*

Cache API

And, considering the possible adverse effects on application performance that we may experience when we start allowing users to add files to text, another important API we need to be considering is the *Cache API*--see `https://docs.moodle.org/dev/Cache_API`. A *cache* is a place to store data--especially data that is the result of some complex processing--so that it can be retrieved and served more quickly the next time it is requested. Moodle supports the concept of cache plugins and provides an API to access a cache in order to (potentially) free developers from the need to worry about how exactly data is in fact cached. So why cache data at all? A database is designed to manage the effective storing of data but if the data needs to be manipulated and subsequently shared between web pages or between users then rather than repeatedly reading and writing to and from the database, we can cache the data instead. There are three basic types of cache:

- **Application**: Application is for data that is shared by all users across the application
- **Session**: Session is for user-specific data that is stored in the PHP session
- **Request**: Request is only available to the user owning the page request and only alive until the end of the request

Output renderers

In the final section of this chapter, we briefly consider interfaces for outputting data to the browser. See `https://docs.moodle.org/dev/Output_renderers` for details on Moodle's rendering framework. Our new enhanced choice plugin will need to include a `renderer.php` script. This will contain the code needed to display the activity itself--not only the choices but also the results. The `renderer.php` file will contain a declaration of a new class based on `plugin_renderer_base`:

```
                              19    * Moodle renderer used to display special elements of the enhanced choice module
 ▷ 🗐 message                  20    *
 ▷ 🗐 mnet                     21    * @package    mod_enhancedchoice
 ▲ 🗐 mod                      22    * @copyright 2010 Rossiani Wijaya
    ▷ 🗐 assign                23    * @license   http://www.gnu.org/copyleft/gpl.html GNU GPL v3 or later
    ▷ 🗐 assignment            24    **/
    ▷ 🗐 book                  25   define ('DISPLAY_HORIZONTAL_LAYOUT', 0);
    ▷ 🗐 chat                  26   define ('DISPLAY_VERTICAL_LAYOUT', 1);
    ▷ 🗐 choice                27
    ▷ 🗐 data                  28   class mod_enahncedchoice_renderer extends plugin_renderer_base {
    ▲ 🗐 enhancedchoice        29
       ▷ 🗐 backup             30      /**
       ▷ 🗐 classes            31       * Returns HTML to display choices of option
       ▷ 🗐 db                 32       * @param object $options
       ▷ 🗐 lang               33       * @param int  $coursemoduleid
       ▷ 🗐 pix                34       * @param bool $vertical
       ▷ 🗐 tests              35       * @return string
       ▷ 📄 index.php          36       */
       ▷ 📄 lib.php            37      public function display_options($options, $coursemoduleid, $vertical = false, $multiple = false) {
       ▷ 📄 mod_form.php       38          $layoutclass = 'horizontal';
                              39          if ($vertical) {
                              40              $layoutclass = 'vertical';
                              41          }
```

We will be investigating--and developing--this code in much more detail in `Chapter 4`, *Course Management*.

Summary

In this chapter, we investigated core Moodle interfaces. In the first half, we enhanced the dual language local plugin we developed in `Chapter 1`, *Getting to Grips with the Moodle 3 Architecture* in order to allow a Moodle administrator to configure a primary and a secondary language and also to specify a reading order (either left to right or right to left). We saw how a new settings page can be built and added to the Site administration menu.

In the rest of the chapter, we refactored the "choice" activity into an "enhanced" choice activity--a new teaching interaction based on the "choice" activity but one that allows a teacher to include multimedia (specifically images in this example) in the choice options. Doing so allowed us to consider the internal APIs required to support plugins, such as the *Form API*, *Events API*, and the *File Storage API*. This work forms the introduction to `Chapter 5`, *Creative Teaching - Developing Custom Resources and Activities*, where we will continue to develop new teaching interactions. In the next chapter, we will be learning how to manage courses using plugins--starting with the course layouts.

4
Course Management

In Chapter 3, *Internal Interfaces*, we investigated core Moodle application programming interfaces--that is, libraries of functions provided to developers that ensure third-party plugins interface with Moodle in a coherent and consistent way. In this chapter, we will be developing plugins to enhance course layout and structure. We will be focusing on three different types of course plugin:

- Course formats
- Blocks
- Text filters

Developing these plugin types will allow us to further explore Moodle's internal APIs--and allows us to see just how plugins can be used to alter Moodle's default behavior.

By the end of this chapter, you will have done the following:

- Developed a new course format that will reveal activities depending on your GPS location
- Investigated the intricacies of Moodle's file handling API (the File API) by developing a novel QR Code block
- Explored how text filters can be used to manipulate onscreen text

The **instructional designers (IDs)** working on courses for the resilience project have identified the need for a course format that reveals activities depending on your location. Generic courses are being developed that require subtle differences depending on which country the learner is in. It was quickly realized that one could take this idea further, to revealing resources and activities depending on where in the country you were located--for example, where you might find local infrastructure resources.

The IDs also want to use QR Codes to provide links to further information that can only be accessed through secure means (this is, in fact, a dedicated QR Code reader app that provides a secure link to information on critical infrastructure that is not publicly available on the internet). In a separate work package, the harmonization of critical infrastructure terminology is being investigated. As terminology is being changed and updated, the ability to substitute words and phrases before they are displayed on the page will become more important (rather than having to repeatedly alter course content). Rather than going into too much detail with this specific requirement, we will be developing a simple Moodle text filter (but certainly one upon which more complex filters can be built).

Let us start by creating the new location-based course format.

Course formats

The layout of a course page is managed through the selection of the relevant course format plugin. See `https://docs.moodle.org/dev/Course_formats` for details. Our IDs are willing to display resources and activities based on the user's location. A search through the Moodle plugins directory revealed the GPS Format plugin--see `https://moodle.org/plugins/format_gps`-- originally developed by *Jürgen Kappus*, *Barry Oosthuizen*, and *Ralf Krause*. However, our designers were looking for something simpler and have asked us to investigate further.

What's great about this plugin is that it allows us to also investigate how we can go about incorporating JavaScript and AJAX into our Moodle plugins. Recall that PHP scripts run server-side and JavaScript runs client-side. Advantages of running code client-side include the following:

- There are some things about the client that the server can't know about (such as the client's location)
- Processing takes place on the client machine not on the server, saving the server's resources
- Because it is executed client-side, it is relatively fast for the end user
- Javascript is a simple language that allows developers to extend web pages more easily

Of course, code running on the client side may well need to communicate with the server, and this is where AJAX comes in: AJAX allows us to obtain data from the server without having to reload the page.

GPS location - background to the project

Discussions with our IDs highlighted the possibility of revealing links to resources and course activities depending on your location within a planned emergency response camp. Planned camps tend to follow the guidelines laid down by the UN Refugee Agency, meaning fire safety, drainage, first aid facilities, and so on, are easy to locate. If we could specify the location of facilities in a Moodle course and have resources automatically revealed to learners depending on their location (determined via GPS on their mobile devices) then this could help keep course content focused on the learner's needs.

Obtaining device location

How are we going to determine a learner's location? This is something that would definitely need to be achieved client-side--it will need JavaScript. Luckily, there is a JavaScript application programming interface we can use: the Geolocation API. Full documentation for this API is available at `https://www.w3.org/TR/geolocation-API/`.

Device location - security issues

One can appreciate that a web application knowing the location of a device has its own inherent security issues (see `https://www.w3.org/TR/geolocation-API/#security`), and therefore one of the basic requirements of any application using the Geolocation API is that it will need to be hosted on a secure website--that is, using `https://` and not simply `http://`. This means that before we start developing any Moodle code we need to know how to configure an `https://` site in WampServer.

Configuring SSL on WampServer

We are going to use OpenSSL to generate the keys needed to make https operational. See `https://www.openssl.org/` for details on the OpenSSL project. The OpenSLL project provides the source code rather than binaries and installers, but the wiki does provide links to third-party projects at `https://wiki.openssl.org/index.php/Binaries`. Let's download the latest version of the Windows installer from `https://slproweb.com/products/Win32OpenSSL.html`. Remember to run the installer as a Windows administrator.

The OpenSSL binaries are often shipped with other tools (such as source control clients or file transfer tools) so, rather than installing the binaries to the Windows System directory, install them to a separate bin folder. Once installed, make sure your PATH environment variable is set so that the location of your newly installed OpenSSL libraries is specified first:

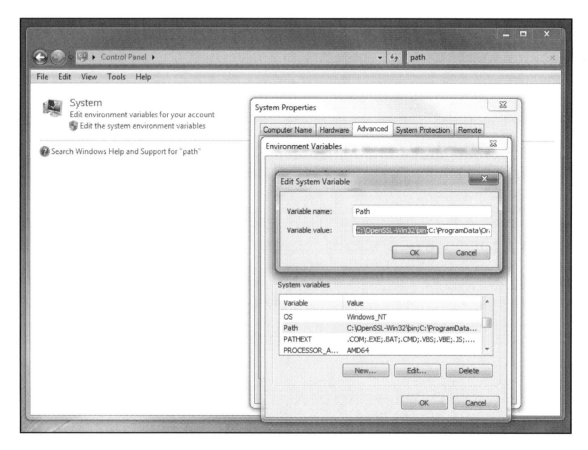

To create the certificate, we need to open a Windows command prompt and navigate to our Wamp installation's Apache \bin folder. For example, mine is at C:\wamp\bin\apache\apache2.4.9\bin. The first step is to create an RSA key.

Type the following at the command line to create an RSA key:

```
openssl genrsa -out server.key 2048
```

You will be asked for a passphrase when the new key is generated. Leave this blank.

The next step is to create a self-signed, X509 format **Certificate Signing Request (CSR)**. The process requires various pieces of information, but we need to be very specific with the **Common Name (CN)**. The CN is the name of the website we need to secure so, for example, my local development site is currently at `http://moodle313.localhost` so the CN will need to be `moodle313.localhost`. Type the following at the command line:

```
openssl req -new -key server.key -out server.csr
```

Your Apache `bin` directory will now contain a `server.key` file and a `server.csr` file:

The certificate signing request (`.csr`) file would normally be sent off to a certificate signing authority, such as Verizon or GoDaddy (see `https://en.wikipedia.org/wiki/Certificate_authority`). The signing authority would carry out due diligence on our request (attempt to confirm that we are who we say we are and charge us a nominal fee for the privilege), and by return send us our certificate. As this is our own development site we are wanting to secure (and remember: this is so we can experiment with the Geolocation API), then we can sign the certificate ourselves. Clearly, browsers are going to warn that our test site is using a self-signed certificate, but that is not going to be a problem for development. Therefore, the next step is to sign our CSR. At the command line, type the following:

```
openssl x509 -req -days 365 -in server.csr -signkey server.key -out
server.crt
```

Here is a screenshot of the entire command-line process:

The Apache \bin directory will now contain a server private key (.key), a certificate signing request (.csr), and, finally, the actual certificate (.crt).

Now we need to install the certificate. In Apache's \conf folder, create two more folders, called \ssl.key and \ssl.crt:

Copy the `server.key` file to `\ssl.key` and the `server.crt` file to `ssl.crt`.

That done, we need to reconfigure Apache and PHP to enable HTTPS. We need to ensure the Apache `ssl_module` is enabled. This we can do directly through the WampServer notification icon by clicking on it with the mouse, selecting **Apache** from the menu, sliding across to **Apache modules**, and then ensuring `ssl_module` is enabled. Also, make sure `socache_shmcb_module` is enabled (this caches SSL session data).

While in the Wamp configuration menu, we can also configure **PHP**. Click on **PHP**, then on **PHP extensions**, and ensure the `php_openssl` extension is loaded.

Next, we need to edit Apache's `httpd-ssl.conf` file, located in `\extra`. Find the line that says `<VirtualHost _default_:443>` and ensure that the `DocumentRoot` variable immediately after that line specifies your Moodle directory and the `ServerName` variable specifies your local Moodle URL. Note that it is also worthwhile ensuring the access and error log paths are specified correctly. Here is my configuration:

```
81
82   <VirtualHost _default_:443>
83
84   #   General setup for the virtual host
85   DocumentRoot "C:/wamp/www/moodle313"
86   ServerName moodle313.localhost:443
87   ServerAdmin admin@example.com
88   ErrorLog "C:/wamp/bin/apache/apache2.4.9/logs/ssl_error.log"
89   TransferLog "C:/wamp/bin/apache/apache2.4.9/logs/ssl_access.log"
90
91   #   SSL Engine Switch:
92   #   Enable/Disable SSL for this virtual host.
93   SSLEngine on
94
```

Now find the line that specifies the SSLCertificateFile variable. Set it to the path to your server.crt file. You will find the SSLCertificateKeyFile variable in the following image. Likewise, set this to the path to your server.key file:

```
 94
 95   #     Server Certificate:
 96   #     Point SSLCertificateFile at a PEM encoded certificate.  If
 97   #     the certificate is encrypted, then you will be prompted for a
 98   #     pass phrase.  Note that a kill -HUP will prompt again.  Keep
 99   #     in mind that if you have both an RSA and a DSA certificate you
100   #     can configure both in parallel (to also allow the use of DSA
101   #     ciphers, etc.)
102   #     Some ECC cipher suites (http://www.ietf.org/rfc/rfc4492.txt)
103   #     require an ECC certificate which can also be configured in
104   #     parallel.
105   SSLCertificateFile "C:/wamp/bin/apache/apache2.4.9/conf/ssl.crt/server.crt"
106   #SSLCertificateFile "c:/Apache24/conf/server-dsa.crt"
107   #SSLCertificateFile "c:/Apache24/conf/server-ecc.crt"
108
109   #     Server Private Key:
110   #     If the key is not combined with the certificate, use this
111   #     directive to point at the key file.  Keep in mind that if
112   #     you've both a RSA and a DSA private key you can configure
113   #     both in parallel (to also allow the use of DSA ciphers, etc.)
114   #     ECC keys, when in use, can also be configured in parallel
115   SSLCertificateKeyFile "C:/wamp/bin/apache/apache2.4.9/conf/ssl.key/server.key"
116   #SSLCertificateKeyFile "c:/Apache24/conf/ser/ver-dsa.key"
117   #SSLCertificateKeyFile "c:/Apache24/conf/server-ecc.key"
118
```

Now, in httpd.conf ensure the following lines are uncommented:

```
LoadModule authn_socache_module modules/mod_authn_socache.so
LoadModule socache_shmcb_module modules/mod_socache_shmcb.so
```

And to enable SSL, uncomment the following line:

```
Include conf/extra/httpd-ssl.conf
```

Before we restart Apache, we can test to ensure we haven't made any spelling mistakes or misconfigured any Apache modules. At the command line, type httpd -t. If all is well, then Apache will report Syntax OK. Otherwise, check out the preceding steps to ensure you have typed things in correctly.

Your development Moodle `config.php` file will also need to be updated to reflect the new root URL. This is simply a matter of updating the `wwwroot` variable:

```
$CFG->wwwroot    = 'https://moodle313.localhost';
```

Now we can restart Apache and navigate to your development Moodle, in my case `https://moodle313.localhost`. As discussed earlier, because we have created a self-signed certificate, the browser (in my case Chrome) is going to complain--but still we should be able to test our site:

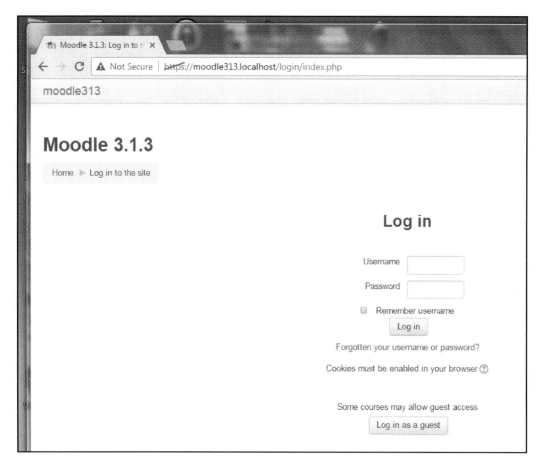

Now we can get to grips with developing our new course format.

Understanding renderers

Renderers manage most things you see on the screen when you visit a Moodle site. In Eclipse, take a look in `\lib\outputrenderers.php`:

The two classes of interest are `renderer_base` and `plugin_renderer_base` (which actually extends `renderer_base`). You will see from the comments in the code that all plugins should extend `plugin_renderer_base` and our new course format will be, ultimately, no exception. I say ultimately because course formats that consist of sections can be rendered via the `format_section_renderer_base` class (which is a helper class that makes displaying sections easier) declared in `/course/format/renderer.php`. Our new course format will construct the course page using a renderer based on `format_section_renderer_base`. As described in the user story, course sections will be configured with longitudes and latitudes, and sections will only be displayed when a user is located in that section's region. So how do we determine the location?

Finding a user's location with the Geolocation API

Let's use some simple JavaScript to determine firstly if the user's browser actually supports the Geolocation API and, if it does, attempt to obtain the location. The code is based on **YUI (Yahoo User Interface)**--and if you go ahead and adapt a Moodle plugin as we are here then chances are you may find yourself modifying YUI.

YUI is no longer being developed by Yahoo. This means any new Moodle plugin should be employing jQuery. We'll be investigating employing jQuery in new plugins in later chapters.

Let's study the code we will be using. Firstly, we need an `initializer` function. This will determine if geolocation services are available:

```
initializer : function ()
{
    Y.Geo = {
            getCurrentPosition: navigator.geolocation?
            getCurrentPositionByAPI:console.log("Geolocation services
            are not supported by your web browser.")
            };
```

If `navigator.geolocation` returns a geolocation object, then we can call `getCurrentPositionByAPI`. This, in turn, calls the `navigator.geolocation.getCurrentPosition()` method in the Geolocation API. Here is the function in detail:

```
// call to geolocation API
function getCurrentPositionByAPI(callback, scope, opts)
{
    navigator.geolocation.getCurrentPosition(
    function(data)
    {
        callback.call(scope,
        {
                success: true,
                coords:
                {
                        latitude: data.coords.latitude,
                        longitude: data.coords.longitude,
                        accuracy: data.coords.accuracy,
                        altitude: data.coords.altitude,
                        altitudeAccuracy:
                        data.coords.altitudeAccuracy,
                        heading: data.coords.heading,
                        speed: data.coords.speed
                },
        timestamp: data.timestamp,
        source: "native"
        }
    );
    },
```

```
                function(error)
                {
                        callback.call(scope,
                        {
                                code: error.code
                        });
                },
                opts
        );}
        }
}
```

Moodle supports the YUI JavaScript framework, so our code will need to be wrapped in a YUI class. Also, see that we are posting the location data from our JavaScript back to PHP using the YUI `io` function:

```
Y.io(M.cfg.wwwroot+'/course/format/location/geo.php',
{
method: 'POST', data: build_querystring(params),
context: this
```

The `geo.php` script simply needs to check the `POST` parameters:

```
$userlatitude = optional_param('latitude', null, PARAM_FLOAT);
$userlongitude = optional_param('longitude', null, PARAM_FLOAT);
```

Including JavaScript

Luckily, the Page API provides a simple method for loading YUI-wrapped JavaScript into pages. For details, take a look at the Moodle documentation here:
https://docs.moodle.org/dev/YUI/Modules

When Moodle displays a course using the specified format, it will attempt to load the plugin's `format.php` file, so it is in here that we will need to load our JavaScript:

```
$PAGE->requires->yui_module('moodle-format_location-geo',
'M.format_location.init_geo', null, null, true);
```

Note the format of the module name: `moodle-format_location-geo`. The naming convention is called **Frankenstyle** (a term coined by *Martin Dougiamas*--see https://docs.moodle.org/dev/Frankenstyle). This is a *moodle* script that belongs to a *format* plugin called *location* and the script is called *geo*--hence it is identified by `moodle-format_location-geo`.

Specifying location settings

We now need to add extra configuration options to each section. Here is how the finished page will look to the end user:

The file lib.php contains a declaration of the format_location class, which itself extends format_base. See https://docs.moodle.org/dev/Course_formats#Developing_course_formats_for_Moodle _2.4_and_above for more details on the format_base class. Essentially, the lib.php file contains a set of callback functions, one of which, create_edit_form_elements(), can be used to add extra configuration settings--either for the format itself or the layout sections it contains. You will see from the code that the create_edit_form_elements() method displays configuration options for both the course and for a section. We need to edit the code that displays settings for the section. We need to add options to determine if visibility of the section is limited to GPS location:

```
$mform->addElement('header', 'gpssettings', new
lang_string('editsection_geo_heading', 'format_location'));
$mform->addHelpButton('gpssettings', 'gpshelp', 'format_location');
      if ($validationerror == 'yes')
      {
      $error = html_writer::div(new lang_string('validationerror',
      'format_location'), 'bold red error');
      $errorlabel = html_writer::div(new lang_string('error'), 'bold
      red error');
      $mform->addElement('static', 'validationerror', $errorlabel,
      $error);
      $mform->addHelpButton('validationerror', 'errorhelp',
      'format_location');
      }
$mform->addElement('checkbox', 'format_location_restricted', new
lang_string('active', 'format_location'));
$mform->setDefault('format_gps_restricted', FORMAT_LOCATION_UNRESTRICTED);
```

```
$attributes = array('size' => '100', 'width' => '500', 'maxlength' =>
'100');
```

Next, we need to include new settings to allow the user to specify the location at which the section should be visible:

```
$mform->addElement('text', 'format_location_address', new
lang_string('address', 'format_location'), $attributes);
$mform->setType('format_location_address', PARAM_TEXT);
$mform->addElement('text', 'format_location_latitude', new
lang_string('latitude', 'format_location'));
$mform->addElement('text', 'format_location_longitude', new
lang_string('longitude', 'format_location'));
$mform->addRule('format_location_address', null, 'maxlength', 255,
'client');
$mform->addRule('format_location_longitude', null, 'numeric', null,
'client');
$mform->addRule('format_location_longitude', null, 'numeric', null,
'client');
$mform->addRule('format_location_latitude', null, 'numeric', null,
'client');
$mform->setType('format_location_latitude', PARAM_RAW);
$mform->setType('format_location_longitude', PARAM_RAW);
$mform->disabledIf('format_location_address', 'format_location_restricted',
'notchecked');
$mform->disabledIf('format_location_latitude',
'format_location_restricted', 'notchecked');
$mform->disabledIf('format_location_longitude',
'format_location_restricted', 'notchecked');
```

Displaying sections based on location

Recall that the location data is passed into PHP via a YUI callback--`geo.php`:

```
/**
 * GPS Format free. Restrict access to topics according to user's
 geolocation.
 *
 * @package format_location
 * @copyright 2013 Barry Oosthuizen
 * @author Barry Oosthuizen
 * @license http://www.gnu.org/copyleft/gpl.html GNU GPL v3 or later
 */
define('AJAX_SCRIPT', true);

require_once(dirname(dirname(dirname(dirname(__FILE__)))) . '/config.php');
```

```
require_sesskey();
require_login();

$userlatitude = optional_param('latitude', null, PARAM_FLOAT);
$userlongitude = optional_param('longitude', null, PARAM_FLOAT);

$location = new stdClass();
$location->userid = $USER->id;
$location->latitude = $userlatitude;
$location->longitude = $userlongitude;
$location->timemodified = time();

global $DB;

    if ($currentrecord = $DB->get_record('format_location_user',
    array("userid" => $USER->id)))
    {
        $location->id = $currentrecord->id;
        try
        {
            $DB->update_record('format_location_user', $location);
        }
        catch (dml_exception $e)
        {
            echo json_encode($e->debuginfo . ', ' . $e-
            >getTraceAsString());
        }

    }
    else
    {
        try
        {
            $DB->insert_record('format_location_user', $location);
        }
        catch (dml_exception $e)
        {
            echo json_encode($e->debuginfo. ', ' . $e-
            >getTraceAsString());
        }
    }
```

You can see from the preceding code that the Data Manipulation API, through the $DB object, is used to store or update the user's current location in the database

So far, we can determine the current user's location and we can configure a course section with a latitude and longitude. Now, we need to add some math that determines how far away the user is from a section's position (within a certain radius from a given point) and logic that decides whether to display a section. In `locallib.php`, you will find the math used to determine the distance between two points. This uses the Haversine formula (see `https://en.wikipedia.org/wiki/Haversine_formula`)--if you think this calculation looks complicated then remember that the earth is a squashed sphere and not, contrary to popular belief perhaps (see `http://blackbag.gawker.com/the-earth-is-flat-explained-1755002534`), flat:

```php
// Based on C++ code by Jochen Topf <jochen@topf.org>
// See http://osmiumapi.openstreetmap.de/haversine_8hpp_source.html
// Translated into PHP and extended to cater for different distance
units by Barry Oosthuizen
class format_location_haversine
{

    public $radius;
    public $distance;

 public function __construct($x1, $y1, $x2, $y2) {

     $this->radius = 6378100; // Meters.
     $this->distance = $this->get_distance($x1, $y1, $x2, $y2);
 }

 public function get_distance($x1, $y1, $x2, $y2)
 {
     $lon_arc = deg2rad(($x1 - $x2));
     $lat_arc = deg2rad(($y1 - $y2));
     $lonh = sin($lon_arc * 0.5);
     $lonh *= $lonh;
     $lath = sin($lat_arc * 0.5);
     $lath *= $lath;
     $tmp = cos(deg2rad($y1)) * cos(deg2rad($y2));
     $distance = 2 * $this->radius * asin(sqrt($lath + $tmp *
     $lonh));
     return $distance;
 }
```

Once we have the distance between the user's location and a course section's position then we can decide if we should display the section or display a warning. Here is the function from `locallib.php` to check a user's proximity to a given location:

```
function format_location_check_proximity($topic, $location)
{

    $proximity = new stdClass();

    $locationlatitude = $topic->format_location_latitude;
    $locationlongitude = $topic->format_location_longitude;
    $locationradius = 50;
    $userlatitude = $location->latitude;
    $userlongitude = $location->longitude;
    $userlocation = new format_location_haversine($userlatitude,
    $userlongitude, $locationlatitude, $locationlongitude);

    if ($userlocation->distance > $locationradius) {
        // User is to far away.
        $proximity->status = 'toofar';
    } else {
        // User is within allowed radius.
        $proximity->status = 'ok';
    }
    return $proximity;

}
```

This function is used in `renderer.php`--check out the `print_multiple_section_page()` function--to determine if a section should be shown:

```
// Show the section if the user is permitted to access it, OR if it's not
available.
// but showavailability is turned on (and there is some available info
text).
$proximity = new stdClass();
if ($thissection->format_location_restricted ==
   FORMAT_LOCATION_RESTRICTED)
{
    if ($location)
    {
            $proximity =
            format_location_check_proximity($thissection,
            $location);
    }
    else
    {
            $proximity->status = 'notallowed';
```

```
        }
}
else
{
        $proximity->status = 'ok';
}
```

From here, we can choose what to display to the user:

```
if (!$showsection || $proximity->status == 'toofar' || $proximity->status
== 'notallowed')
{
        if ($PAGE->user_is_editing() &&
           has_capability('moodle/course:update', $context))
        {
        // Do nothing.
        }
        else
        {
                $thissection->visible = false;
                // Hidden section message is overridden by
                'unavailable' control
                // (showavailability option).
                if ($proximity->status == 'toofar')
                {
                        if (!$course->hiddensections && $thissection-
                          >available)
                        {
                            echo $this-
                            >location_section_hidden($section);
                        }
                }
                else if ($proximity->status == 'notallowed')
                {
                        if (!$course->hiddensections && $thissection-
                          >available)
                        {
                                echo $this->location_section_notallowed
                                        ($section);
                        }
                }
        else
        {
                if (!$course->hiddensections && $thissection->available)
                {
                        echo $this->section_hidden($section);
                }
        }
  }
```

```
continue;
        }
}
```

The code discussed in this section is available from GitHub here: `https://github.com/ian davidwild/moodle-format_location`.

Try it yourself

Try experimenting with the code to add in new features of your own:

- Add a new section configuration setting that allows the course creator to specify the proximity radius
- Allow the user to specify a proximity radius in either kilometres or miles

Course blocks

From an initial requirement to access critical infrastructure data securely, the resilience project IDs want to include QR Codes as a novel means to include supplementary information, such as maps of critical infrastructure or answers to knowledge checks. Here is the user story:

In this section, we will be building a dedicated QR Code block--based on the *QR Links* plugin by Catalyst IT (see `https://moodle.org/plugins/local_qrlinks`). You can download the code described in this section from `https://github.com/iandavidwild/moodle-block_qr_code`. Here is the block in action:

Scanning the code will provide a link to a geographically accurate map of the London Underground.

Let's now start developing our new block. Firstly, we need to create a new folder under `blocks` called `qr_code`:

That done, there are four files we need to create in order to implement our new Moodle block. The first is `\block_qr_code.php`. This will contain a declaration of a new class called `block_qr_code`, an extension of `block_base`:

```
class block_qr_code extends block_base
{

    function init()
    {
        $this->title = get_string('pluginname', 'block_qr_code');
    }
}
```

We are initializing the block by setting the title with a string loaded from the block's language file. Next let's create the language file. Create a new folder called `\lang\en`, and in it create a new file called `block_qr_code.php`. Add the new string, `pluginname`:

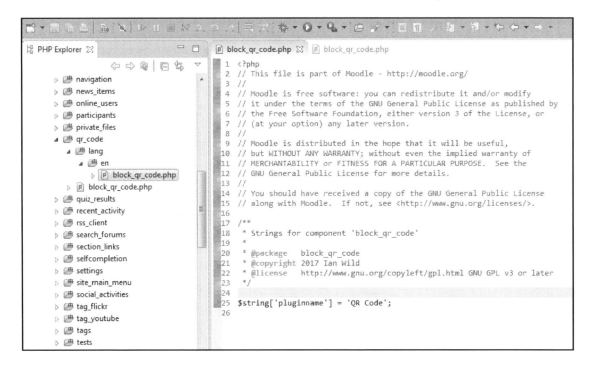

Next, our plugin needs to tell Moodle about who can do what to our block, based on role capabilities using the Access API (see `https://docs.moodle.org/dev/Access_API`). At the very least, we need to specify which Moodle roles can add a new instance to a course (the `addinstance` capability) and which roles can add the block to their My Moodle pages (the `myaddinstance` capability). Create a new folder called `db` and add a new file called `access.php`:

Then, add the following code:

```php
defined('MOODLE_INTERNAL') || die();
$capabilities = array(

    'block/qr_code:myaddinstance' => array(
    'captype' => 'write',
    'contextlevel' => CONTEXT_SYSTEM,
    'archetypes' => array(
    'user' => CAP_ALLOW
     ),

        'clonepermissionsfrom' => 'moodle/my:manageblocks'
    ),

    'block/qr_code:addinstance' => array(
        'riskbitmask' => RISK_SPAM | RISK_XSS,

        'captype' => 'write',
        'contextlevel' => CONTEXT_BLOCK,
        'archetypes' => array(
            'editingteacher' => CAP_ALLOW,
            'manager' => CAP_ALLOW
        ),

        'clonepermissionsfrom' => 'moodle/site:manageblocks'
    ),
);
```

Finally, we need to add versioning information. Create a new file called `version.php`:

Then, add the following code:

```
defined('MOODLE_INTERNAL') || die();

$plugin->version   = 2017011700;          // The current plugin version
(Date: YYYYMMDDXX)
$plugin->requires  = 2016051900;          // Requires this Moodle version
$plugin->component = 'block_qr_code';      // Full name of the plugin (used
for diagnostics)
```

That done, we now have a basic Moodle block we can install. To install it, from the **Administration block** click on **Site administration** and select **Notifications**.

Configuring the QR Code block

Here is the agreed wireframe for the configuration screen:

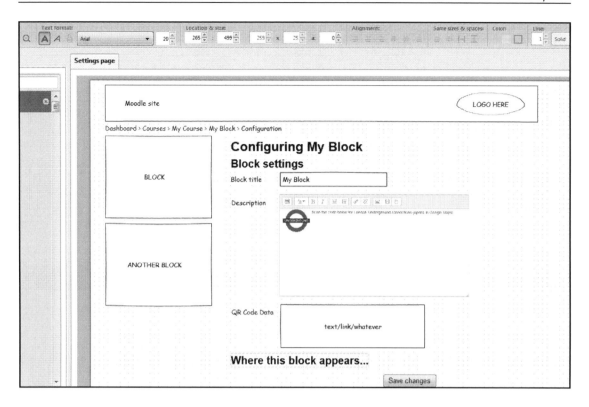

The configuration page includes an HTML Description field, which will allow the user to include images (and in fact any other supported multimedia files), which we will also need to store in the file storage area.

Block settings are specified in a new class based on the `block_edit_form` class. The configuration page itself is declared in the `specific_definition()` function. Here is the code to create the configuration screen:

```
protected function specific_definition($mform)
{
        global $CFG;

        // Fields for editing QR code block title and contents.
        $mform->addElement('header', 'configheader',
                        get_string('blocksettings', 'block'));
        $mform->addElement('text', 'config_title',
                        get_string('configtitle', 'block_qr_code'));
        $mform->setType('config_title', PARAM_TEXT);
        $editoroptions = array('maxfiles' => EDITOR_UNLIMITED_FILES,
                        'noclean'=>true, 'context'=>$this->block-
                        >context);
```

```
$mform->addElement('editor', 'config_description',
                    get_string('configdescription',
                    'block_qr_code'), null, $editoroptions);
$mform->setType('config_description', PARAM_RAW);
// XSS is  prevented when printing the block contents and
serving files

$mform->addElement('textarea', 'config_data',
                    get_string('configdata', 'block_qr_code'),
                    'wrap="virtual" rows="5" cols="50"');
$mform->addRule('config_data', null, 'required', null,
                    'client');
$mform->setType('config_data', PARAM_RAW);
if (!empty($CFG->block_qr_code_allowcssclasses))
{
        $mform->addElement('text', 'config_classes',
                            get_string('configclasses',
                            'block_qr_code'));
        $mform->setType('config_classes', PARAM_TEXT);
        $mform->addHelpButton('config_classes', 'configclasses',
        'block_qr_code');
}
}
```

Including the QR Code library

We will use a third-party library to generate the QR Code, rather than attempt to write something ourselves. The code we will be using is the same as that used in the QR Links plugin--see https://github.com/endroid/QrCode. This library is straightforward to use. Firstly, we need to include the code and, as in the QL Links plugin, I'm going to put the library in a new folder called thirdparty:

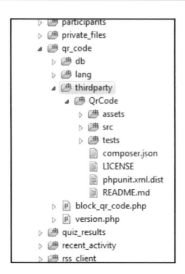

Manipulating files with the File API

The QR Code library we are using generates an image that we need to display in our block. But what is the best way of handling the image? It doesn't make sense to generate a QR Code image every time a user views the page (as this would be very inefficient). It would clearly be far better to create the image file and then import it into Moodle's file storage area using the File API then display the image there. In this section, we explore how.

Each block will have one QR code, meaning code images can be identified by each block's instance ID (the instance ID is the ID of the row in Moodle's block table). We can generate the QR Code in Moodle's \temp directory. Then we can import the file into Moodle's file store using the File API's `create_file_from_pathname()` function. This function not only requires the instance ID, but also the context ID (this is the ID of the row in Moodle's context table that describes where the block fits in the system). Here is the function we will need to generate the QR Code image file in Moodle's \moodledata\temp directory and then load it into the file storage area:

```
function generate_qrcode($instanceid, $contextid, $data)
{
    global $CFG;
    $code = new QrCode();
    $code->setText($data);
    $code->setSize(250);
    $code->setPadding(6);
    $code->setErrorCorrection('high');
    $code->setForegroundColor(array('r' => 0, 'g' => 0, 'b' => 0, 'a'
```

```
                                          => 0));
          $code->setBackgroundColor(array('r' => 255, 'g' => 255, 'b' =>
                                          255,'a' => 0));
          $code->setLabelFontSize(16);
          // generate file path
          $filename = 'qr_code_' . $instanceid . '.png';
          $sourcepath = $CFG->dataroot . '/temp/' . $filename;
          $code->render($sourcepath, 'png');
          $fs = get_file_storage();
          $file_record = array(
                              'contextid'=>$contextid,
                              'component'=>'block_qr_code',
                              'filearea'=>'qr_code',
                              'itemid'=>$instanceid,
                              'filepath'=>'/',
                              'filename'=>$filename,
                              'timecreated'=>time(),
                              'timemodified'=>time());
          $result = $fs->create_file_from_pathname($file_record,
                  $sourcepath);
          // delete file from temp directory...
          @unlink($sourcepath);
          return $result;
    }
```

Let's implement some lazy loading and only create the image if and when we need it. Aside from a function to generate the code, we will need three more supporting functions:

- A function to determine if the code image is already in the file store
- A function to retrieve the image from the file store
- A function to delete the file store image when the block is deleted

Here are the functions in question:

```
function qr_code_exists($instanceid, $contextid)
{
    $fs = get_file_storage();
    $filename = 'qr_code_' . $instanceid . '.png';
    $result = $fs->file_exists($contextid, 'block_qr_code',
            'qr_code', $instanceid, '/', $filename);
    return $result;
}
function get_qrcode_from_filestore($instanceid, $contextid)
{
    $fs = get_file_storage();
    $filename = 'qr_code_' . $instanceid . '.png';
    // Generate file URL
```

```
        return moodle_url::make_pluginfile_url($contextid,
        'block_qr_code', 'qr_code', $instanceid, '/', $filename);
}

function delete_qrcode_from_filestore($instanceid, $contextid)
{
        $fs = get_file_storage();
        $filename = 'qr_code_' . $instanceid . '.png';
        // Prepare file record object
        $fileinfo = array(
                        'component' => 'block_qr_code',
                        'filearea' => 'qr_code', // usually = table name
                        'itemid' => $instanceidd,// usually = ID of row
                                                       in table
                        'contextid' => $contextid, // ID of context
                        'filepath' => '/', // any path beginning and
                                                 ending in /
                        'filename' => $filename); // any filename
                        // Get file
                        $file = $fs->get_file($fileinfo['contextid'],
                        $fileinfo['component'], $fileinfo['filearea'],
                        $fileinfo['itemid'], $fileinfo['filepath'],
                        $fileinfo['filename']);
                        // Delete it if it exists
        if ($file)
        {
                $file->delete();
        }
}
```

Let's implement these in a separate `locallib.php` file and call on them from the `block_qr_code` class.

Block contents are generated by the `get_content()` function, a member of the `block_qr_code` class. Here is the complete `get_content()` function, as implemented in the sample code available on GitHub:

```
function get_content()
{
        global $CFG;
        require_once($CFG->libdir . '/filelib.php');
        // have we loaded the block's content already?
        if ($this->content !== NULL)
        {
                return $this->content;
        }
        // have we created a new QR code image?
```

```
if(isset($this->config->data))
{
     if(!qr_code_exists($this->instance->id, $this->context-
       >id))
     {
          generate_qrcode($this->instance->id, $this->context-
                          >id, $this->config->data);
     }
}
$filteropt = new stdClass;
$filteropt->overflowdiv = true;
if ($this->content_is_trusted())
{
     // fancy html allowed only on course, category and system
     blocks.
     $filteropt->noclean = true;
}

$this->content = new stdClass;
$this->content->footer = '';
if (isset($this->config->description))
{
     // rewrite url
     $this->config->description =
     file_rewrite_pluginfile_urls($this->config->description,
     'pluginfile.php', $this->context->id, 'block_qr_code',
     'content', NULL);
     // Default to FORMAT_HTML which is what will have been
     used before the
     // editor was properly implemented for the block.
     $format = FORMAT_HTML;
     // Check to see if the format has been properly set on
     the config
     if (isset($this->config->format))
     {
          $format = $this->config->format;
     }
     $this->content->text = format_text($this->config-
                                        >description, $format,
                                        $filteropt);
}
else
{
     $this->content->text = '';
}

if(qr_code_exists($this->instance->id, $this->context->id))
{
```

```
                // Send the QR code from the file store
                $this->content->text .=
                                        '<div class="qr_code"><img
                                        src="'.get_qrcode_from_filestore(
                                        $this->instance->id,$this->context-
                                        >id).'"/></div>';
        }
        unset($filteropt); // memory footprint

        return $this->content;
    }
```

Serving files from the file store

Notice how the link to the QR Code image is generated by the
`moodleurl::make_pluginfile_url()` function. This creates a link to the
`pluginfile.php` file serving script, referencing the required file.

In order to serve files from the file store, we need to implement the `pluginfile` function in
`lib.php`. This is a callback function that Moodle uses to serve files from the file store, but
one that is specific to this block. This function is described in the Moodle documentation at
`https://docs.moodle.org/dev/File_API#Serving_files_to_users`.

Let's now explore the file serving method in full. The function opens with the following
code:

```
function block_qr_code_pluginfile($course, $birecord_or_cm, $context,
$filearea, $args, $forcedownload, array $options=array())
{
        global $DB, $CFG, $USER;
        if ($context->contextlevel != CONTEXT_BLOCK)
        {
                send_file_not_found();
        }
}
```

If the block is in course context, then check if the user can access the course:

```
        if ($context->get_course_context(false))
        {
                require_course_login($course);
        }
        else if ($CFG->forcelogin)
        {
            require_login();
        }
```

```
else
{
        // Get parent context and see if user have proper
        permission.
        $parentcontext = $context->get_parent_context();
        if ($parentcontext->contextlevel === CONTEXT_COURSECAT)
        {
                // Check if category is visible and user can view
                this
                category.
                $category = $DB->get_record('course_categories',
                array('id' => $parentcontext->instanceid), '*',
                    MUST_EXIST);
                if (!$category->visible)
                {
                        require_capability('moodle/category:
                                        viewhiddencategories',
                                        $parentcontext);
                }
        }
        else if ($parentcontext->contextlevel === CONTEXT_USER &&
                $parentcontext->instanceid != $USER->id)
        {
                // The block is in the context of a user, it is only
                visible to the user who it belongs to.
                send_file_not_found();
        }
// At this point there is no way to check SYSTEM context, so
ignoring it.
}
```

Next, we need to check our sanity and ensure that we are serving files from the right file area:

```
if (($filearea !== 'content') && $filearea !== 'qr_code')
{
        send_file_not_found();
}
$fs = get_file_storage();
$itemid = 0;
if($filearea === 'qr_code')
{
        $itemid = array_shift($args); // The first item in the
                                        $args array.
        $filepath = '/';
        $filename = array_pop($args);
}
else
```

```
{
    $filename = array_pop($args);
    $filepath = $args ? '/'.implode('/', $args).'/' : '/';
}
if (!$file = $fs->get_file($context->id, 'block_qr_code',
    $filearea, $itemid, $filepath, $filename) or $file-
    >is_directory())
{
    send_file_not_found();
}

if ($parentcontext = context::instance_by_id($birecord_or_cm-
    >parentcontextid, IGNORE_MISSING))
{
    if ($parentcontext->contextlevel == CONTEXT_USER)
    {
        // force download on all personal pages including
        /my///because we do not have reliable way to find out
        from where this is used
        $forcedownload = true;
    }
}
else
{
    // weird, there should be parent context, better force
    download then
    $forcedownload = true;
}

// NOTE: it would be nice to have file revisions here, for now
rely on standard file lifetime,
//do not lower it because the files are displayed very often.
\core\session\manager::write_close();
send_stored_file($file, null, 0, $forcedownload, $options);
}
```

Try it yourself

The dimensions of the QR Code, their foreground and background colors are all currently hardcoded. Can you add new configuration settings that allow the user to choose their own settings?

Text filters

One of the tasks of the organizational resilience project is the standardization of language--in other words, ensuring there is standardization of common terms and definitions across the project. There was some discussion as to whether Moodle could be used to filter text and check for the appearance of specified terms. As a proof of concept, we can finish this chapter by having some fun with text filters. The idea discussed is that we are able to use Moodle to filter text displayed on a page to (potentially) replace words and phrases as they are harmonized across the resilience project. Let's demonstrate how this can be done by creating a Swedish Chef text filter. The code we will be using is based on the ezborktranslator--see

`https://github.com/patrickallaert/ezpublish-legacy-php7/blob/master/lib/ezi18n/classes/ezborktranslator.php.`

For details on how filters are constructed, check out the Moodle documentation: `https://docs.moodle.org/dev/Filters#Creating_a_basic_filter.`

The plugin itself can be downloaded from GitHub, at `https://github.com/iandavidwild/moodle-filter_swedishchef.` Download the complete package now and install it to the `filter` folder:

```
          ▷ 🗐 mathjaxloader
          ▷ 🗐 mediaplugin
          ▷ 🗐 multilang
          ▲ 🗐 swedishchef
              ▲ 🗐 lang
                  ▲ 🗐 en
                      ▷ 📄 filter_swedishchef.php
              ▷ 📄 filter.php
                 📄 README.txt
              ▷ 📄 version.php
          ▷ 🗐 tex
          ▷ 🗐 tidy
          ▷ 🗐 urltolink
             📄 index.html
          ▷ 📄 local_settings_form.php
          ▷ 📄 manage.php
```

Take a look in `filter.php` and see that there is a declaration of a new class called
`filter_swedishchef` that extends `moodle_text_filter`. Within this class, we need to
implement the `filter` function:

```
class filter_swedishchef extends moodle_text_filter
{
    function filter($text, array $options = array())
    {
        global $CFG;

        if (empty($text) or is_numeric($text)) {
            return $text;
        }

        $text = preg_replace( "/a\B/", "e", $text );
        $text = preg_replace( "/an/", "un", $text );
        $text = preg_replace( "/au/", "oo", $text );
        $text = preg_replace( "/en\b/", "ee", $text );
        $text = preg_replace( "/\Bew/", "oo", $text );
        $text = preg_replace( "/\Bf/", "ff", $text );
        $text = preg_replace( "/\Bi/", "ee", $text );
        $text = preg_replace( "/\Bir/", "ur", $text );
        $text = preg_replace( "/\bo/", "oo", $text );
        $text = preg_replace( "/ow/", "oo", $text );
        $text = preg_replace( "/ph/", "f", $text );
        $text = preg_replace( "/th\b/", "t", $text );
        $text = preg_replace( "/\Btion/", "shun", $text );
        $text = preg_replace( "/\Bu/", "oo", $text );
        $text = preg_replace( "/\bU/", "Oo", $text );
        $text = preg_replace( "/y\b/", "ai", $text );
        $text = preg_replace( "/v/", "f", $text );
```

```
        $text = preg_replace( "/w/", "v", $text );
        $text = preg_replace( "/ooo/", "oo", $text );

        if(strlen($text) > 20) {
            $text .= " Børk! Børk! Børk!";
        }

        return $text;
    }
}
```

Note that this initial implementation is rather clunky--repeated calls to preg_replace aren't necessarily very efficient. Our function will be called for nearly every fragment of text that is displayed on screen, so an inefficient filter() function might well cause a big performance hit. The problem with relying on baked-in PHP functions to handle strings is that we are then at the mercy of the author of the underlying code that the function exercises. For example, we can re-implement the function using a single call to preg_replace(). Let's replace multiple calls to preg_replace() with the following:

```
$patterns = array (
                    "/a\B/",
                    "/an/",
                    "/au/",
                    "/en\b/",
                    "/\Bew/",
                    "/\Bf/",
                    "/\Bi/",
                    "/\Bir/",
                    "/\bo/",
                    "/ow/",
                    "/ph/",
                    "/th\b/",
                    "/\Btion/",
                    "/\Bu/",
                    "/\bU/",
                    "/y\b/",
                    "/v/",
                    "/w/",
                    "/ooo/");
$replacements = array (
                    "e",
                    "un",
                    "oo",
                    "ee",
                    "oo",
                    "ff",
                    "ee",
```

```
                                "ur",
                                "oo",
                                "oo",
                                "f",
                                "t",
                                "shun",
                                "oo",
                                "Oo",
                                "ai",
                                "f",
                                "v",
                                "oo");
    $text = preg_replace($patterns, $replacements, $text );
```

But is this single call actually more efficient? If we are unsure of the efficiency of an algorithm then we can bracket our process with the PHP `microtime()` function--see `http://php.net/manual/en/function.microtime.php`. For string replacement functions, it might be cheaper to use the `strops()` function to check if the string we are needing to replace is present before using a regular expression function.

Also, don't forget that we can use the Cache API to store values rather than, say, repeated calls to the database through the Data Manipulation API--although this isn't necessary in this simple example.

The following screenshot demonstrates how the filter operates on content and headings:

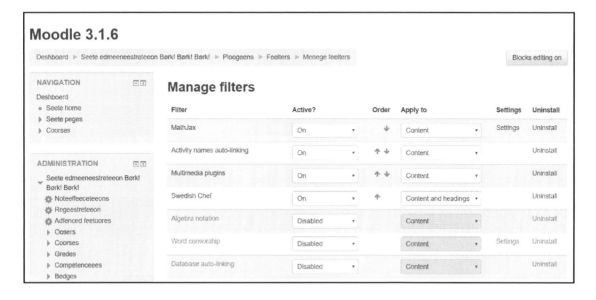

Subscribing to a text changed event

There may well be an instance where another plugin (including other filters) has used an AJAX (JavaScript) callback to change text on the screen, but your filter still needs to know about it. In this scenario, we need to hook a JavaScript event. See the documentation at `https://docs.moodle.org/dev/Filters#Dynamic_content` for details. The first step to enabling this function is to create a new YUI module to listen out for changes. Create a new file called `loader.js`, nested inside a `\yui\loader\` folder:

The YUI module that listens for a change event, and subsequently handles it (albeit it doesn't actually do anything yet), is given here:

```
YUI.add('moodle-filter_swedishchef-loader', function (Y, NAME)
{
        M.filter_swedishchefloader = M.filter_swedishchefloader ||
        {
                /**
                * Boolean used to prevent configuring Swedish Chef twice.
                * @property _configured
                * @type Boolean
                * @default ''
                * @private
                */
                _configured: false,
                /**
                * Called by the filter when it is active on any page.
                * Subscribes to the filter-content-updated event so MathJax
                can respond to content loaded by Ajax.*
                * @method typeset
                * @param {Object} params List of optional configuration
                params.
                */
                configure: function(params)
                {
                        // Listen for events triggered when new text is added
```

```
                    to a page that needs
                    // processing by a filter.
                    Y.on(M.core.event.FILTER_CONTENT_UPDATED,
                    this.contentUpdated,
                    this);
            },

            /**
            * Handle content updated events - typeset the new content.
            * @method contentUpdated
            * @param Y.Event - Custom event with "nodes" indicating the
            root of the updated nodes.*/
            contentUpdated: function(event) {
            var self = this;
            event.nodes.each(function (node)
            {
            // Do something with the node
            });
            }

        };
}, '@VERSION@', {"requires": ["moodle-core-event"]});
```

Next, we need to implement the `moodle_text_filter::setup()` function to load the new script. Add the following function to the `filter_swedishchef` class:

```
/*
* Add the javascript to enable swedish chef language processing on
this page.
*
* @param moodle_page $page The current page.
* @param context $context The current context.
*/
public function setup($page, $context)
{
    // This only requires execution once per request.
    static $jsinitialised = false;
    if (empty($jsinitialised))
    {
        $page->requires->yui_module('moodle-filter_swedishchef-
        loader', 'M.filter_swedishchefloader.configure');
        $jsinitialised = true;
    }
}
```

The best method of testing your new JavaScript code is in the browser--all modern browsers have a developer mode you can enable to test your code. To test if the AJAX event is being fired, we can add a glossary activity to a course (see) as the pop-up glossary entry uses AJAX to display the glossary entry popup:

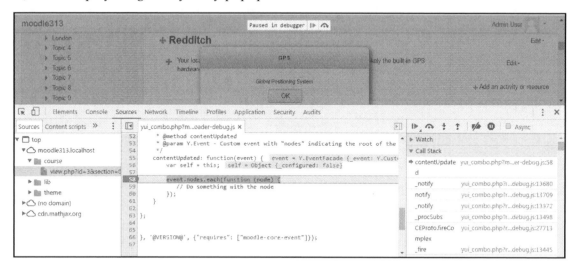

Try it yourself

Can you write a JavaScript function to replace the inner texts of the event nodes passed into `contentUpdated()`?

Summary

In this chapter, we investigated how courses can be enhanced by custom plugins. We developed a course format plugin that revealed sections depending on your GPS location. We also developed a block that displays a QR Code on a course. Finally, we developed a text filter plugin to manipulate on-screen text.

By deconstructing the GPS Format plugin, which displays resources and activities dependant on your location, we learned how to incorporate JavaScript into our plugins, and how to wrap JavaScript in YUI code (YUI is the JavaScript library currently supported by Moodle, although Moodle is transitioning away from YUI to jQuery--see `https://docs.moodle.org/dev/YUI`).

Courses can be enhanced with the inclusion of blocks, and also in this chapter we learned how to construct a QR Code block, using the third-party QR Code image library employed by the *QL Links* plugin. By doing so, we learned how to handle files using Moodle's File API--we created files in Moodle's \temp directory, importing them into the file store, and serving files from the file store to users.

In the final section, we had some fun with text filters. We saw how easy it is to manipulate onscreen text before it is displayed. We did learn, however, the need to be aware that we could seriously impair Moodle performance if our plugins handle their output inefficiently.

Having mastered course layout, we now turn our attention to teaching interactions and the design and development of resources and activities, which is the subject of the next chapter.

5
Creative Teaching - Developing Custom Resources and Activities

Having created plugins to enhance the structure and layout of courses in Chapter 4, *Course Management*, in this chapter we will be learning how to develop new teaching interactions. Recall that Moodle comes with a range of teaching interactions baked in. For example, there are interactions that allow teachers to add quizzes, self-directed lessons, glossaries, discussion forums, and much more, to courses. But there are many instances where you, or your instructional designers, will wish that Moodle included an interaction to support a particular aspect of teaching and/or learning. This is where the possibility to develop custom teaching interactions gives Moodle the edge. Not only does this provide greater opportunities for teaching but it also enhances the experience for our learners.

Moodle supports two types of teaching interactions: *resources* and *activities*. Both of these are types of course module plugins and we begin this chapter with a more thorough exploration of how we can map the requirements for a given teaching interaction onto a suitable type of plugin.

We then get to grips with the development of a novel three-dimensional model viewer. This uses the JavaScript library, three.js, to render a Wavefront 3D model--as well as allowing a user to interact with it. We continue our investigations into the most suitable methods to include JavaScript in our plugins now that YUI is no longer being developed by Yahoo!

This chapter will also help you gain a more thorough understanding of the File API (which we first encountered in `Chapter 3`, *Internal Interfaces*) and how file storage and retrieval works. This understanding is vital as any file a teacher or learner uploads to Moodle will be accessed through this API. We learn more about the scripts we need to prepare in order for our module to install cleanly, and we finish with a brief overview of the things to check before you make your final release.

At the end of this chapter, you will understand how Moodle course plugins work, which scripts need to be present in order for your plugin to behave correctly, and you will know how to modify course plugins to fit your needs.

This chapter will cover the following points:

- Knowing if a user story requires a resource or an activity
- How to manage files (including ZIP compressed files) using the File API
- The scripts required for course plugin installation and an understanding of their structure
- Knowing how to include JavaScript in your plugins--including passing parameters to JavaScript AMD modules
- How to support course backup and restore
- Introducing resources and activities

Let us start with learning the difference between *resources* and *activities*.

Teaching interactions

I am sure that by this stage you will have investigated the **Add an activity or resource** link on a course page (remember that you will need to turn editing on to see this link):

If not, then click on one of these links now to display the **Add an activity or resource** popup dialog:

Resources and activities are the building blocks of Moodle courses. Before continuing, look at the variety of resource and activity plugins a plain vanilla Moodle install supports. See that an *activity* provides teaching interactions--this is Moodle in transmit/receive mode. An activity (at least in the Moodle sense of the word) is something that demands some form of response from the learner (and, ideally, one that will make knowledge stick and/or develop competency in some way). A *resource*, on the other hand, is Moodle in transmit mode. Moodle resources provide access to information and do not necessarily require any further interaction back from the learner. It should be noted that, although resources and activities exhibit very different behaviors, they are built in very similar ways (their PHP scripts are similarly structured), as you will discover in this chapter.

The plugins we will be developing in this chapter are in response to two scenarios--called *User Stories* in Agile. The first describes how the online learning needs to contain 3D models with which a user can interact:

A user should be able to click on a model; zoom in and out, tilt, and rotate it.

The second user story describes what is essentially, a Moodle choice activity but with multimedia in the choice text:

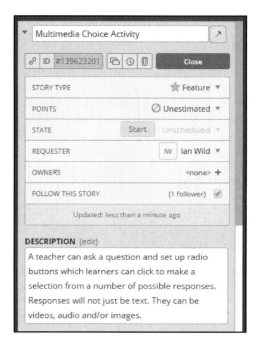

We first encountered the development of an enhanced choice plugin in `Chapter 3`, *Internal*

Interfaces. If you haven't yet read `Chapter 3`, *Internal Interfaces* then it might be worth doing so before continuing with this chapter. What's great about studying this particular plugin is that, in a broader context, it will give you a good understanding of how multimedia files can be handled in any plugin. Likewise, the development of the three-dimensional model viewer plugin--also explained in this chapter--will give you a thorough understanding of how to include third-party (specifically JavaScript) libraries in your plugins.

Let us start with developing the three-dimensional model viewer. Before we start, you might want to download the latest version of this code from GitHib at: `https://github.com/iandavidwild/moodle-mod_wavefront`.

Developing a Resource plugin

As mentioned, although used in very different ways to support teaching, as far as plugin structure is concerned, there is little difference between a resource and an activity plugin. Each one has a similar folder and file structure--which by now I'm sure you are becoming more familiar with. We will explore the details later in this section. First, let us understand how we can actually render a three-dimensional model in the browser.

Rendering a three-dimensional model

Thanks mainly to the gaming community, tools to create and render three-dimensional models are both plentiful and free. For example, there is a whole community dedicated to creating new 3D Mobs models in Minecraft using the open source tool Blender (check out *Blender 2.5 Materials and Textures Cookbook*, also from Packt, at:
`https://www.packtpub.com/hardware-and-creative/blender-25-materials-and-texture`
`s-cookbook`). To render the models in the browser, we will be using a JavaScript library called `three.js`--see `https://threejs.org/` for details, as well as *Learning Three.js - the JavaScript 3D Library for WebGL - Second Edition*, also from Packt (more details can be found at
`https://www.packtpub.com/web-development/learning-threejs-%E2%80%93-javascript-`
`3d-library-webgl-second-edition`).

Three-dimensional models must be described in some mathematical form and there are many file standards that do so. The one we are to support is called **wavefront**. A wavefront .OBJ file is a text file that contains the locations of model vertices (a vertex is a point where two or more lines meet), and shows how the texture of the model fits over each flat surface of the model. Then we will also need information on the model's surface texture. This is stored in a *Materials* .MTL file (which can also contain information on the physical properties of the surface, such as friction), which we will also need to load. Finally, we will need a .PNG image file containing images of surface textures.

As well as `three.js`, our module will need the following JavaScript libraries to support both the rendering and the manipulation of the model:

- `Detector.js`: determines if the browser and/or the graphics card supports WebGL
- `MTLLoader.js`: loads material data
- `OBJLoader.js`: loads the model data
- `OrbitControls.js`: allows the user to manipulate the model on screen using the mouse and keyboard

These scripts, as well as the `three.js` library, can be downloaded from the `threejs.org` website.

Note that it is beyond the scope of this book to describe the technology that makes all this possible--all we need to appreciate is that JavaScript libraries are required and we will:

- Need to locate them within our plugin
- Pass the relevant data to them from our PHP scripts

Assuming you are using the Eclipse IDE (`http://www.eclipse.org/pdt`), in Eclipse, create a new folder under `mod` named `wavefront`. Within the `wavefront` directory, create a folder called `thirdparty` and drop our `three.js` JavaScript files into it:

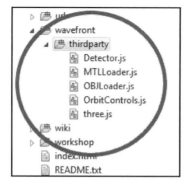

It often makes sense to start developing modules from the backend first (it certainly stops our managers from thinking that we have finished development when they see a mocked-up frontend).

The instructional designer responsible for this user story has mentioned that we need to have learners able to upload models. That would make adding a model to a course a two-step process: first, a course creator would add a `wavefront` resource to a course and then, second, a user with the correct privileges could edit or upload their model for other users to view.

Remember that it is easier to create wireframes of the module configuration and model editing pages and have these agreed with our instructional designer before you start coding.

Module configuration

In Eclipse, create a new file called /mod_form.php. This will contain the form definition class, given in full in the following code:

```php
class mod_wavefront_mod_form extends moodleform_mod
{
    public function definition()
    {
        global $CFG;
        $mform =& $this->_form;
        // General options.
        $mform->addElement('header', 'general',
        get_string('general', 'form'));
        $mform->addElement('text', 'name', get_string('name'),
                            array('size' => '48', 'maxlength' =>
                            '255'));
        $mform->setType('name', PARAM_TEXT);
        $mform->addRule('name', null, 'required', null, 'client');
        $mform->addRule('name', get_string('maximumchars', '',
                        255), 'maxlength', 255, 'client');
        $this->standard_intro_elements();
        // Advanced options.
        $mform->addElement('header', 'wavefrontoptions',
                            get_string('advanced'));
        $yesno = array(0 => get_string('no'), 1 =>
                        get_string('yes'));
        $mform->addElement('select', 'captionfull',
                            get_string('captionfull', 'wavefront'),
                            $yesno);
        $captionposopts = array('0' =>
                                get_string('position_bottom',
                                'wavefront'),
                                '1' => get_string('position_top',
                                'wavefront'),
                                '2' => get_string('hide'),
                                );
        $mform->addElement('select', 'captionpos',
                            get_string('captionpos', 'wavefront'),
                            $captionposopts);
        $mform->addElement('select', 'comments',
                            get_string('allowcomments',
                            'wavefront'), $yesno);
        $mform->setType('comments', PARAM_INT);
        $mform->addElement('select', 'ispublic',
                            get_string('makepublic', 'wavefront'),
                            $yesno);
        $mform->setType('ispublic', PARAM_INT);
```

```
        // Module options.
        $features = array('groups' => false, 'groupings' => false,
        'groupmembersonly' => false,
        'outcomes' => false, 'gradecat' => false, 'idnumber' =>
        false);
        $this->standard_coursemodule_elements($features);
        $this->add_action_buttons();
    }
}
```

See how we are using the Moodle Forms API to construct the page. The only extra function to mention here is `standard_coursemodule_elements()`. This displays the "standard" settings associated with all resource and activity plugins at the bottom of our form,

dependent on the features we are supporting.

Once a `wavefront` resource has been added to a course, we need then to provide a means of configuring the model. In Eclipse, let's add two new files: `mod/edit_model.php` and `mod/edit_model_form.php`:

More on file handling

Firstly, we need to provide a means for the user to upload the three model files: the wavefront .OBJ file, the materials .MTL file, and the .PNG texture image file (described previously). Luckily, the File API and Form API together provide functions to manage these files for us. The first is `file_prepare_standard_filemanager()`. We call this File API function in `edit_model.php` to associate files (if any) in Moodle's file store with the corresponding form element declared in `edit_model_form.php`. In our plugin, we have the following line in `edit_model.php`:

```
$model = file_prepare_standard_filemanager($model, 'model', $modeloptions,
$context, 'mod_wavefront', 'model', $model->id);
```

The preceeding line prepares the files for the following form element added in
`edit_model_form.php`:

```
$mform->addElement('filemanager', 'model_filemanager',
get_string('modelfiles', 'wavefront'), null, $modeloptions);
```

Note that we need to be careful to make sure the form element name (in this case "model")
is appended with "_filemanager" so that the API can associate our model files with the
correct element.

The model also has an optional description and this, potentially, can have files embedded in
it (for example, images). To prepare a standard text editor, we can call the
`file_prepare_standard_editor()` function in `edit_model.php`:

```
$model = file_prepare_standard_editor($model, 'description',
$descriptionoptions, $context, 'mod_wavefront', 'description', $model->id);
```

Similar to the file manager form element, we need to add an editor element called
description_editor (that is, the name specified in the second parameter *description* appended
with *_editor*) to the form:

```
$mform->addElement('editor', 'description_editor',
get_string('modeldescription', 'wavefront'), null, $descriptionoptions);
```

Plugin library callbacks

The next step is to create a new file, `/lib.php`, which will contain the plugin's library
callback functions:

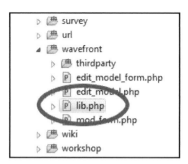

---

[143]

Each function in this script will be prefixed with the name of the module *wavefront_*. For example, the `wavefront_supports()` function is called by the module framework to determine what features our wavefront renderer provides:

```
function wavefront_supports($feature)
{
    switch($feature)
    {
        case FEATURE_MOD_ARCHETYPE:
            return MOD_ARCHETYPE_RESOURCE;
        case FEATURE_GROUPS:
            return false;
        case FEATURE_GROUPINGS:
            return false;
        case FEATURE_MOD_INTRO:
            return true;
        case FEATURE_COMPLETION_TRACKS_VIEWS:
            return true;
        case FEATURE_GRADE_HAS_GRADE:
            return false;
        case FEATURE_GRADE_OUTCOMES:
            return false;
        case FEATURE_BACKUP_MOODLE2:
            return true;
    default:
    return null;
    }
}
```

There are also callback functions for adding, updating, and deleting wavefront renderer activities (note that's not the model but the activity). Firstly, the method to add a new wavefront instance is as follows:

```
/**
 * Given an object containing all the necessary data,
 * (defined by the form in mod_form.php) this function
 * will create a new instance and return the id number
 * of the new instance.
 *
 * @param object $model An object from the form in mod_form.php
 * @return int The id of the newly inserted newmodule record
 */
function wavefront_add_instance($wavefront)
{
    global $DB;
    $wavefront->timemodified = time();
    wavefront_set_sizing($wavefront);
```

```
        return $DB->insert_record('wavefront', $wavefront);
    }
```

Then there is the function to update a current instance. This will need to update the correct record in the database:

```
/**
 * Given an object containing all the necessary data,
 * (defined by the form in mod_form.php) this function
 * will update an existing instance with new data.
 *
 * @param object $model An object from the form in mod_form.php
 * @return boolean Success/Fail
 */
function wavefront_update_instance($wavefront)
{
        global $DB;
        $wavefront->timemodified = time();
        $wavefront->id = $wavefront->instance;
        wavefront_set_sizing($wavefront);
        return $DB->update_record('wavefront', $wavefront);
    }
```

Finally, we need to provide a method to delete a current wavefront instance. This will need to remove the relevant record from the database:

```
/**
 * Given an ID of an instance of this module,
 * this function will permanently delete the instance
 * and any data that depends on it.
 *
 * @param int $id Id of the module instance
 * @return boolean Success/Failure
 */
function wavefront_delete_instance($id)
{
        global $DB;
        if (!$wavefront = $DB->get_record('wavefront', array('id' =>
            $id)))
        {
            return false;
        }
        $cm = get_coursemodule_from_instance('wavefront', $wavefront-
                                             >id);
        $context = context_module::instance($cm->id);
        // Files.
        $fs = get_file_storage();
        $fs->delete_area_files($context->id, 'mod_wavefront');
```

```
            // Delete all the records and models.
            $DB->delete_records('wavefront_comments', array('wavefrontid' =>
                            $wavefront->id) );
            $DB->delete_records('wavefront_model', array('wavefrontid' =>
                            $wavefront->id));
            // Delete the instance itself.
            $DB->delete_records('wavefront', array('id' => $id));
            return true;
    }
```

Note that we are using the Data Manipulation API (via the $DB global variable) to store and retrieve activity and model data in the preceding functions. I tend to add tables (and the necessary columns) as I am developing and then rationalize afterwards. This is discussed later in this section.

Rendering the Model

We will be relying on three files to render the model. The first is /view.php. This PHP script is loaded by the framework when it's time to display the activity. This script calls on the Page API (via the $PAGE global variable) to, among other things, set the page URL and to load up the necessary JavaScript files:

```
    // The javascript this page requires
    // The code we are using is neat javascript so load each script one at a
    time
    //
    $PAGE->requires->js('/mod/wavefront/thirdparty/three.js', true);
    $PAGE->requires->js('/mod/wavefront/thirdparty/Detector.js', true);
    $PAGE->requires->js('/mod/wavefront/thirdparty/OrbitControls.js', true);
    $PAGE->requires->js('/mod/wavefront/thirdparty/OBJLoader.js', true);
    $PAGE->requires->js('/mod/wavefront/thirdparty/MTLLoader.js', true);
```

Notice that I am loading each JavaScript file one at a time, initially, at least, in order to improve readability, rather than using a module loader such as RequireJS (which Moodle 3.1 does also support--see

https://docs.moodle.org/dev/Javascript_Modules#Loading_modules_dynamically).

The construction of the page HTML--that is, page header, footer, and the actual rendering of the model--should be handled by an output renderer (see `https://docs.moodle.org/dev/Output_renderers`). For that, we need our second script: `/renderer.php`. This script is a declaration of the `mod_wavefront_renderer()` class, which itself contains two public functions and one private helper function:

1. `display_model()`: outputs the HTML needed to display the model. Note that the model is rendered using JavaScript so all that is needed at this stage is a DIV tag for `three.js` to output into (more about this shortly).
2. `display_comments()`: display any user comments.
3. `print_comments()`: a private helper function that prints an individual comment.

We load the renderer in `/view.php` and call on it to display the necessary HTML:

```
$output = $PAGE->get_renderer('mod_folder');
echo $output->header();
$heading = get_string('displayingmodel', 'wavefront', $wavefront->name);
echo $output->heading($heading);
echo $output->display_model($wavefront, $editing);
echo $output->display_comments($wavefront);
echo $output->footer();
```

We need to call upon JavaScript to display the model and, for that, we will need not only to call the relevant functions in the three.js library but also we will need to pass to the script file the URLs of the model files and the relevant configuration settings (such as the model stage size). This is described in the next section.

More on JavaScript

As mentioned in `Chapter 4`, *Course Management*, Moodle supports both YUI and jQuery JavaScript modules. Recall that in `Chapter 4`, *Course Management*, we used YUI to load geolocation scripts for our geolocation course format. However, Yahoo! have stopped developing YUI and so Moodle is now recommending that any new modules load JavaScript using the *Asynchronous Module Definition API*--see `https://docs.moodle.org/dev/Javascript_Modules`.

Asynchronous Module Definition (AMD) API

In Eclipse, create a new folder called `/amd/src` and a new file called `model_renderer.js`:

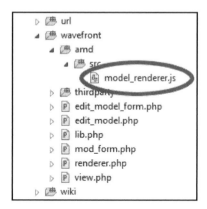

The structure of AMD modules is described in the Moodle documentation at: `https://docs.moodle.org/dev/Javascript_Modules`.

Within `model_renderer.js`, we will implement what is, in essence, a single closure function that will be called from `view.php`. Within the close, we can implement an init() function to initialize the wavefront renderer and allow the user to manipulate the model. Rather than repeat the code here, check out the complete declaration at `https://github.com/iandavidwild/moodle-mod_wavefront/blob/develop/amd/src/model_renderer.js`.

Note that the `init()` function accepts the following parameters:

- `stage`: the ID of the DIV tag within which the model will be rendered (the three.js library will append a CANVAS entity to it).
- `obj_file`: the URL of the .OBJ model description file
- `mtl_file`: the URL of the .MTL
- `baseurl`: the URL at which the .PNG file will be found
- `width`: the onscreen width of the CANVAS entity
- `height`: the onscreen height of the CANVAS entity

These parameters are passed from `/view.php` through a call to `js_call_amd()`. The following is the complete code:

```
if ($model = $DB->get_record('wavefront_model', array('wavefrontid' =>
$wavefront->id)))
{
```

```
$fs = get_file_storage();
$fs_files = $fs->get_area_files($context->id, 'mod_wavefront',
        'model', $model->id);
// A Wavefront model contains three files
$mtl_file = null;
$obj_file = null;
$baseurl = null;
foreach ($fs_files as $f)
{
     // $f is an instance of stored_file
     $pathname = $f->get_filepath();
     $filename = $f->get_filename();
     $ext = strtolower(pathinfo($filename, PATHINFO_EXTENSION));
     // what type of file is this?
          if($ext === "mtl")
          {
               $mtl_file = moodle_url::make_pluginfile_url
                         ($context->id,'mod_wavefront',
                         'model', $model->id, $pathname,
                         $filename);
          }
          elseif ($ext === "obj")
          {
               $obj_file = moodle_url::make_pluginfile_url
                         ($context->id, 'mod_wavefront',
                         'model', $model->id, $pathname,
                         $filename);
          }
          elseif ($ext === "png")
          {
               $baseurl = moodle_url::make_pluginfile_url
                         ($context->id, 'mod_wavefront',
                         'model', $model->id, $pathname, '');
          }
}
$js_params = array('wavefront_stage', $obj_file->__toString(),
$mtl_file->__toString(), $baseurl->__toString(), $model->width,
$model->height);
$PAGE->requires->js_call_amd('mod_wavefront/model_renderer',
'init', $js_params);
}
```

See how the base URL and the URLs of the .OBJ and .MTL files are constructed using the `make_pluginfile_url()` function. To support these URLs, we will need to implement another callback function in `/lib.php` called `wavefront_pluginfile()`:

```
 * Serves model files.
 *
 * @param object $course
 * @param object $cm
 * @param object $context
 * @param string $filearea
 * @param array $args
 * @param bool $forcedownload
 * @return bool false if file not found, does not return if found - just
send the file
 */
function wavefront_pluginfile($course, $cm, $context, $filearea, $args,
$forcedownload)
{
        global $CFG, $DB, $USER;
        require_once($CFG->libdir.'/filelib.php');
        $wavefront = $DB->get_record('wavefront', array('id' => $cm-
                    >instance));
        if (!$wavefront->ispublic)
        {
                require_login($course, false, $cm);
        }
        $relativepath = implode('/', $args);
        $fullpath = '/'.$context-
                    >id.'/mod_wavefront/'.$filearea.'/'.$relativepath;
        $fs = get_file_storage();
        if (!$file = $fs->get_file_by_hash(sha1($fullpath)) or $file-
            >is_directory())
        {
                return false;
        }
        send_stored_file($file, 0, 0, true); // Download MUST be forced
                                              - security!
        return;
}
```

Reporting events

However a user interacts with both the Wavefront activity and the model it contains, it is important that we record these events in the Moodle log.

In Eclipse, create a new folder called `/classes/event`:

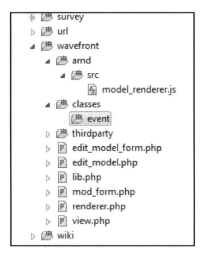

For each interaction we wish to log, we implement a new PHP event class and trigger it. See the documentation at `https://docs.moodle.org/dev/Event_2` for details on the Moodle events system. The Moodle events system is a powerful way for us to track most types of activity taking place in the platform--both activities instigated by the user (such as viewing an activity) or activities engaged in automatically (for example, instigated by a cron job).

In the following example, we want to log when a user views a model. So we create a new PHP script in `/classes/event` called `course_module_viewed.php`:

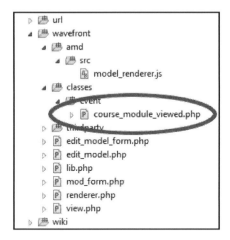

Within this, we need to implement a class that extends the `course_module_viewed` class:

```
/**
 * The mod_wavefront viewed event class.
 *
 * @property-read array $other {
 * Extra information about event.
 *
 *- int wavefrontid: the id of the wavefront activity.
 * }
 *
 * @package    mod_wavefront
 * @copyright  2017 Ian Wild
 * @license    http://www.gnu.org/copyleft/gpl.html GNU GPL v3 or later
 */
class course_module_viewed extends \core\event\course_module_viewed
{
        /**
         * Init method.
         *
         * @return void
         */
        protected function init()
        {
                $this->data['crud'] = 'r';
                $this->data['edulevel'] = self::LEVEL_PARTICIPATING;
                $this->data['objecttable'] = 'wavefront';
        }
```

```
/**
 * Get URL related to the action.
 *
 * @return \moodle_url
 */
public function get_url()
{
        return new \moodle_url('/mod/wavefront/view.php',
                                array('l' => $this->objectid));
}
/**
 * Return the legacy event log data.
 *
 * @return array|null
 */
protected function get_legacy_logdata()
{
        return array($this->courseid, 'wavefront', 'view',
                        'view.php?l=' . $this->objectid,
                        $this->objectid, $this->->
                        contextinstanceid);
}
}
```

By nature of its location in the file system, its name, and the name of the class declaration it contains, this class is automatically loaded by Moodle when it is needed (see https://docs.moodle.org/dev/Automatic_class_loading).

To fire the event, we have to trigger it. Here is the fragment of code to do so:

```
$params = array( 'context' => $context,
                'objectid' => $wavefront->id);
$event = \mod_wavefront\event\course_module_viewed::create($params);
$event->add_record_snapshot('course_modules', $cm);
$event->add_record_snapshot('course', $course);
$event->add_record_snapshot('wavefront', $wavefront);
$event->trigger();
```

Firstly, we create the event we want to fire, making sure we create the right event by specifying the correct namespace, in this case \mod_wavefront\event.

It's not only the Moodle log that listens out for events, so the add_record_snapshot() function adds data that other event listeners might be interested in hearing.

To improve maintainability, I have implemented each event class in its own PHP script:

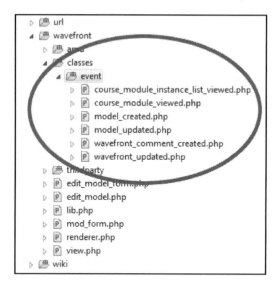

Other files

In this section, we quickly run through the other PHP script files we will need to implement in order to make the plugin function.

Script file	Details
/index.php	Lists all the wavefront modules which have been added to the current course.
/version.php	Contains version information--not only the current version of the plugin but also the minimum version of Moodle this plugin supports.
/pix/icon.svg	The plugin's main icon.
lang/en/wavefront.php	This contains the relevant English language strings and other languages.

With these files included in the plugin, we now have in place the framework for a working three-dimensional model viewer. In the next section, we will describe the scripts we will need to implement within the plugin to install it.

Installation scripts

In Eclipse, create a new folder called /db. Our first issue is user permissions: which user has the capability to perform what actions? This is described in access.php:

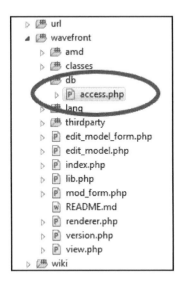

The script access.php contains an array of uniquely named capabilities, and the risks associated with each capability--for example, the risk of spam or of a **Cross-Site Scripting (XSS)** attack. The complete list of capabilities from our new module can be seen on GitHub at https://www.github.com.

For example, we can specify who is allowed to add a comment:

```
$capabilities = array(
    'mod/wavefront:addcomment' => array(
        'riskbitmask' => RISK_SPAM,
        'captype' => 'write',
        'contextlevel' => CONTEXT_MODULE,
        'legacy' => array(
            'student' => CAP_ALLOW,
            'teacher' => CAP_ALLOW,
            'editingteacher' => CAP_ALLOW,
            'manager' => CAP_ALLOW
        )
    )
```

The next two files are installation log and upgrade support files, `log.php` and `upgrade.php`:

The `upgrade.php` script contains a single function, `xmldb_wavefront_upgrade()`, which is called during the upgrade process. As this is a new module, `upgrade.php` need only contain a placeholder. I have also included a few comments for future reference:

```
function xmldb_wavefront_upgrade($oldversion)
{
        global $CFG;
        // Moodle v2.8.0 release upgrade line.
        // Put any upgrade step following this.
        // Moodle v2.9.0 release upgrade line.
        // Put any upgrade step following this.
        // Moodle v3.0.0 release upgrade line.
        // Put any upgrade step following this.
        // Moodle v3.1.0 release upgrade line.
        // Put any upgrade step following this.
        return true;
}
```

XMLDB editor

Finally, we need to implement the means by which the necessary database tables are created at install time: the `install.xml` file. This is done through a special built-in tool called **XMLDB Editor**--see `https://docs.moodle.org/dev/XMLDB_editor`. In Moodle, from the **Administration** block, click on **Site administration**, slide down to **Development,** and then click on **XMLDB editor**. A list of all the installed modules will appear--including our wavefront module:

Click on **[Create]** to create a new `install.xml` file. Next, we need to click on **[Load]** to load the file (even though it is currently empty) and then click on **[Edit]** to begin to author it. When developing modules, I tend to create the database tables as I am going along. This is fine as it means you can load the tables into the editor using the **New table from MySQL** option:

In the **New table from MySQL** page, select the database table you want to create from the drop-down menu and where in the `install.xml` script you want the table declaration to appear:

Specify the table you wish to create the XML file from, and the table which will precede it. Then press the **Create** button. On subsequent pages, you can edit the configuration. More details are available at `https://docs.moodle.org/31/en/admin/tool/xmldb/index`.

Allowing user comments

As far as completing the functionality is concerned, the final piece of the jigsaw is to allow users to make comments on models. A new comments form is created in much the same way as described just now. Let us add two new PHP scripts, `/comment.php` and `/comment_form.php`:

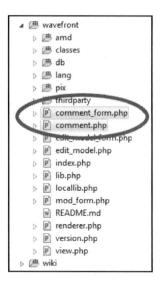

In `comment_form.php`, we declare a simple form that allows the user to specify a comment:

```
/**
 * Form for adding comments on a model
 *
 * @package    mod_wavefront
 * @copyright 2017 Ian Wild
 * @license    http://www.gnu.org/copyleft/gpl.html GNU GPL v3 or later
 */
require_once($CFG->libdir.'/formslib.php');
class mod_wavefront_comment_form extends moodleform
{
    public function definition()
    {
        $mform =& $this->_form;
        $wavefront = $this->_customdata;
        $straddcomment = get_string('addcomment', 'wavefront');
        $mform->addElement('editor', 'comment', $straddcomment,
                            array('cols' => 85, 'rows' => 18));
        $mform->addRule('comment', get_string('required'),
                        'required', null, 'client');
        $mform->setType('comment', PARAM_RAW);
        $mform->addElement('hidden', 'id', 0);
        $mform->setDefault('id', $wavefront->id);
        $mform->setType('id', PARAM_INT);
        $this->add_action_buttons(true, $straddcomment);
    }
}
```

This form is supported by comment.php, which stores the comment text (note that we are not providing support for embedded multimedia) along with details of when, who, and to which instance of the wavefront plugin the comment is associated. It also manages the deleting of comments--and again for this we have to be careful: we should only have users with the correct privileges able to delete comments. The following is the relevant code fragment from comment.php which ensures the current user has the capability to delete a comment:

```
if ($delete && has_capability('mod/wavefront:edit', $context))
{
        if ($confirm && confirm_sesskey())
        {
                $DB->delete_records('wavefront_comments', array('id' =>
                                    $comment->id));
                redirect($wavefronturl);
        }
        else
        {
                echo $OUTPUT->header();
                wavefront_print_comment($comment, $context);
                echo('<br />');
                $paramsyes = array('id' => $wavefront->id, 'delete' =>
                $comment->id, 'sesskey' => sesskey(), 'confirm' => 1);
                $paramsno = array('id' => $cm->id);
                echo $OUTPUT->confirm(get_string('commentdelete',
                'wavefront'),
                new moodle_url('/mod/wavefront/comment.php', $paramsyes),
                            new moodle_url('/mod/wavefront/view.php',
                            $paramsno));
                echo $OUTPUT->footer();
                die();
        }
}
```

More on file handling

Rather than having to upload individual .OBJ, .MTL, and .PNG files, would it not be easier if we could ZIP up the files we need and upload them in a single file to the wavefront module? We can then have the plugin unzip them automatically. In this section, we learn how.

Firstly, let us create a new file called `/locallib.php`, within which we can add local library functions (for example, library functions to be used only by the wavefront plugin):

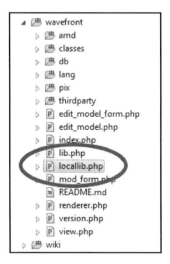

In `locallib.php`, we add a new function called `wavefront_check_for_zips()`:

```
/**
 * Checks for ZIP files to unpack.
 *
 * @param context $context
 * @param cm_info $cm
 * @param $model
 * @return void
 */
function wavefront_check_for_zips($context, $cm, $model)
{
        $fs = get_file_storage();
        $files = $fs->get_area_files($context->id, 'mod_wavefront',
                'model', $model->id, "itemid, filepath, filename",
                false);
        foreach ($files as $storedfile)
        {
                if ($storedfile->get_mimetype() == 'application/zip')
                {
                        // Unpack.
                        $packer = get_file_packer('application/zip');
                        $fs->delete_area_files($context->id, 'mod_wavefront',
                        'unpacktemp', 0);
                        $storedfile->extract_to_storage($packer, $context-
                                >id, 'mod_wavefront', 'unpacktemp', 0,
```

```
                                   '/');
            $tempfiles = $fs->get_area_files($context->id,
                    'mod_wavefront', 'unpacktemp', 0,
                    "itemid, filepath, filename", false);
        if(count($tempfiles) > 0)
        {
                $storedfile->delete(); // delete the ZIP file.
                foreach ($tempfiles as $storedfile)
                {
                        $filename = $storedfile->get_filename();
                        $fileinfo = array(
                                        'contextid'     =>
                                        $context->id,
                                        'component'     =>
                                        'mod_wavefront',
                                        'filearea'      =>
                                        'model',
                                        'itemid'        =>
                                        $model->id,
                                        'filepath'      => '/',
                                        'filename'      =>
                                        $filename
                                        );
                        $storedfile = $fs->
                                        create_file_from_storedfile
                                        ($fileinfo, $storedfile);

                }
        }
        $fs->delete_area_files($context->id, 'mod_wavefront',
                                'unpacktemp', 0);


                }
        }
    }
```

In this function, we introduce the get_file_packer() and extract_to_storage()
functions. These aren't too well documented but are fairly self-explanatory. Basically, this
function looks for ZIP files and, if it finds one, extracts the contents to a temporary area.
Once extracted, the files in the temporary area are copied into the correct file area for the
given module instance and, once the process is complete, everything is cleared down.

All that is left is for us to call this function from /edit_model.php, immediately after the
call to file_postupdate_standard_filemanager().

Styling

Each module comes with its own style sheet named /styles.css. Let's create this now in Eclipse:

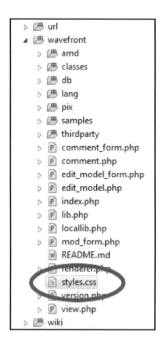

We only need concern ourselves with basic styling at this stage, as detailed styling is implemented in the **theme**. For example, to provide default styling to the model caption, we can include suitable styling in styles.css:

```
.wavefront .wavefront-model-frame
{
    background-color: #fff;
    display: inline-block;
    margin: 10px auto;
    text-align:      center;
    border: 1px solid #ccc;
    border-radius: 5px;
    transition: box-shadow 150ms, border-color 150ms, background-
               color 150ms, color 150ms;
    -webkit-transition: box-shadow 150ms, border-color 150ms,
    background-color 150ms, color 150ms;
    color: #696969;
}
.wavefront .wavefront-model-caption
```

```
{
      font-weight: bold;
      word-wrap: break-word;
}
```

The following ensures the spacing is correct when the caption is displayed above the model:

```
.wavefront .wavefront-model-caption.top
{
      margin-bottom: -3px;
}
```

The model and description (with the description configured to be displayed at the top) now looks like this:

We also include a hover glow so that the user knows when the model has focus:

```
.wavefront .wavefront-model-container .wavefront-model-frame:hover
{
      transition: box-shadow 150ms, border-color 150ms;
      text-decoration:none;
      box-shadow: 0 0 15px #ccc;
      -webkit-box-shadow: 0 0 15px #ccc;
      border-color: #999;
      background-color: #f6f6f6;
      color: #333;
}
```

Moodle theming is covered in detail in `Chapter 7`, *Creating a Dashboard - Developing a Learner Homepage*.

In the next section, we will introduce two new APIs--Backup and Restore.

Backup and Restore API

When a course is backed up, then, quite sensibly, it is the responsibility of each individual plugin to handle the backing up and the restoring of each instance of that plugin belonging to the course. To register that we support Backup and Restore, in the `/lib.php` callback function `wavefront_supports($feature)`, we need to ensure we set the `FEATURE_BACKUP_MOODLE2` flag to true (refer to the section, *Plugin library callbacks*, earlier in this chapter).

In order to implement the functionality, there are four scripts we need to create:

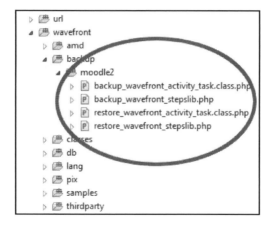

Backup API

For more information on the Backup API (as it applies to activities), refer to the Moodle documentation here:

`https://docs.moodle.org/dev/Backup_API#API_for_activity_modules`.

The documentation describes the functioning of these scripts very well so there isn't much need to go into too much detail here. Of interest is the `define_structure()`, function contained in the `backup_wavefront_steps.php` script, as this implements the actual backing up. The following is the complete function:

```php
protected function define_structure()
{
        // To know if we are including userinfo.
        $userinfo = $this->get_setting_value('userinfo');
        // Define each element separated.
        $wavefront = new backup_nested_element('wavefront', array('id'),
                                        array('course', 'folder',
                                        'name', 'comments',
                                        'timemodified',
                                        'ispublic',
                                        'intro', 'introformat'
                                        ));
        $comments = new backup_nested_element('usercomments');
        $comment = new backup_nested_element('comment', array('id'),
                                        array('wavefrontid',
                                        'userid', 'commenttext',
                                        'timemodified'
                                        ));
        // currenty one model per wavefront
        $model = new backup_nested_element('model', array('id'), array(
                                        'wavefrontid',
                                        'description',
                                        'descriptionformat',
                                        'descriptionpos',
                                        'stagewidth', 'stageheight',
                                        'camerax', 'cameray',
                                        'cameraz', 'cameraangle',
                                        'camerafar',
                                        'model', 'timemodified'
                                        ));

        // Build the tree.
        $wavefront->add_child($model);
        $wavefront->add_child($comments);
        $comments->add_child($comment);
        // Define sources.
        $wavefront->set_source_table('wavefront', array('id' =>
                backup::VAR_ACTIVITYID));
        $model->set_source_table('wavefront_model', array('wavefrontid'
                => backup::VAR_ACTIVITYID));
        // All the rest of elements only happen if we are including
        user info.
```

```
        if ($userinfo)
        {
                $comment->set_source_table('wavefront_comments',
                        array('wavefrontid' => backup::VAR_PARENTID));
        }
        // Define file annotations.
        $wavefront->annotate_files('mod_wavefront', 'model', null);
        $wavefront->annotate_files('mod_wavefront', 'intro', null);
        $comment->annotate_ids('user', 'userid');
        // Return the root element (wavefront), wrapped into standard
        activity structure.
        return $this->prepare_activity_structure($wavefront);
}
```

See that we are only including user data (for example, comments users have added to the model) if user data is included in the backup (there is an option to include--or not--user data when a backup is requested).

Restore API

As one can imagine, restoring is essentially the reverse of backing up. Details of the Restore API are to be found in the developer documentation at: `https://docs.moodle.org/dev/Re store_API#API_for_activity_modules`.

The `restore_wavefront_activity_structure_step` class defined in `restore_wavefront_stepslib.php` needs to provide one function per database table that describes how data should be taken from the backup and inserted back into the database. The following example covers user comments:

```
protected function process_wavefront_comment($data)
{
        global $DB;
        $data = (object)$data;
        $data->wavefront = $this->get_new_parentid('wavefront');
        $data->userid = $this->get_mappingid('user', $data->userid);
        $data->timemodified = $this->apply_date_offset($data-
                                >timemodified);
        if (isset($data->comment))
        {
                $data->commenttext = $data->comment;
        }
        $DB->insert_record('wavefront_comments', $data);
}
```

Roles and permissions

Remember we specify default roles and permissions in `access.php`--refer to the section, Installation scripts, earlier in this chapter. Capabilities are reasonably straightforward to understand. Take a look at `https://docs.moodle.org/dev/Access_API` for an explanation of how we can use the Access API to determine if the current user can, for instance, edit a model (from `/view.php`):

```
if ($editing)
{
        require_capability('mod/wavefront:edit', $context);
}
```

With the wavefront module almost complete, now it is time to consider the final steps before release.

Preparing for release

There are two main considerations for releasing a module. The first concerns maintainability. You may understand how your plugin functions but will anyone else? Will you understand it if you need to come back to it in six months' time? Maintainability and readability go hand in hand. For more information on the coding style that is expected of you, check out `https://docs.moodle.org/dev/Coding_style`.

Minimising JavaScript

Another factor to consider in the Wavefront plugin is that we are including JavaScript. Both the AMD script and the third-party `three.js` libraries we are deploying with our module will need to be minified. Check the Moodle documentation at `https://docs.moodle.org/dev/Javascript_Modules` for details on how **Grunt** can be used to minify JavaScript.

Taking things further

Here are some more ideas for further developments to the model viewer plugin:

1. Create a gallery of 3D models. The plugin's tables have been structured such that a model refers to an instance of a wavefront plugin. This allows us to have more than one model belonging to a wavefront instance.
2. Provide extra settings for lighting effects. Currently, lighting is fixed.
3. Provide a debugging option that displays extra information to the user. For instance, the viewer's roll, pitch, and yaw can be posted to a debug window.

Activities

Moodle activity plugins support teaching interactions. If we are working on a user story that describes some form of learner input, then it is a safe bet that we need to create an activity to support that.

In terms of structure, there is little difference between an activity and a resource--an activity will be listed as such in the **Add an activity or resource** dialog if the xxxx_supports() library callback function doesn't specify the module archetype as a resource (as described earlier in this chapter).

Recall that the user story we have been provided with, describes the choice activity (https://docs.moodle.org/31/en/Choice_activity) with the choices, potentially, enhanced with multimedia.

Enhanced choice

Using a development environment such as Eclipse will make the transformation of the choice module into the enhanced choice module simple. First we simply right-click on the /mod/choice folder and paste it back in to the /mod folder as enhancedchoice.

Next, we need to modify /version.php to:

* Update the version numbers
* Replace any reference to the word choice with enhancedchoice

Having done this for `/version.php`, we now need to run through the rest of the files to replace all instances of the word `choice` with `enhancedchoice`. Again, the **Find/Replace** option in Eclipse makes this exercise straightforward:

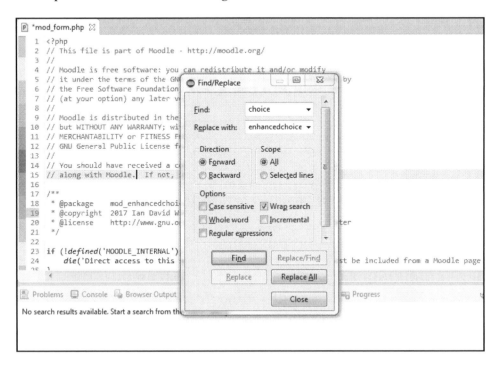

Next, we need to update the names of the Backup/Restore and language scripts:

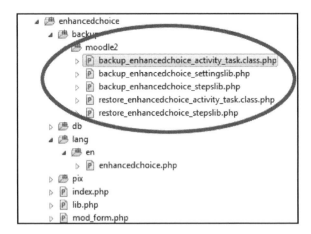

That done, it is worth attempting to install the new module by opening the **Site administration** menu and selecting **Notifications**. Any errors or omissions will be easy to spot at this stage.

Editing choices

The choice activity configuration form /mod_form.php is currently scripted such that choices are specified using text boxes:

```
$repeatarray = array();
$repeatarray[] = $mform->createElement('text', 'option',
                                       get_string('optionno',
                                       'choice'));
$repeatarray[] = $mform->createElement('text', 'limit',
                                       get_string('limitno',
                                       'choice'));
$repeatarray[] = $mform->createElement('hidden', 'optionid', 0);
if ($this->_instance)
{
        $repeatno = $DB->count_records('choice_options',
                                       array('choiceid'=>$this-
                                       >_instance));
        $repeatno += 2;
}
else
{
        $repeatno = 5;
}
$repeateloptions = array();
$repeateloptions['limit']['default'] = 0;
$repeateloptions['limit']['disabledif'] = array('limitanswers', 'eq', 0);
$repeateloptions['limit']['rule'] = 'numeric';
$repeateloptions['limit']['type'] = PARAM_INT;
$repeateloptions['option']['helpbutton'] = array('choiceoptions',
'choice');
```

We need to modify this, so that the user is presented with the HTML editor instead:

```
$repeatarray = array();
$repeatarray[] = $mform->createElement('header', '',
                get_string('option','enhancedchoice').' {no}');
$repeatarray[] = $mform->createElement('editor', 'option',
                get_string('option','enhancedchoice'), null,
                array('maxfiles'=>EDITOR_UNLIMITED_FILES,
                'noclean'=>true, 'context'=>$this->context));
$repeatarray[] = $mform->createElement('text', 'limit',
```

```
                    get_string('limit','enhancedchoice'));
$repeatarray[] = $mform->createElement('hidden', 'optionid', 0);
$menuoptions = array();
$menuoptions[0] = get_string('disable');
$menuoptions[1] = get_string('enable');
$mform->addElement('header', 'timerestricthdr', get_string('limit',
                    'enhancedchoice'));
$mform->addElement('select', 'limitanswers', get_string('limitanswers',
                    'enhancedchoice'), $menuoptions);
$mform->addHelpButton('limitanswers', 'limitanswers',
                    'enhancedchoice');
if ($this->_instance)
{
      $repeatno = $DB->count_records('enhancedchoice_options',
                                array('choiceid'=>$this->
                                _instance));
      $repeatno += 2;
}
else
{
      $repeatno = 5;
}
$repeateloptions = array();
$repeateloptions['limit']['default'] = 0;
$repeateloptions['limit']['disabledif'] = array('limitanswers', 'eq', 0);
$repeateloptions['limit']['rule'] = 'numeric';
$repeateloptions['limit']['type'] = PARAM_INT;
$repeateloptions['option']['helpbutton'] =
array('enhancedchoice_options', 'enhancedchoice');
```

The data_preprocessing() function will need to be modified so that any multimedia files added to a choice are copied from the file store into the draft file area for each text editor included in the choice configuration form. Recall that we do so by calling the file_get_submitted_draft_itemid() File API function:

```
function data_preprocessing(&$default_values)
{
      global $DB;
      if (!empty($this->_instance) && ($options = $DB->
          get_records('enhancedchoice_options',array('choiceid'=>$this-
          >_instance), 'id', 'id,text,textformat'))
          && ($options2 = $DB->
          get_records_menu('enhancedchoice_options',
          array('choiceid'=>$this->_instance), 'id', 'id,maxanswers'))
        )
      {
            $choiceids=array_keys($options);
            $options=array_values($options);
```

```
        $options2=array_values($options2);
        $editoroptions = enhancedchoice_get_editor_options();
        $idx = 0;
        foreach (array_keys($options) as $key)
        {
                $draftid = file_get_submitted_draft_itemid
                        ('option['.$key.']');
                $defaulttext = file_prepare_draft_area($draftid,
                        $this->context->id,
                        'mod_enhancedchoice',
                        'option',
                        !empty($choiceids[$key]) ? (int)
                $choiceids[$key] : null, // Itemid.,
                $editoroptions,
                $options[$key]->text);
                $default_values['option['.$key.']']['text'] =
                $defaulttext;
                $default_values['option['.$key.']']['itemid'] =
                $draftid;

                $default_values['limit['.$key.']'] = $options2[$key];
                $default_values['optionid['.$key.']'] =
                $choiceids[$key];
                $idx++;
        }
    }
    if (empty($default_values['timeopen']))
    {
            $default_values['timerestrict'] = 0;
    }
    else
    {
            $default_values['timerestrict'] = 1;
    }

}
```

We now need to modify /lib.php to serve any multimedia files included in the choice text. Remember that the library callback function we should implement will be called enhancedchoice_pluginfile():

```
/**
 * Serves the folder files.
 *
 * @package   mod_enhancedchoice
 * @category  files
 * @param stdClass $course course object
 * @param stdClass $cm course module
```

```
 * @param stdClass $context context object
 * @param string $filearea file area
 * @param array $args extra arguments
 * @param bool $forcedownload whether or not force download
 * @param array $options additional options affecting the file serving
 * @return bool false if file not found, does not return if found -just
send the file
 */
function enhancedchoice_pluginfile($course, $cm, $context, $filearea,
$args, $forcedownload, array $options=array())
{
      global $CFG, $DB;
      if ($context->contextlevel != CONTEXT_MODULE)
      {
            return false;
      }
      require_course_login($course, true, $cm);
            if ($filearea !== 'option')
            {
                  // intro is handled automatically in pluginfile.php
                  return false;
            }
      $optionid = array_shift($args); // ignore revision - designed to
                                      prevent caching problems only
      $fs = get_file_storage();
      $relativepath = implode('/', $args);
      $fullpath = "/$context->id/mod_enhancedchoice/$filearea/$optionid
              /$relativepath";
      if (!$file = $fs->get_file_by_hash(sha1($fullpath)) or $file->
              is_directory())
      {
            return false;
      }
      // finally send the file
      // for folder module, we force download file all the time
      send_stored_file($file, 86400, 0, true, $options);
}
```

The following is a screen grab of the enhanced choice module in action:

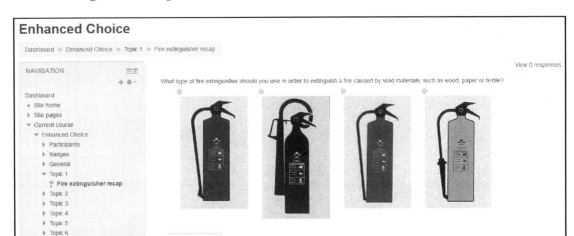

Notice that each choice has an image included in it--this is what puts the "Enhanced" in the Enhanced Choice activity.

Summary

In this chapter, we developed two types of teaching interaction. First, we developed a course resource-type plugin that allows a teacher to include complex three-dimensional models in their courses. In developing this plugin, we explored the Moodle File API, and the Backup and Restore APIs--as well as learning how events are logged, how roles and permissions are managed, and much, much more. Second, we revisited the enhanced choice activity we first encountered in Chapter 3, *Internal Interfaces*. By enhancing Moodle's choice activity to allow teachers to include, for example, images in their choices (rather than choices being just text) we learned in detail how Moodle manages user files.

In the next chapter, you will learn how to manage users--from account provisioning to role assignment; we will investigate how to create new user accounts and have those users assigned to the correct courses.

6
Managing Users - Letting in the Crowds

We have our courses structured and we have our teaching interactions developed, so now it is time to start introducing our users--both to the system itself through the provision of user accounts and to our courses through enrolment. Moreover, it is not just letting the crowds in. We need to consider how to manage them while they are in and how to see them out in an orderly fashion. There are privacy laws in the US (**the Family Educational Rights and Privacy Act--FERPA**) and the EU (the **General Data Protection Regulation--GDPR**) that provide the reasons why authentication (and its associated user data) has to be managed in specific ways--you will need to confirm how privacy laws affect you in your region. In addition, what of archiving user interactions and retrieving that data from the archives? This is an important consideration for our project--not just for the sake of monitoring which organizations are compliant with the agreed resilience framework (see `Chapter 1`, *Getting to Grips with the Moodle 3 Architecture*, for more details on this project) but also for other purposes (for example, to assess the quality of our training or in the event of mistakes being made).

At the end of this chapter, you will understand how we can adapt Moodle to manage users in a variety of contexts. We will investigate how to integrate account creation with third-party systems (including single sign on). Our resilience project has a portal based on WordPress and in this chapter we will be working together to develop two novel plugins to manage users: one to authorize users through WordPress and the other to enroll users directly onto courses when they connect to Moodle via WordPress.

With regards to the management of learning, we will be focusing on competency frameworks, which are generally used to satisfy general education requirements and, in the case of the resilience project, used to ensure aid workers have reached a base level of understanding of the issues associated with societal resilience. We are going to create a new administration tool plugin which synchronizes a Moodle competency framework with an external database.

In this chapter, we will cover:

- How to design and develop new authentication plugins
- The enrolment of users onto courses through the development of new course enrolment plugins
- Introducing Admin Tool plugins through the development of a new competency framework plugin

Let us start with learning how to create new user accounts.

Authentication

Luckily, Moodle supports a range of different authentication protocols out of the box, each one supported by its own plugin. We should say at the outset that this means that it is unlikely to be necessary for you to create a new plugin. So, before you do decide to create a new authentication plugin, it is best to make absolutely certain that your authentication requirements can't already be accommodated. To go to the list of available plugins, from the **Administration** block, click on **Site administration**, click **Plugins**, then click **Authentication**, and finally click on **Manage authentication**. The list of currently installed authentication plugins is displayed:

Available authentication plugins

Name	Users	Enable	Up/Down	Settings	Test settings	Uninstall
Manual accounts	3			Settings		
No login	0			Settings		
Email-based self-registration	0	⊙		Settings		Uninstall
CAS server (SSO)	0	⊘		Settings		Uninstall
External database	0	⊘		Settings	Test settings	Uninstall
FirstClass server	0	⊘		Settings		Uninstall
IMAP server	0	⊘		Settings		Uninstall
LDAP server	0	⊘		Settings		
LTI	0	⊘		Settings		Uninstall
MNet authentication	0	⊘		Settings		
NNTP server	0	⊘		Settings		Uninstall
No authentication	0	⊘		Settings		Uninstall
PAM (Pluggable Authentication Modules)	0	⊘		Settings		Uninstall
POP3 server	0	⊘		Settings		Uninstall
RADIUS server	0	⊘		Settings		Uninstall
Shibboleth	0	⊘		Settings		Uninstall
Web services authentication	0	⊘		Settings		

Each plugin interfaces with the Access API--see the Moodle developer documentation for details at: `https://docs.moodle.org/dev/Access_API`.

Authentication - general principles

The authentication process begins either because the user has attempted to log in directly at the login page (`/login/index.php`), or because the user has attempted to navigate to a Moodle page that requires them to log in. A page requiring a user to have logged in will include a call to either `require_login()` or `require_course_login()`, usually immediately after the call `$PAGE->set_url()` to specify the page URL. The steps taken to determine if a user login is required can be somewhat elaborate as this can depend on the visibility of a course. For example, is the course public? Do you need to be enrolled on the course to access it? Such courses are referred to as *protected resources*. In the next section, we will investigate further.

Getting logged in

In Moodle, there are two ways of prompting the authentication process:

- Attempting to log in from the login page
- Clicking on a link to a protected resource (for example, a page or file that you can't view or download before you log in)

Attempting to log in from the login page is the process with which you are probably familiar. Take a look at the overview in the developer documentation at `https://docs.moodle.org/dev/Authentication_plugins#Overview_of_Moodle_authentic ation_process`, and open `/login/index.php` in Eclipse. After checks to determine if an upgrade is required (or if we are part way through the upgrade process), there is a short fragment of code that loads the configured authentication plugins and for each one calls the `loginpage_hook()` function:

```
$authsequence = get_enabled_auth_plugins(true); // auths, in sequence
foreach($authsequence as $authname)
{
        $authplugin = get_auth_plugin($authname);
        $authplugin->loginpage_hook();
}
```

The `loginpage_hook()` function gives each authentication plugin the chance to intercept the login (compare this to `pre_loginpage_hook()`, which gives us the opportunity to perform any pre-login checks, such as determining our location if the login is prevented if we are attempting to log in from a particular place). Assuming that the login has not been intercepted, then the process continues with a check to ensure the supplied username conforms to the configured standard before calling `authenticate_user_login()`, which, if successful, returns a `$user` object.

But if, instead of clicking on a login link and being redirected to the login page, the user clicks on a link to a protected resource, what then is the process? In fact, it is much the same and it relies on us handling the login process in `loginpage_hook()`.

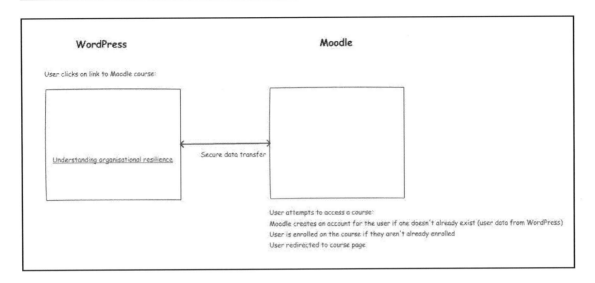

Single sign on

The resilience platform we are helping to develop contains a range of different features that no one platform supports completely. However, our business analyst has identified a number of different open source platforms that can support the various features required of this project. The content management part of the platform will be implemented in WordPress (`https://wordpress.com/`) while the courses will be managed in Moodle (see the preceding diagram).

Of course, WordPress and Moodle are two different applications each requiring a user to have their own login credentials. However, what we want to avoid is the user needing to log in to WordPress and then having to log into Moodle to access a training course.

This means that, as far as the end user is concerned, they will be navigating between different parts of the resilience platform whilst, unbeknown to them, they will actually be accessing completely different web applications. It is also important to note that, given the international nature of the project, our users might well be accessing different applications which are themselves running on different servers in completely different countries.

During this project's foundations stage, it became clear that the minimum useable subset of features requires the deployment of some form of content management system as well as a learning platform. Therefore, after a thorough analysis of all of the options, we have decided at the very minimum to implement a WordPress-based portal and a Moodle-based learning platform. However, a "must have" is **Single Sign On (SSO)**--being able to seamlessly navigate from one platform to the next.

In the next section, we investigate options for the WordPress to Moodle SSO.

WordPress to Moodle - SSO options

As described, the intention is that a page in WordPress may contain a link to a Moodle course and when clicked, this should authenticate the user in Moodle and then navigate the user to the course. The user should be automatically authenticated in Moodle with their WordPress login details. Let us explore some of the possible ways we could implement SSO with WordPress. Of course, the issues we explore here will apply to any content management system-based portal.

Calling WordPress code directly

The first option we investigate is to call WordPress code directly. Of course, this will only work if your code is residing on the same server and can access the WordPress core. To load the core, we would need to require `wp-load.php`; for example:

```
include_once("/var/www/yourdomain.com/htdocs/wp-load.php");
```

However, both Moodle and WordPress contain a global function called `get_users()`. This collision of function names can, in theory, be handled by renaming the functions using runkit (`http://php.net/manual/en/book.runkit.php`) or similar.

If you aren't familiar with tools to modify PHP's behavior (such as function renaming), then look at the PHP documentation at: `http://php.net/manual/en/refs.basic.php.php`. These toolkits are designed for testing purposes and it is strongly recommended that you don't use them to accommodate poor architectural design.

Let us now move our investigation on to how WordPress authenticates its own users.

Cookie authentication

WordPress handles two types of user authentication: cookies and OAuth. If you are not familiar with them, cookies are packets of data stored at the client end (for example, the browser). By default, WordPress uses cookies to cache the basic details of the currently logged in user. Could we access this information to determine who the current user is and authenticate them in Moodle? The short answer is no--and when considering what a massive security issue cookies are then you will understand why: it simply isn't possible (and nor would it be prudent) for an application running in one domain to directly access the data of an application running in another. OAuth, however, is a topic we will return to shortly.

Links from WordPress to Moodle

Another authentication mechanism you will see used frequently is the use of *special* links. Imagine we have a WordPress page in which we have included a link to a Moodle course:

`http://moodle313.localhost/course/view.php?id=6.`

We could add to this some extra user details: `http://moodle313.localhost/course/view.php?id=6&user=admin&email=admin%40example.com.`

Of course, passing user details in this way is not particularly secure so we could encrypt this extra data. There is also an architectural issue: this kind of link is called an HTTP *GET* and GET is all about retrieving data. We want to send user data over to Moodle to allow for automatic authentication. So it would be better to encrypt the user data and, rather than adding the data to the end of the URI (*GET*), we add the data to the body of the HTTP request. This is called an HTTP *POST*--see `https://en.wikipedia.org/wiki/POST_(HTTP)` for details. We would need to implement a mechanism for including POST data within the request, which would require a new WordPress plugin--as well as a new Moodle plugin to receive the request at the other end.

Again, as an approach, this is quite common and you will find more than one freely available implementation of this idea (for an example, see `https://github.com/frumbert/wp2moodle-moodle`). However, the authentication is only one way. Imagine you tried accessing a link to a Moodle course without currently being logged into Moodle. Without having the correct user data added to the request then, obviously, authentication would fail.

External Web Services APIs

So far we have spent a good deal of time investigating Moodle's internal APIs but did you know that both Moodle and WordPress implement their own externally facing APIs? We will be investigating Moodle's Web Services API later in Chapter 9, *Moodle Analytics*. The WordPress API, WP-API, is documented at: http://v2.wp-api.org/. By employing web services, we can have Moodle delegate authentication to WordPress (regardless of--within reason--where in the world WordPress is running). Our WordPress installation then becomes our single sign on *authority*.

However, how do we authenticate against WordPress? Recall that WordPress uses both cookie and OAuth authentication. In the next section, we learn more about OAuth.

OAuth overview

A thorough investigation of the OAuth mechanism is beyond the scope of this book. You will find a description of the authentication process in Wikipedia at: https://en.wikipedia.org/wiki/OAuth. In outline, what OAuth provides is *secure delegated access*. OAuth supports a number of scenarios, including:

- A client requests access from a server and the server responds with either a *confirm* or *deny*. This is called *two-legged authentication*.
- A client requests access from a server and the server then pops up a confirmation dialog so that the user can authorize the access, and then it finally responds with either a *confirm* or *deny*. This is called *three-legged authentication*.

It is three-legged authentication we will be implementing in this chapter. Such a mechanism means, in practice, that:

- An authentication server will only talk to configured clients
- No passwords are exchanged between server and client--only tokens are exchanged, which are meaningless on their own
- By default, users need to give permission before resources are accessed

Having given an overview, here is the process again described in a little more detail:

1. A new client is configured in the authentication server. A client is allocated a unique *client key*, along with a secret token (referred to as *client secret*).
2. The client POSTs an HTTP request to the server (identifying itself using the *client key* and *client secret*) and the server responds with a temporary *access token*.

3. This token is used to request authorization to access *protected resources* from the server. In this case, "protected resources" means the WordPress API. Access to the WordPress API will allow us to determine details of the currently logged in user.

4. The server responds, not with an HTTP response, but by POSTing new permanent tokens back to the client via a *callback* URI (that is, the server talks to the client directly in order to ensure security).

5. The process ends with the client possessing permanent authorization tokens that can be used to access WP-API functions.

Obviously, the most effective way of learning about this process is to implement it, so let's go ahead and do that now.

Installing the WordPress OAuth 1.0a server

The first step will be to add the OAuth 1.0a server plugin to WordPress. Why not the more recent OAuth 2.0 server plugin? This is because 2.0 only supports `https://` and not `http://`. Also, internally (at least at the time of writing), WordPress will only authenticate internally using either OAuth 1.0a or cookies.

Log into WordPress as an administrator and, from the Dashboard hover the mouse over the **Plugins** menu item and click on **Installed Plugins**. The **Plugins** page is displayed. At the top of the page, press the **Add New** button:

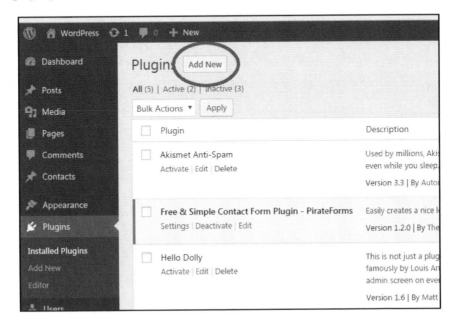

As stated already, ensure that you install version 1.0a and not 2.0:

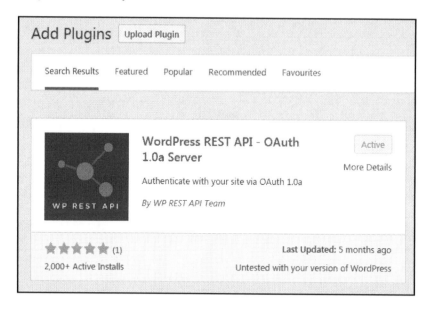

Once installed, we need to configure a new client. From the Dashboard menu, hover the mouse over **Users** and you will see a new **Applications** menu item has been added. Click on this to display the **Registered Applications** page. Click the **Add New** button to display the **Add Application** page:

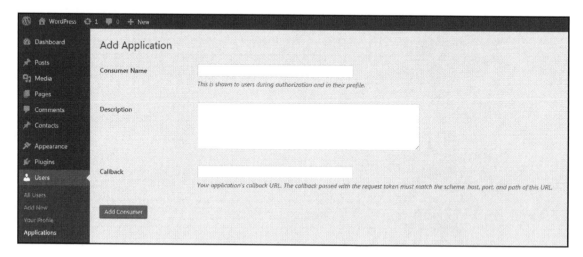

The **Consumer Name** is the title for our client that will appear in the **Add Application** page, and **Description** is a brief explanation of that client to aid with the identification. The **Callback** is the URI that WordPress will talk to (refer to the outline of the preceding OAuth authentication steps). As we have not yet developed the Moodle/OAuth client end yet you can specify `oob` in **Callback** (this stands for *out of band*). Once configured, WordPress will generate new OAuth credentials, a *Client Key*, and a *Client Secret*:

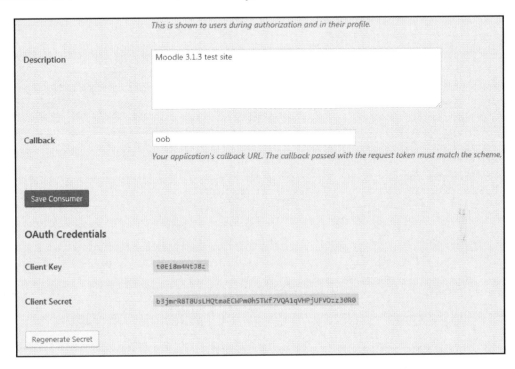

Having installed and configured the server end, now it's time to develop the client.

Creating a new Moodle auth plugin

Our new Moodle authentication plugin will determine if a new user account needs to be created and, if so, will obtain the relevant user data from WordPress. It will update an existing account if required. This is all to ensure a user can access the necessary courses.

Before we begin, download the finished plugin from `https://github.com/iandavidwild/moodle-auth_wordpress` and install it in your local development Moodle instance.

The development of a new authentication plugin is described in the developer documentation at `https://docs.moodle.org/dev/Authentication_plugins`. As described there, let us start with copying the *none* plugin (the "no login" authentication method) and using this as a template for our new plugin. In Eclipse, I'm going to copy the *none* plugin to a new authentication method called `wordpress`:

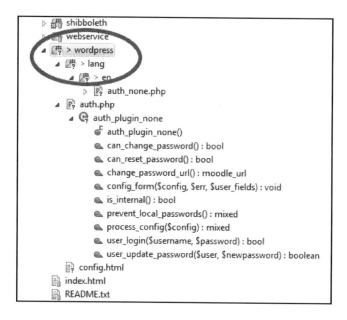

That done, we need to update the occurrences of `auth_none` to `auth_wordpress`. Firstly, rename `/auth/wordpress/lang/en/auth_none.php` to `auth_wordpress.php`. Then, in `auth.php`, we need to rename the class `auth_plugin_none` to `auth_plugin_wordpress`. As described in previous chapters, the Eclipse **Find/Replace** function is great for updating scripts:

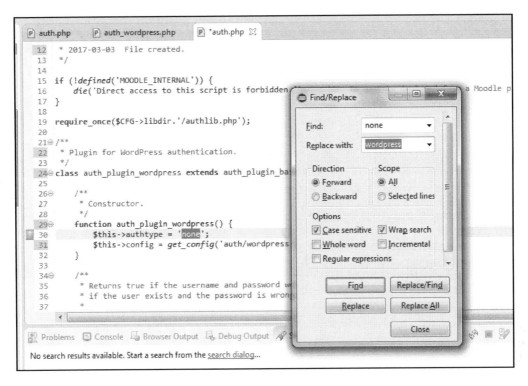

Next, in order for Moodle to reload our new plug in--and for us to be able to know which version of the plugin a user has installed in the event of there being any issues with it--we need to update version information in `version.php`:

```
/**
 * Version information
 *
 * @package    auth_wordpress
 * @copyright  2017 Ian Wild (http://skodak.org)
 * @license    http://www.gnu.org/copyleft/gpl.html GNU GPL v3 or later   */

defined('MOODLE_INTERNAL') || die();

$plugin->version    = 2017030300;      // The current plugin version
(Date: YYYYMMDDXX)
$plugin->requires   = 2016051900;      // Requires this Moodle version
$plugin->component  = 'auth_wordpress'; // Full name of the plugin (used
for diagnostics)
```

Finally, we can check that Moodle recognizes our new plugin by navigating to the Site administration menu and clicking on Notifications. If installation is successful, our new plugin will be listed on the **Available authentication plugins** page:

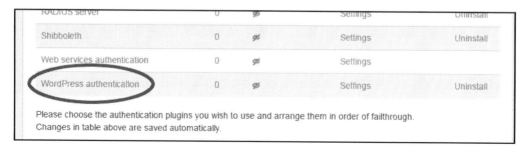

Configuration

Let us start by considering the plugin configuration. We will need to allow a Moodle administrator to configure the following:

- The URL of the WordPress installation
- The *client key* and *client secret* provided by WordPress

There is very little flexibility in the design of an authentication plugin configuration page so, at this stage, rather than creating a wireframe drawing, we can simply go ahead and write the code. The configuration page is defined in /config.html. Firstly, there will be a fragment of PHP to set any defaults:

```php
<?php

// Set to defaults if undefined
if (!isset($config->wordpress_host))
{
    $config->wordpress_host = '';
}
if (!isset($config->client_key))
{
    $config->client_key = '';
}
if (!isset($config->client_secret))
{
    $config->client_secret = '';
}
?>
```

What follows is an HTML table containing one row for each setting. For example, to allow the administrator to configure the WordPress host URL, we would define a new table row as follows:

```
<tr valign="top" class="required">
    <td align="right">
        <label for="wordpress_host"><?php print_string('wordpress_host',
'auth_wordpress') ?></label>
    </td>
    <td>
        <input id="wordpress_host" name="wordpress_host" type="text"
value="<?php echo $config->wordpress_host ?>" />
        <?php if (isset($err['wordpress_host'])) { echo
$OUTPUT->error_text($err['wordpress_host']); } ?>
    </td>
    <td>
        <?php print_string('wordpress_host_help', 'auth_wordpress') ?>
    </td>
</tr>
```

See that we are displaying language strings using `print_string()`, which means we need to start declaring the relevant strings in `/lang/en/auth_wordpress.php`.

Configuration settings themselves will be managed by the framework by calling the `auth_plugin_wordpress' process_config()` method. Here is the declaration:

```
/**
 * Processes and stores configuration data for this authentication
plugin.
 *
 * @return @bool
 */
function process_config($config)
{
    // Set to defaults if undefined
    if (!isset($config->wordpress_host))
    {
        $config->wordpress_host = '';
    }
    if (!isset($config->client_key))
    {
        $config->client_key = '';
    }
    if (!isset($config->client_secret))
    {
        $config->client_secret = '';
    }
```

```
        set_config('wordpress_host', trim($config->wordpress_host),
        'auth/wordpress');
        set_config('client_key', trim($config->client_key),
        'auth/wordpress');
        set_config('client_secret', trim($config->client_secret),
        'auth/wordpress');
        return true;
    }
```

Having dealt with the configuration, now let us start managing the actual OAuth process.

Handling OAuth calls

Rather than going into the details of how we can send HTTP (or HTTPS) requests to WordPress, let's use a free third-party library to do this work. The code I'm going to use is based on *Abraham Williams' twitteroauth* library (see https://github.com/abraham/twitteroauth). The two files we need are OAuth.php and BasicOAuth.php. To use the library, you will need to add the following lines to the top of /wordpress/auth.php:

```
require_once($CFG->dirroot . '/auth/wordpress/OAuth.php');
require_once($CFG->dirroot . '/auth/wordpress/BasicOAuth.php');
use \OAuth1\BasicOauth;
```

Always attribute any third-party library you include with your plugin. That means including a thirdpartylibs.xml file that specifies the libraries we are bundling with our plugin. Here is what we need to include:

```xml
<?xml version="1.0"?>
<libraries>
  <library>
    <location>BasicOAuth</location>
    <name>OAuth</name>
    <license>MIT</license>
    <version>v1</version>
    <licenseversion>1</licenseversion>
  </library>
  <library>
    <location>OAuth</location>
    <name>OAuth</name>
    <license>CC0</license>
    <version>v1</version>
    <licenseversion>1</licenseversion>
  </library>
</libraries>
```

The BasicOAuth library is released under the MIT permissive free software license (see `http s://en.wikipedia.org/wiki/MIT_License`) and the OAuth library under the CC0 "no rights reserved" Creative Commons license. Both are compatible with Moodle's own software license--Moodle is released under the GNU version 3 license (see `https://docs.moodle.org/dev/License`)--meaning we can use these libraries without flouting copyright.

Now that copyright issues have been dealt with, let's start work on handling the Moodle login event.

Handling the Moodle login event

Recall that when a user clicks on a link to a protected resource, Moodle calls `loginpage_hook()` in each enabled authentication plugin. To handle this, let us first implement `loginpage_hook()`. In Eclipse, add the following lines to `auth.php`:

```
/**
 * Will get called before the login page is shown.
 *
 */
function loginpage_hook() {
    $client_key = $this->config->client_key;
    $client_secret = $this->config->client_secret;
    $wordpress_host = $this->config->wordpress_host;
    if( (strlen($wordpress_host) > 0) && (strlen($client_key) > 0) &&
(strlen($client_secret) > 0) ) {
        // kick ff the authentication process
        $connection = new BasicOAuth($client_key, $client_secret);
        // strip the trailing slashes from the end of the host URL to
avoid any confusion (and to make the code easier to read)
        $wordpress_host = rtrim($wordpress_host, '/');
        $connection->host = $wordpress_host . "/wp-json";
        $connection->requestTokenURL = $wordpress_host .
"/oauth1/request";
        $callback = $CFG->wwwroot . '/auth/wordpress/callback.php';
        $tempCredentials = $connection->getRequestToken($callback);
        // Store temporary credentials in the $_SESSION
    }// if
}
```

This implements the first leg of the authentication process and the variable `$tempCredentials` will now contain a temporary access token. We will need to store these temporary credentials and then call on the server to ask the user to authorize the connection (leg two). Add the following lines immediately after the `// Store temporary credentials in the $_SESSION` comment:

```
$_SESSION['oauth_token'] = $tempCredentials['oauth_token'];
$_SESSION['oauth_token_secret'] = $tempCredentials['oauth_token_secret'];
$connection->authorizeURL = $wordpress_host . "/oauth1/authorize";
$redirect_url = $connection->getAuthorizeURL($tempCredentials);
header('Location: ' . $redirect_url);
die;
```

Next, we need to implement the OAuth callback. Let us create a new script called `callback.php`:

The callback script will:

- "Sanity" check (that is, check the validity of) the data being passed back from WordPress and fail gracefully if there is an issue
- Get the WordPress authentication plugin instance (an instance of `auth_plugin_wordpress`)
- Call on a handler method that will perform the authentication (which we will then need to implement)

The following is the code:

```
require_once('../../config.php');
require_once($CFG->dirroot . '/auth/wordpress/auth.php');
defined('MOODLE_INTERNAL') || die();
// checks to ensure that we have come here via WordPress...
if(!isset($_REQUEST['oauth_verifier']))
```

```
{
    print_error('missingverifier', 'auth_wordpress');
}
// get the wordpress plugin instance
$authplugin = get_auth_plugin('wordpress');
if(isset($authplugin))
{
// call the callback handler
$authplugin->callback_handler();
}
```

Now, in the auth.php script, add the following method to auth_plugin_wordpress:

```
/**
* Called externally as the third and final leg of three legged
authentication. This function performs the final
* Moodle authentication.
*
*/
function callback_handler()
{
    global $CFG, $DB, $SESSION;
    $client_key = $this->config->client_key;
    $client_secret = $this->config->client_secret;
    $wordpress_host = $this->config->wordpress_host;
    // strip the trailing slashes from the end of the host URL to
    avoid any confusion (and to make the code easier to read)
    $wordpress_host = rtrim($wordpress_host, '/');
    // at this stage we have been provided with new permanent token
    $connection = new BasicOAuth($client_key, $client_secret,
    $_SESSION['oauth_token'], $_SESSION['oauth_token_secret']);
    $connection->host = $wordpress_host . "/wp-json";
    $connection->accessTokenURL = $wordpress_host . "/oauth1/access";
    $tokenCredentials = $connection->
    getAccessToken($_REQUEST['oauth_verifier']);
    if(isset($tokenCredentials['oauth_token']) &&
    isset($tokenCredentials['oauth_token_secret']))
    {
        $perm_connection = new BasicOAuth($client_key,
        $client_secret, $tokenCredentials['oauth_token'],
        $tokenCredentials['oauth_token_secret']);
        $account = $perm_connection->get($wordpress_host . '/wp-
                json/wp/v2/users/me?context=edit');
        if(isset($account))
        {
            // firstly make sure there isn't an email collision:
            if($user = $DB->get_record('user',
                array('email'=>$account->email)))
            {
```

```
                    if($user->auth != 'wordpress')
                    {
                            print_error('usercollision',
                            'auth_wordpress');
                     }
          }
    // check to determine if a user has already been
    created...
    if($user = authenticate_user_login($account->username,
        $account->username))
    {
          // TODO update the current user with the latest
          first name and last name pulled from WordPress?
          if (user_not_fully_set_up($user, false))
          {
                  $urltogo = $CFG->wwwroot.'/user/edit.php?
                  id='.$user->id.'&amp;course='.SITEID;
                  // We don't delete $SESSION->wantsurl yet,
                  so we get there later
          }
    }
    else
    {
          require_once($CFG->dirroot . '/user/lib.php');
          // we need to configure a new user account
          $user = new stdClass();
          $user->mnethostid = $CFG->mnet_localhost_id;
          $user->confirmed = 1;
          $user->username = $account->username;
          $user->password = AUTH_PASSWORD_NOT_CACHED;
          $user->firstname = $account->first_name;
          $user->lastname = $account->last_name;
          $user->email = $account->email;
          $user->description = $account->description;
          $user->auth = 'wordpress';
          $id = user_create_user($user, false);
          $user = $DB->get_record('user',
                  array('id'=>$id));
    }
    complete_user_login($user);
     if (isset($SESSION->wantsurl) and (strpos($SESSION-
        >wantsurl, $CFG->wwwroot) === 0))
     {
          $urltogo = $SESSION->wantsurl;      /// Because
          it's an address in this site
          unset($SESSION->wantsurl);
     }
     else
```

```
        {
            $urltogo = $CFG->wwwroot.'/';        /// Go to the
            standard home page
            unset($SESSION->wantsurl);           /// Just in
                                                     case
        }
        /// Go to my-moodle page instead of homepage if
        defaulthomepage enabled
        if (!has_capability('moodle/site:config',
            context_system::instance()) and
            !empty($CFG->defaulthomepage) && $CFG-
            >defaulthomepage == HOMEPAGE_MY and !isguestuser())
        {
            if ($urltogo == $CFG->wwwroot or $urltogo ==
                $CFG->wwwroot.'/' or $urltogo == $CFG-
                >wwwroot.'/index.php')
            {
                $urltogo = $CFG->wwwroot.'/my/';
            }
        }
        redirect($urltogo);
        exit;
        }
    }
}
```

We are not going to go into details here, as the flow of execution in the callback handler is easy to follow. The final steps are to ensure that the plugin handles passwords correctly. Passwords won't be stored in the Moodle database, so we need to ensure the prevent_local_passwords() method returns true.

Lastly, let us add a fragment of code to the loginpage_hook() method that allows us to turn off WordPress authentication in config.php. Add the following to the very beginning of the loginpage_hook() function:

```
global $CFG;
if(isset($CFG->disablewordpressauth) && ($CFG->disablewordpressauth ==
true))
{
    return;
}
```

Taking things further

Rather than a global setting in `config.php`, can you think of a way of determining if the user has clicked on a link to a protected resource or the *Log in* link? If you can differentiate between clicking on the Log in link and a link to a course, for instance, then you could ensure that Moodle authenticates against WordPress only when a user attempts to access a protected resource (hint: look out for the `$SESSION->wantsurl` variable).

In the preceding example, we implemented *three-legged* authentication. Try investigating *two-legged* authentication. This would involve removing the need for the user to authorize access to the resource. Can you think of a way of implementing this? (Hint: this may require changes to the WordPress server end).

Course Enrolment

Our new WordPress authentication plugin allows us to click on a link to a Moodle course in WordPress and have us automatically logged into Moodle. It also creates a new user account in Moodle if this is the first time the user has attempted to log in. Which is fine as far as it goes, but it still doesn't allow us to access the protected resource because the user isn't yet enrolled on a course. If you have WordPress OAuth authentication set up, then attempting to access a course will, by default, present you with the following (or similar) page:

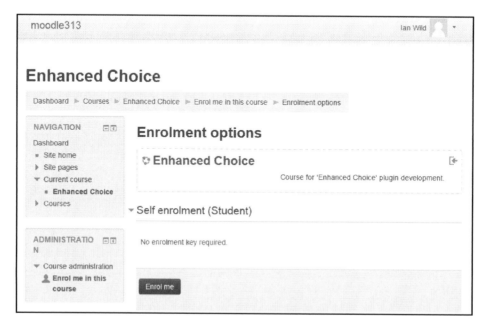

What would be much more preferable is if, when clicking on a link to a protected resource in WordPress, you are enrolled automatically in the relevant Moodle course. In this section, we learn how.

A WordPress course enrolment plugin

Let us start the development of our new WordPress `enrolment` plugin by creating a clone of the self `enrolment` plugin. In Eclipse, right click on `/enrol/self` and paste back into the `/enrol` folder renaming it `wordpress`:

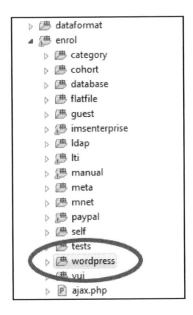

Next, search through each script replacing *self* with *wordpress* where relevant. Finally, update the `version.php` script accordingly. Finally, you will be able to click on **Notifications** in the **Site administration** menu to install the new plugin. (As part of the installation process, you will be asked to specify a number of global settings. Simply accept the defaults for now.)

To test the new plugin, we first need to enable it. Open the **Site administration** menu and click on **Plugins**, then Enrolments, and finally **Manage enrol plugins**. On the **Manage enrol plugins** page, you will see the WordPress enrolment plugin listed. Ensure this is enabled by poking it in the eye (the "eye" icon needs to be open):

Manage enrol plugins

Available course enrolment plugins

Name	Instances / enrolments	Version	Enable	Up/Down	Settings	Test settings	Uninstall
Manual enrolments	6 / 1	2016052300	👁	↓	Settings		
Guest access	6 / 0	2016052300	👁	↑ ↓	Settings		Uninstall
Self enrolment	6 / 0	2016052301	👁	↑ ↓	Settings		Uninstall
Cohort sync	0 / 0	2016052300	👁	↑ ↓	Settings		Uninstall
WordPress enrolment	1 / 0	2017032001	👁	↑	Settings		Uninstall
Category enrolments	0 / 0	2016052300	👁🚫		Settings		Uninstall
External database	0 / 0	2016052300	👁🚫		Settings	Test settings	Uninstall
Flat file (CSV)	0 / 0	2016052300	👁🚫		Settings		Uninstall

Having enabled our new plugin, we can now go ahead and add it to a course. Create a new course and, under the **Course administration** menu, click on Users and then **Enrolment methods** to display the **Enrolment method** page. Disable **Manual enrolments** and enable **WordPress enrolment**. As this will be the primary (or only) enrolment method for this course, we can shuffle it to the top of the list of course enrolment methods (by clicking on the up and down arrow icons):

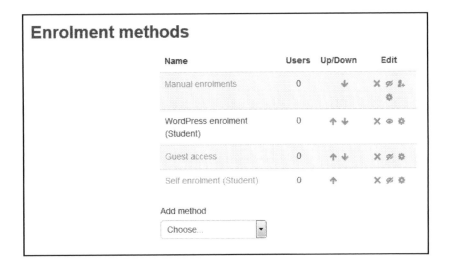

In our new plugin, there are two functions we will need to investigate: `can_wordpress_enrol()` and `enrol_page_hook()`. Both of these functions are located in `enrol/wordpress/lib.php`. Firstly, we need to determine if the current user authenticated via WordPress. Add the following code fragment to the bottom of the `can_wordpress_enrol()` function:

```
if ($userauth = $DB->get_record('user', array('id' => $USER->id), 'auth'))
{
    if($userauth->auth !== 'wordpress')
    {
        return get_string('canntenrol', 'enrol_wordpress');
    }
}
```

Next we need to re-engineer `enrol_page_hook()` so that the enrolment form is only displayed when an enrolment key has been specified. Here is the complete function:

```
public function enrol_page_hook(stdClass $instance)
{
    global $CFG, $OUTPUT, $USER;
    require_once("$CFG->dirroot/enrol/wordpress/locallib.php");
    $enrolstatus = $this->can_wordpress_enrol($instance);
    if (true === $enrolstatus)
    {
    // only display the enrolment form if we need to - i.e. if there
    is an enrolment key to be specified
        if ($instance->password)
        {
            // This user can wordpress enrol using this instance.
```

```
            $form = new enrol_wordpress_enrol_form(null,
                    $instance);
            $instanceid = optional_param('instance', 0,
                        PARAM_INT);
            if ($instance->id == $instanceid)
            {
                if ($data = $form->get_data())
                {
                        $this->enrol_wordpress($instance, $data);
                }
            }
    }
    else
    {
            $this->enrol_wordpress($instance);
            $data = new stdClass();
            $data->header = $this->get_instance_name($instance);
            $data->info = $enrolstatus;
            $form = new enrol_wordpress_empty_form(null, $data);
    }
    }
    else
    {
        // This user can not wordpress enrol using this
        instance. Using an empty form to keep
        // the UI consistent with other enrolment plugins that
        returns a form.
        $data = new stdClass();
        $data->header = $this->get_instance_name($instance);
        $data->info = $enrolstatus;

        // The can_self_enrol call returns a button to the
        login page if the user is a
        // guest, setting the login url to the form if that is
        the case.
        $url = isguestuser() ? get_login_url() : null;
        $form = new enrol_wordpress_empty_form($url, $data);
    }
    ob_start();
    $form->display();
    $output = ob_get_clean();
    return $OUTPUT->box($output);
}
```

Taking things further

By cloning and adapting the "self" `enrolment` plugin, we have included some already useful features, such as providing enrolment keys for extra security (only those users with the key can actually enroll on a course--see `https://docs.moodle.org/31/en/Enrolment_key`).

With WordPress plugins, for instance `https://en-gb.wordpress.org/plugins/groups/`, we are able to group users and manage their capabilities and access to content in WordPress. There is the potential to use the WP-API to allow us to map Moodle roles to groups in WordPress. Remember that you will need to store the OAuth access tokens in the current PHP session in order to continue to use the API. Moodle also has the concept of course groups (`https://docs.moodle.org/31/en/Groups`). How might we determine, via the WP-API, which course groups to add our users to?

Management of Competencies

Having provided our users with access to courses--through the process of authentication and enrolment--we can now think about how to manage their learning in terms of the skills and knowledge they have attained. Let us now focus our attention on competencies (`https://docs.moodle.org/31/en/Competencies`) and in particular the automatic management of competency frameworks in Moodle.

It is beyond the scope of this book to describe competency frameworks in detail but, in outline, they describe for instance:

- A minimum level of understanding that a learner must achieve in order to qualify for an award

However, more typically, they describe:

- The minimum level of understanding that an employee must have in order to do their job

In some cases, both are required and, as an example take a look at the Care Certificate (`http://www.skillsforhealth.org.uk/standards/item/216-the-care-certificate`)--a means to ensure UK care workers all possess the minimum standards of knowledge and exhibit the necessary behaviors.

For information on Moodle competency frameworks see
`https://docs.moodle.org/31/en/Competency_frameworks`. In this section, we will be developing a new plugin to automatically map competencies in an external system (in this case, an external database, although this might just as easily be an external API) to Moodle. Our project demands that, rather than having an administrator update competency frameworks manually, these are managed automatically. Our customer is happy to allow us to connect to the database that contains their framework--and they are happy to modify the data to suit the Moodle structure. As a demonstration of this principle, let us create a new plugin that we could potentially call on using *cron* (see
`https://docs.moodle.org/31/en/Cron`). Let us create the plugin first and then briefly investigate cron.

The plugin we find ourselves developing is to satisfy a purely administration-based need. That being the case, it is an *admin tool* plugin we will be creating. See `https://docs.moodle.org/31/en/Admin_tools`for an overview. A test admin tool plugin containing the code on which the samples in this section are based is available from GitHub at `https://github.com/iandavidwild/moodle-tool_lpsync`.

Before we go ahead and develop the plugin, on a final architectural note, we need to ensure that the attributes and behaviors of the plugin itself are encapsulated in a single class in order for the functionality to be exercised by a CLI/cron job. That point made, let us get on and start development.

Creating a new admin tool plugin

Competencies are managed site-wide via the **Site administration** menu:

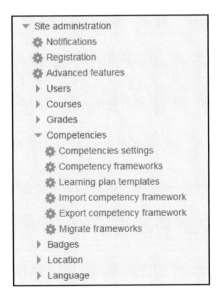

The importing and exporting of competencies is managed through the `lpinportcsv` admin plugin located in `/admin/tool`. This plugin was originally developed by *Damyon Wiese* and it is his work that we will base our new plugin on. Let us start by cloning Damyon's competency framework import/export plugin and making the necessary adjustments to refactor (rename) our new admin plugin to `lpsync`:

Start with our new plugin's configuration. Firstly, we need to connect to an external database and for that we will need to store the database type, where it is hosted, the username and password to allow us to access the data, the name of the database itself and, finally, the table that the data is stored in. Then we will need to store the mapping between fields in the external database and the corresponding `branch/leaf/attribute` in Moodle's competency tree.

As you can see in the preceding screen grab, I have created a new folder called db and in this I'm going to create a new install.xml script:

```xml
<?xml version="1.0" encoding="UTF-8" ?>
<XMLDB PATH="admin/tool/lpsync/db" VERSION="20172403" COMMENT="XMLDB file
for Moodle admin/tool/lpsync"
    xmlns:xsi="http://www.w3.org/2001/XMLSchema-instance"
    xsi:noNamespaceSchemaLocation="../../../../lib/xmldb/xmldb.xsd"
>
  <TABLES>
    <TABLE NAME="tool_lpsync" COMMENT="General database configuration and
mapping of required headers to external database headers.">
      <FIELDS>
        <FIELD NAME="id" TYPE="int" LENGTH="10" NOTNULL="true"
SEQUENCE="true"/>
        <FIELD NAME="name" TYPE="text" LENGTH="255" NOTNULL="false"
SEQUENCE="false" COMMENT="Name of setting"/>
        <FIELD NAME="value" TYPE="text" LENGTH="255" NOTNULL="false"
SEQUENCE="false" COMMENT="Setting value"/>
      </FIELDS>
      <KEYS>
        <KEY NAME="primary" TYPE="primary" FIELDS="id"/>
      </KEYS>
    </TABLE>
  </TABLES>
</XMLDB>
```

This new table will simply store a list of configuration settings by name and value:

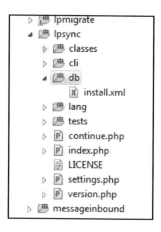

Next, we need to ensure the configuration settings are managed correctly. In the **classes** folder, let us add in the code required to support our new settings. Firstly, we will need a new form, via which the administrator can configure these settings:

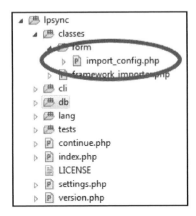

There is no underlying framework support for configuration settings in admin tool plugins, so we will need to handle this ourselves. Luckily, we can pass custom data to a form using the _customdata variable. We can pass in an associative array of settings ('name' => 'value'). For example, here is a code fragment showing the declaration of a new import_config class, including the start of the form's definition() function:

```
/**
 * Import Competency framework database and mapping form.
 *
 * @package    tool_lpsync
 * @copyright 2017 Ian Wild
 * @license    http://www.gnu.org/copyleft/gpl.html GNU GPL v3 or later
 */
class import_config extends moodleform
{
/**
* Define the form - called by parent constructor
*/
        public function definition()
        {
                global $CFG;
                $mform = $this->_form;
                $config = $this->_customdata;
                // External database settings
                $mform->addElement('header', 'extdb',
                get_string('db_header', 'tool_lpsync'));
                $dbtypes = array("access","ado_access", "ado", "ado_mssql",
                "borland_ibase", "csv", "db2", "fbsql", "firebird",
```

```
"ibase", "informix72", "informix", "mssql", "mssql_n",
"mssqlnative", "mysql", "mysqli", "mysqlt", "oci805",
"oci8", "oci8po", "odbc", "odbc_mssql", "odbc_oracle",
"oracle", "postgres64", "postgres7", "postgres", "proxy",
"sqlanywhere", "sybase", "vfp");
 foreach ($dbtypes as $dbtype)
 {
        $dboptions[$dbtype] = $dbtype;
 }
$mform->addElement('select', 'type', get_string('db_type',
'tool_lpsync'), $dboptions);
$mform->addRule('type', null, 'required');
$mform->setDefault('type', $config['type']);
$mform->addElement('text', 'host', get_string('db_host',
'tool_lpsync'), array('size'=>'48'));
$mform->setType('host', PARAM_HOST);
$mform->addRule('host', null, 'required');
$mform->setDefault('host', $config['host']);
 ...
```

As mentioned, because we are going to be synchronizing our competency frameworks via a cron job, we need to ensure all of the plugin's functionality is encapsulated in a single class. This is declared in the /classes/framework_importer.php script. Because we have based our plugin on the CSV importer code, we don't need to concern ourselves with understanding how competency data is processed and stored in Moodle (that is left as an exercise for the reader). In the following sections, we will be dealing with configuration, accessing external databases, and finally, how to run the synchronization process via a CLI script.

Synchronisation settings

Storing and retrieving settings will need to be managed by the framework_importer class. We can implement a new function that attempts to load settings from our new database table and, if it fails to do so, stores a set of defaults (so-called "lazy" loading). The following is the init() function in its entirety:

```
function init()
{
        global $DB;
        // Get details of external database from our config. Currently we
        do this one record at a time, which is a little clunky:
        $records = $DB->get_records('tool_lpsync', null, null);
        // if there aren't any entries in the table then we need to
        prepare them:
        if(count($records) == 0)
        {
```

```
            $rows = array(  'type' => 'mysqli',
                            'host' => 'localhost',
                            'user' => '',
                            'pass' => '',
                            'name' => '',
                            'table' => '',
                            'parentidnumber' => 'parentidnumber',
                            'idnumber' => 'idnumber',
                            'shortname' => 'shortname',
                            'description' => 'description',
                            'descriptionformat' => 'descriptionformat',
                            'scalevalues' => 'scalevalues',
                            'scaleconfiguration' =>
                            'scaleconfiguration',
                            'ruletype' => '',
                            'ruleoutcome' => '',
                            'ruleconfig' => '',
                            'relatedidnumbers' => 'relatedidnumbers',
                            'isframework' => 'isframework',
                            'taxonomy' => 'taxonomy'
                            );
                foreach($rows as $name => $value)
                {
                        $object = new stdClass();
                        $object->name = $name;
                        $object->value = $value;
                        $DB->insert_record('tool_lpsync', $object);
                }
                // try that again
                $records = $DB->get_records('tool_lpsync');
        }
        foreach($records as $record)
        {
                $this->config[$record->name] = $record->value;
        }
    return true;
    }
```

We then need to make sure that the init() method is called when this plugin is
instantiated, so add a call to init() the framework_importer class constructor:

```
/**
 * Constructor - initialise this instance.
 */
public function __construct()
{
        $this->init();
}
```

In order to store the settings back into the Moodle database, we will need to implement a new `framework_importer` method, to which we can pass the form configuration data. Here is the complete function:

```
/**
 * Stores importer configuration
 *
 * @param stdClass $data - form data
 */
public function update_config($data)
{
        global $DB;
        // what settings do we need to store?
        $settings = array('type', 'host', 'user', 'pass', 'name',
        'table', 'parentidnumber',
        'idnumber', 'shortname', 'description', 'descriptionformat',
        'scalevalues', 'scaleconfiguration',
        'ruletype', 'ruleoutcome', 'ruleconfig', 'relatedidnumbers',
        'isframework', 'taxonomy');
        foreach($settings as $setting)
        {
                // only update a current record
                $sql = 'UPDATE {tool_lpsync} SET `value` = ? WHERE `name` =
                        ?';
                $params = array($data->{$setting}, $setting);
                $DB->execute($sql, $params);
        }
}
```

To determine if the user has pressed the Submit button and, if that is the case, store the data, we implement the following in /index.php:

```
if (!$form->is_cancelled()) {
    // store the new config if necessary
    $form_data = $form->get_data();
    if($form_data != null) {
        $importer->update_config($form_data);
    }
}
```

To allow the administrator to configure these settings, we will need to add a new menu option to the Site administration menu. This we do in /settings.php:

```
/**
 * Links and settings
 *
 * This file contains links and settings used by tool_lpsync
 *
```

```
 * @package    tool_lpsync
 * @copyright  2017 Ian Wild
 * @license    http://www.gnu.org/copyleft/gpl.html GNU GPL v3 or later
 */
defined('MOODLE_INTERNAL') || die;

// Manage competency frameworks page.
$temp = new admin_externalpage(
        'toollpsync',
        get_string('pluginname', 'tool_lpsync'),
        new moodle_url('/admin/tool/lpsync/index.php'),
        'moodle/competency:competencymanage'
        );
$ADMIN->add('competencies', $temp);
// No report settings.
$settings = null;
```

This will add a new menu item under **Site administration**, **Competencies**:

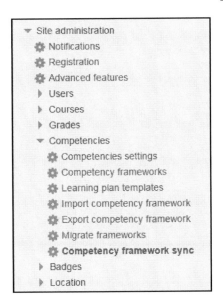

Clicking on this link will run /index.php, so we need to implement code in there to instantiate a new instance of the framework_importer class and then load the configuration form. In /index.php, we have:

```
$importer = new \tool_lpsync\framework_importer();
$form = new \tool_lpsync\form\import_config(null, $importer->config);
```

We can then check the return status of the form (using the `$form->is_cancelled()` method) and, if necessary, store any changes.

Connecting to external databases

Because we don't know what kind of database we might be connecting to (recall in our configuration form, we included an array of 32 different database types) that an administrator could potentially synchronize competency frameworks with. In order to connect, let us employ PHP's database abstraction layer API, **ADOdb**. This library is already included in Moodle--we just need to add the following line to the top of the `framework_importer.php` script:

```
require_once($CFG->libdir.'/adodb/adodb.inc.php');
```

Details are given at the ADOdb project's main website at `http://adodb.org`. Luckily, the API itself is straightforward to use. Add the following function to the `framework_importer` class to connect to the database:

```
/**
 * Connect to external database.
 *
 * @return ADOConnection
 * @throws moodle_exception
 */
function db_connect()
{
        global $CFG;
        if ($this->is_configured() === false)
        {
                throw new moodle_exception('dbcantconnect', 'tool_lpsync');
        }
        // Connect to the external database (forcing new connection).
        $authdb = ADONewConnection($this->config['type']);
        if (!empty($CFG->debuglpsync))
        {
                $authdb->debug = true;
                ob_start(); //Start output buffer to allow later use of the
                            page headers.
        }
        $authdb->Connect($this->config['host'], $this->config['user'],
        $this->config['password'], $this->config['name'], true);
        $authdb->SetFetchMode(ADODB_FETCH_ASSOC);
        return $authdb;
}
```

In order to load the framework from the external database, rather than loading each line of a CSV file into memory, we can load all the rows from the database and parse this data as if it were from a CSV file--taking account of the column heading mappings.

Taking things further - Moodle CLI scripts

As mentioned at the start of this section, we can potentially configure Moodle to regularly check for updates to the competency database by the use of a CLI script, as well as displaying the date of the last competency requirements update. For more information on command line scripts, take a look at the documentation at:

`https://docs.moodle.org/31/en/Administration_via_command_line`. We would need to determine if the competency has already been created so that we do not create a duplicate.

Summary

In this chapter, we learned how Moodle plugins are used to authenticate users on the platform and enroll them onto their chosen courses. We investigated implementing a single sign on plugin which allows a WordPress user to access a Moodle course using automatic authentication and enrolment. We developed a Moodle *authentication plugin* which allows a user to log into Moodle from WordPress using OAuth 1.0a (for authentication) and obtain user account information via the WordPress WP-API. We developed a separate Moodle *enrolment plugin* to automatically enroll the user onto a course.

We also studied the management of competencies by developing a new *admin tool plugin* which synchronizes a competency framework to an external database.

In the next chapter, we will develop a custom learner dashboard. This will not only provide a more engaging learner homepage but also a more exciting springboard to learning.

7
Creating a Dashboard - Developing a Learner Homepage

In previous chapters, we learned how to develop new plugins to create new user accounts (authentication) and how to assign users to courses (enrollment). We have also seen how to create custom teaching interactions through the development of new course resources and course activity plugins. In this chapter, we will be taking learning one step further to focus on *learning management*, specifically by developing a learner homepage that motivates and engages learners by tracking progress and incorporating gamification concepts.

Not only (we hope) does a learner need to gain the knowledge and exhibit the behaviors we are teaching, but they also need to have an appreciation of what they need to learn and, to an extent, always require some encouragement to keep learning. How can we achieve this with an online learning environment? In the same way that an automobile's dashboard allows the driver to monitor the performance of the car they are driving, so Moodle also has a learner dashboard to show learning accomplishments. This dashboard, accessible via `http://www.yourwebsite.com/my`, is the subject of this chapter.

In this chapter, we will be working together to create a custom learner homepage. A learner dashboard has a similar structure to a Moodle course. Typically, learner homepages comprise block plugins (see `Chapter 4`, *Course Management*) and so if you have not yet explored the development of Moodle blocks then it is well worth doing so before reading on. Otherwise, in this chapter we will be:

- Investigating how gamification can encourage learning
- Understanding how to apply gamification principles to a learner dashboard

- Learning how to make dashboard plugin content user specific
- Enhancing the visual appeal of blocks with third-party graphics libraries

We start, as all things development-related should, with understanding the requirements of our client.

The client's requirement

During our initial discussions with our client (part of the initial tendering process), there was some concern expressed that one or two of the topics they were wanting to support with online learning might not be particularly engaging. The target audience were busy people, they told us, and some of the training that learners need to complete (for compliance and insurance purposes, for example Information Governance and Fire Safety) was vital in the context of organizational resilience but not particularly engrossing as far as content went. The client wanted to know if there was any way in which we could promote learner engagement, realistically, rather than only going through the motions of completing a training course simply because they have to. Let us take a little time to explore the concept of gamification.

Addicted to learning

If only learning could be as addictive as the latest first person shooter game. If instructional designers and platform developers could use the same psychological techniques and tricks of the mind that games designers use to get players hooked on games then perhaps, so the argument goes, we can get learners hooked on learning in the same way. That, in short, is the foundation of **gamification**. For example, praising a learner for a job well done can promote renewed effort at the next attempt; cheers from the crowd can encourage an exhausted runner over the finish line. It should be stressed that gamification is a slightly misleading term: gamifying learning is not about making it fun. Gamification is about instructional designers and platform developers employing the same psychological tricks that games designers and coders use to get players hooked. In this chapter, we will be encouraging learning through the development of course progress and course availability blocks. Of course, achievement is not based on the number of courses you have completed but on your newly gained understanding and behavior.

Health warning: be aware that not all learners engage with leader boards, badges, and the like in the same way. You will need to be aware of the needs and sensitivities of your audience. You will find many scholarly articles discussing this on the internet; see, for example `http://knowledge.wharton.upenn.edu/article/people-love-games-but-does-gamification-work/`.

Course progress block

In this section, we will be working together to develop a course progress report. The courses being developed for the resilience project are based around a set of core competencies, depending on your role. In Moodle, we can assign competencies to teaching interactions. We can also enable completion tracking on courses (see `https://docs.moodle.org/31/en/Course_completion_settings`). This allows us to set learner goals. The following is a wireframe that demonstrates how the client expects the block to look in a course:

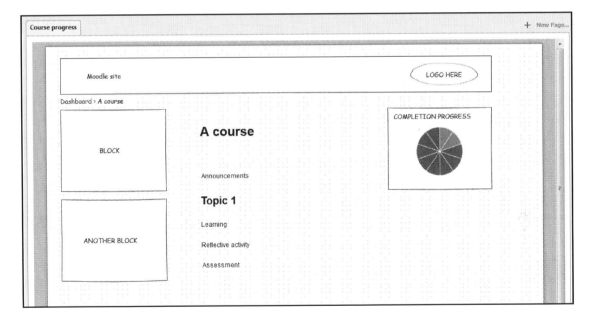

Here is the block as the client wishes it displayed on the learner dashboard:

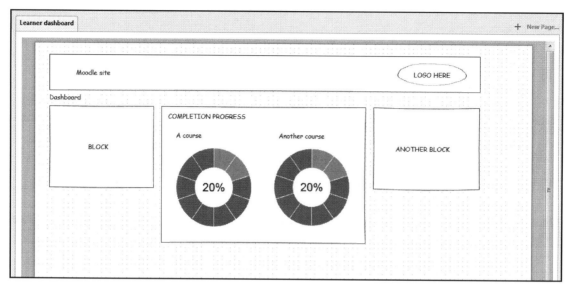

If you have not done so already, read `Chapter 4`, *Course Management,* and in particular the development of the QR Code block, as we will be assuming you are familiar with the structure of a Moodle block plugin (even if you aren't used to developing them).

There are already a number of course progress blocks available. For instance, *Michael de Raadt's Completion Progress block* (`https://moodle.org/plugins/block_completion_progr ess`). As this already contains the code required for determining a learner's progress through a course, let us use this block as the foundation for our new progress block. The code we will be developing in this section is also available at `https://github.com/iandavidwild/moodle-block_completion_progress`. Download Michael de Raadt's original block from GitHub now--and make sure you refresh the Eclipse PHP Explorer so you can see the PHP scripts, and they are ready for editing:

Including graphics libraries

Graphics libraries present a straightforward way for us to create both an attractive and informative dashboard for our users. As we saw in Chapter 5, *Creative Teaching - Developing Custom Resources and Activities,* when we developed a three-dimensional model viewer activity, JavaScript clearly has the potential to create visually appealing content. There are many graphics libraries available but the one we will be focusing on in this section is Chart.js--see http://www.chartjs.org for details.

Download the latest Chart.js file (again, see http://www.chartjs.org for download information). Create a new folder called /thirdparty and copy into that the Chart.js script:

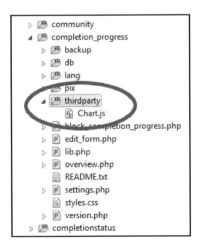

We will need to use the Page API to load the Chart library. In Eclipse, open the `/block_completion_progress.php` script and at the end of the `get_content()` function, add the following line:

```
$this->page->requires->js('/blocks/completion_progress/thirdparty/Chart.js'
, true);
```

This will load the library. Now we need to ensure that the data we need rendering is prepared correctly. Take a look at the `block_completion_progress_bar()` function (in `/lib.php`) to understand how the data provided to that function is displayed. We will need to create a new function that, rather than displaying a progress bar, converts the progress data to a format we can then pass to `Chart.js` to render as a suitable chart. The format we will be using is JSON.

JavaScript Object Notation (JSON)

Recall that our completion chart is to be rendered at the client end (by the browser), which means we will need to transfer the data across the internet from the server to the browser. If you are familiar with data transfer mechanisms then you will be aware that when you transfer data across networks then the data *payload* is packaged inside an *envelope*. The data needs to be sufficiently well described by the sender such that when the receiver unpacks it they know what it is and, potentially, what they can do with it. The packing and unpacking needs to be fast and efficient. At the time of writing, JSON has become the standard data interchange format for data transfer tasks such as the one we face. Luckily, the PHP scripting language has JSON support baked in, with `json_encode()` and `json_decode()` part of the language since version 5.2. For more details, refer to the JSON documentation at `http://www.json.org/`.

Converting progress data to JSON

Make a copy of the `block_completion_progress_bar()` function and rename it `block_completion_progress_json()`:

```
590
591 ⊖ /**
592  * json encode progress data
593  *
594  * @param array     $activities  The activities with completion in the course
595  * @param array     $completions The user's completion of course activities
596  * @param stdClass  $config      The blocks instance configuration settings
597  * @param int       $userid      The user's id
598  * @param int       $courseid    The course id
599  * @param int       instance     The block instance (to identify it on page)
600  * @param bool      $simple      Controls whether instructions are shown below a progress bar
601  * @return string json
602  */
603 ⊖ function block_completion_progress_json($activities, $completions, $config, $userid, $courseid, $instance, $simple = false) {
604     global $OUTPUT, $USER;
605
606     // create a json array of activities
607     $progress = array();
608
609     // Get colours and use defaults if they are not set in global settings.
610     $colornames = array(
611          'completed_colour' => 'completed_colour',
612          'submittednotcomplete_colour' => 'submittednotcomplete_colour',
613          'notCompleted_colour' => 'notCompleted_colour',
614          'futureNotCompleted_colour' => 'futureNotCompleted_colour'
615     );
616     $colors = array();
617     foreach ($colornames as $name => $stringkey) {
```

Next, we need to create an array of data that we need to pass to the browser. We will need to transfer:

- A list of activities, including their names and their completion status
- The colors needed to render the chart

It would also be helpful to the user if they could access an activity by clicking on the progress chart, rather than trying to find it in the course, so we will also pass a link to each activity.

Let us study the code. The function opens with code to load the colors representing the progress status into an array:

```
function block_completion_progress_json($activities, $completions, $config,
$userid, $courseid, $instance, $simple = false)
{
    global $OUTPUT, $USER;
    // create a json array of activities
    $progress = array();
    // Get colours and use defaults if they are not set in global
    settings.
    $colornames = array(
                'completed_colour' => 'completed_colour',
                'submittednotcomplete_colour' =>
                'submittednotcomplete_colour',
                'notCompleted_colour' => 'notCompleted_colour',
                'futureNotCompleted_colour' =>
                'futureNotCompleted_colour'
```

```
                    );
    $colors = array();
    foreach ($colornames as $name => $stringkey)
    {
            $colors[$name] = get_config('block_completion_progress',
            $name) ?: get_string('block_completion_progress',
            $stringkey);
    }
    $progress['colors'] = $colors;
```

Next, we need to determine links to each activity:

```
    // Determine links to activities.
    $alternatelinks =
    block_completion_progress_modules_with_alternate_links();
    $numactivities = count($activities);
    for ($i = 0; $i < $numactivities; $i++)
    {
        if ($userid != $USER->id &&
            array_key_exists($activities[$i]['type'],
            $alternatelinks) &&
            has_capability($alternatelinks[$activities[$i]['type']]
            ['capability'], $activities[$i]['context'])
            )
        {
        $substitutions = array(
                            '/:courseid/' => $courseid,
                            '/:eventid/'  => $activities[$i]
                            ['instance'],
                            '/:cmid/'     => $activities[$i]
                            ['id'],
                            '/:userid/'   => $userid,
                            );
        $link = $alternatelinks[$activities[$i]['type']]['url'];
        $link = preg_replace(array_keys($substitutions),
                array_values($substitutions), $link);
        $activities[$i]['link'] = $CFG->wwwroot.$link;
        }
        else
        {
            $activities[$i]['link'] = $activities[$i]['url'];
        }
    }
```

Finally, we need to create a list of activities, links to those activities, and their status and encode this to JSON so that it is ready to pass to JavaScript:

```
foreach ($activities as $activity)
{
        $activity_details = array();
        $completed = $completions[$activity['id']];
        $activity_details['name'] = s($activity['name']);
        if (!empty($activity['link']) && (!empty($activity['available'])
        || $simple))
        {
                $activity_details['link'] = $activity['link'];
        }
        else
        {
                $activity_details['link'];
        }
        $activity_details['status'] = '';
        if ($completed == COMPLETION_COMPLETE)
        {
                $activity_details['status'] = 'complete';
        }
        else if ($completed == COMPLETION_COMPLETE_PASS)
        {
                $activity_details['status'] = 'passed';
        }
        else if ($completed == COMPLETION_COMPLETE_FAIL)
        {
                $activity_details['status'] = 'failed';
          } else {
                if ($completed === 'submitted') {
                    $activity_details['status'] = 'submitted';
                }
          }
        $progress['activities'][] = $activity_details;
    }
    $data = json_encode($progress);
    return $data;
}
```

Note there are parameters passed to this function; for example, the variables `config` and `simple`, which at this stage we aren't using but we can leave them in place for any future development work.

Once encoded, the data then needs to be transferred to the browser and rendered, which is described in the next section.

Constructing a progress chart

Let us start by creating a new AMD JavaScript module. In Eclipse, create a new folder called /amd/src and, in that, a new file called chart_renderer.js:

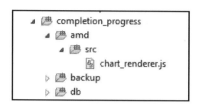

As we did in Chapter 5, *Creative Teaching - Developing Custom Resources and Activities*, where we created a three-dimensional model renderer, we will be creating a new AMD module. However, this time we will be requiring jQuery to help us with the creation of our new progress chart. As described in the Moodle documentation (https://docs.moodle.org/dev/Javascript_Modules#.22Hello_World.22_I_am_a_Javascript_Module), the declaration of our new module opens with the libraries we need to load, specified in the order we need to load them. As with the example given in the docs, we only need to load jQuery:

```
define(['jquery'], function($)
{
    var t = {
            drawChart: function(dataset)
        {
            var completion_data = $.parseJSON(dataset);
        },
};
      return t;
});
```

The preceding stub function loads jQuery (which, recall, ships with Moodle) and specifies the jQuery variable name ('$'). Within the module itself, we declare a function called drawChart() that takes a single parameter called dataset. We then use the jQuery function parseJSON() to decode the data passed to the browser from the server.

At the Moodle end, we need to call the Page API function, js_call_amd():

```
// load the chart using Chart.js
$this->page->requires->js('/blocks/completion_progress/thirdparty/Chart.js'
, true);
$js_params = array($json);
$this->page->requires->js_call_amd('block_completion_progress/chart_rende
r', 'drawChart', $js_params);
```

Historically, Moodle has always included the YUI framework to enable developers to include more effective user experience features (such as drag-and-drop, rendering tree views, implementing AJAX, and so on). However, YUI--although still in use--is no longer being developed.

Creating a chart

To display a chart, we first need to provide an HTML canvas element upon which the chart will be drawn. We can add the following line to the block's `get_content()` function:

```
$this->content->text .= html_writer::empty_tag('canvas',
array('id'=>'myChart'));
```

Now, back in `chart_renderer.js`, we begin by storing the different user configurable colors that represent the various completion statuses:

```
var col_complete = completion_data.colors.completed_colour;
var col_incomplete = completion_data.colors.notCompleted_colour;
var col_submitted = completion_data.colors.submittednotcomplete_colour;
var col_failed = completion_data.colors.futureNotCompleted_colour;
```

Then we establish three arrays to store the status color, the mouse hover labels, and the data:

```
var labels = [];
var data = [];
var background = [];
```

Finally, we can loop through all the activities and store the relevant segment colors and labels:

```
var array_len = completion_data.activities.length;
for (var i = 0; i < array_len; i++) {
labels.push(completion_data.activities[i].name);
    // Note that the pie chart segments will all be the same size
    data.push('1');
    var status = completion_data.activities[i].status;
    switch (status) {
        case 'complete':
                background.push(col_complete);
                break;
        case 'passed':
                background.push(col_complete);
                break;
        case 'failed':
                background.push(col_failed);
```

```
                break;
        case 'submitted':
                background.push(col_submitted);
                break;
        default:
                background.push(col_incomplete);
                break;
        }
    }
```

Notice that we are wanting equal sized pie chart segments so each data value passed in the data array to Chart.js is simply '1'.

To construct the chart proper, first we create a JSON variable containing the relevant configuration settings:

```
var chartData = {
labels: labels,
datasets:[
{
        label: "Completions",
        data: data,
        backgroundColor: background
}
        ]
};
```

Next, we need to get the "drawing context" on which to display the chart (for example, see https://developer.mozilla.org/en/docs/Web/API/HTMLCanvasElement/getContext):

```
var ctx = document.getElementById("myChart").getContext("2d");
```

Finally, we can draw the chart:

```
var myChart = new Chart(ctx,
{
    type: 'pie',
    data: chartData,
    options: {
        legend: {
                display: false
        },
        tooltips: {
                callbacks: {
                        label: function(tooltipItem, data) {
                                        String.prototype.trunc =
                                        function(n){
                                                return
```

```
this.substr(0,n-1)+(this.length>n?'...':'');
                                };
                        var allData =
data.datasets[tooltipItem.datasetIndex].data;
                        var tooltipLabel =
data.labels[tooltipItem.index];
                        // truncate the label to 15
characters plus an ellipsis if necessary:
                        return tooltipLabel.trunc(15);
                    }
                }
    }
        }
});
```

As you can see, we are using a JavaScript callback function to display a label when the user hovers the mouse pointer over a segment. We need to ensure that, if the label is long, it is truncated to fit.

Making the chart clickable

The final step in this section is to allow the user to click on a chart segment to take them to the relevant activity. To achieve this, we need to cache the activity URLs. Add a new `links` array variable to the closure as follows:

```
define(['jquery'], function($)
{
    var links = [];
    var t = {
...
```

Next, find the for loop code that extracts each activity's label and status and add in a line to cache that activity's URL:

```
for (var i = 0; i < array_len; i++)
{
    labels.push(completion_data.activities[i].name);
    // Note that the pie chart segments will all be the same size
    data.push('1');
    links.push(completion_data.activities[i].link);
    var status = completion_data.activities[i].status;
    ...
```

Finally, we can use jQuery to detect when the page has loaded, and in turn, hook the canvas element's `onclick` event:

```
$(document).ready(
function () {
            var canvas = document.getElementById("myChart");
            canvas.onclick = function (evt) {
                var activePoints = myChart.getElementsAtEvent(evt);
                var chartData = activePoints[0]['_chart'].config.data;
                var idx = activePoints[0]['_index'];

                var url = links[idx];
            window.location.href = url;
                return false;
            };
        });
```

It is beyond the scope of this book to discuss the `Chart.js` library in too much detail. For more information, please refer to the online documentation at `http://www.chartjs.org/docs/`.

The following is a screen grab of the block added to a course page:

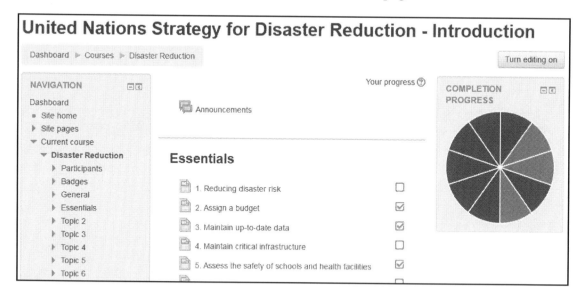

Taking things further

We are adding text to each chart segment so that when the user hovers the mouse pointer over it, a popup label is displayed. It would make sense to make the length to which this chart segment label is truncated configurable. Can you think of a way of implementing this?

Currently, the chart label (Completions) is hardcoded. Try making this a language setting.

Dashboard progress overview

Having created a new block to chart a learner's progress through a course, we now need to develop a set of charts showing the progress through all the courses on which a learner is enrolled. This can then be displayed on their dashboard.

Recall that the dashboard wireframe (agreed by the client) demands doughnut charts, rather than pie charts--with a percentage completion displayed in the center of the chart:

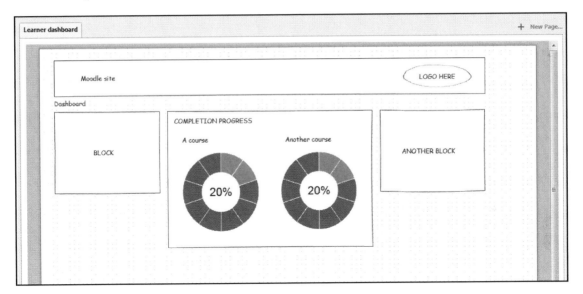

To display text in the center of the chart, we will need to register a new function with the Chart.js library to render the text before the doughnut chart is drawn. We need to take care to ensure that the text resizes with the canvas element in order for the progress block to be responsive. The following is the complete function:

```
Chart.pluginService.register({
beforeDraw: function (chart)
{
        if (chart.config.options.elements.center)
        {
                //Get ctx from string
                var ctx = chart.chart.ctx;
                //Get options from the center object in options
                var centerConfig = chart.config.options.elements.center;
                var fontStyle = centerConfig.fontStyle || 'Arial';
                var txt = centerConfig.text;
                var color = centerConfig.color || '#000';
                var sidePadding = centerConfig.sidePadding || 20;
                var sidePaddingCalculated = (sidePadding/100) *
                (chart.innerRadius * 2)
                //Start with a base font of 30px
                ctx.font = "30px " + fontStyle;
                //Get the width of the string and also the width of the
                element minus 10 to give it 5px side padding
                var stringWidth = ctx.measureText(txt).width;
                var elementWidth = (chart.innerRadius * 2) -
                sidePaddingCalculated;
                // Find out how much the font can grow in width.
                var widthRatio = elementWidth / stringWidth;
                var newFontSize = Math.floor(30 * widthRatio);
                var elementHeight = (chart.innerRadius * 2);
                // Pick a new font size so it will not be larger than the
                height of label.
                var fontSizeToUse = Math.min(newFontSize, elementHeight);
                //Set font settings to draw it correctly.
                ctx.textAlign = 'center';
                ctx.textBaseline = 'middle';
                var centerX = ((chart.chartArea.left +
                chart.chartArea.right) / 2);
                var centerY = ((chart.chartArea.top +
                chart.chartArea.bottom) / 2);
                ctx.font = fontSizeToUse+"px " + fontStyle;
                ctx.fillStyle = color;
                //Draw text in center
                ctx.fillText(txt, centerX, centerY);
        }
}
```

```
});
```

In `block_completion_progress_json()`, we can determine the percentage progress for a course when we loop through the activities. We simply need to keep a count of the number of completed activities, divide by the total number of activities, and then convert to an integer percentage:

```
$percentage = 0;
if ( $numactivities> 0 )
{
        $percentage = round($completed_activities/ ($numactivities/
        100),2);
}
$progress['percentage'] = (string)$percentage;
```

This can then be passed to the AMD module as part of the JSON data.

Finally, for each block instance in each course, we can create a new canvas element (each with a unique id), generate JSON data to plot, and call `drawChart()`:

```
$json = block_completion_progress_json(
$blockinstance->activities,
$completions,
$this->config,
$USER->id,
$courseid,
$this->instance->id);
$chartid = 'progressChart' . $courseid;
$this->content->text .= HTML_WRITER::tag('canvas', '',
array('id'=>$chartid));
$js_params = array($chartid, 'doughnut', $json, true);
$this->page->requires->js_call_amd('block_completion_progress/chart_rendere
r', 'drawChart', $js_params);
```

Styling can be improved and enhanced through the `/styles.css` CSS style sheet. Styling is described in more detail in the next chapter but, in the meantime, the following is the progress block added to a user dashboard:

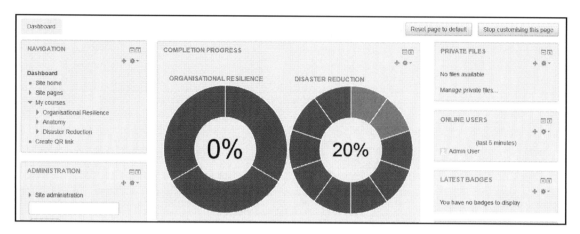

The final aspect of the development of the completion progress block is the **Overview of students**:

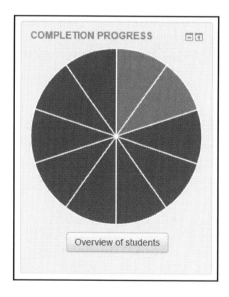

The **Overview of** students button is displayed to users with the `block/completion_progress:overview` capability. The fragment of code responsible for displaying the button is to be found at the end of `get_content()`:

```
// Allow teachers to access the overview page.
if (has_capability('block/completion_progress:overview', $this->context)) {
    $parameters = array('instanceid' => $this->instance->id, 'courseid' =>
$COURSE->id, 'sesskey' => sesskey());
    $url = new moodle_url('/blocks/completion_progress/overview.php',
$parameters);
    $label = get_string('overview', 'block_completion_progress');
    $options = array('class' => 'overviewButton');
$this->content->text .= $OUTPUT->single_button($url, $label, 'post',
$options);
}
```

The client wants a color-coded list of activities to be displayed for each student, along with their overall progress:

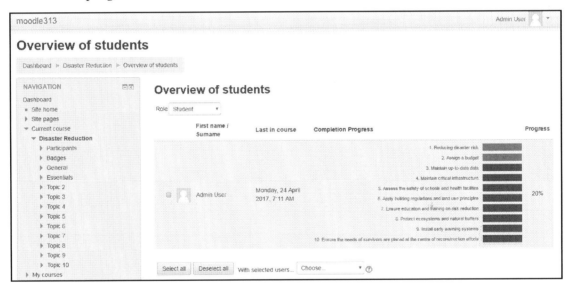

Color coded list of activities

This is a horizontal stacked bar chart, with limited functionality compared to the pie or doughnut charts. In order to display the chart, we will need to implement a second function in chart_render.js. Let us call this new function drawbar():

```
drawBar: function(chartEl, dataSet)
{
        var completion_data = $.parseJSON(dataSet);
        var array_len = completion_data.activities.length;
        var labels = [];
        var data = [];
        var background = [];
        // only handle complete and incomplete at the moment
        var col_complete = completion_data.colors.completed_colour;
        var col_incomplete = completion_data.colors.notCompleted_colour;
        var col_submitted =
        completion_data.colors.submittednotcomplete_colour;
        var col_failed =
        completion_data.colors.futureNotCompleted_colour;
        for (var i = 0; i < array_len; i++)
        {
                labels.push(completion_data.activities[i].name);
                // Note that the pie chart segments will all be the same
                size
                data.push('1');
                links.push(completion_data.activities[i].link);
                var status = completion_data.activities[i].status;
                switch (status)
                {
                        case 'complete':
                        background.push(col_complete);
                        break;
                        case 'passed':
                        background.push(col_complete);
                        break;
                        case 'failed':
                        background.push(col_failed);
                        break;
                        case 'submitted':
                        background.push(col_submitted);
                        break;
                        default:
                        background.push(col_incomplete);
                        break;
                }
        }
    var chartData = {
            labels: labels,
            datasets:[
```

```
            {
                label: "Completions",
                data: data,
                backgroundColor: background
            }
    ]};
// Get the context of the canvas element we want to select
var ctx = document.getElementById(chartEl).getContext("2d");
Chart.defaults.global.tooltips.enabled = false;
// Instantiate a new chart
var myChart = new Chart(ctx, {
    type: 'horizontalBar',
    data: chartData,
    options: {
        scales: {
        xAxes: [{
            ticks: {
            fontFamily: "'Open Sans Bold', sans-serif",
            fontSize:11,
            display: false,
            },
            scaleLabel:{
                display:false
            },
            gridLines: {
                display:false
            },
            stacked: true
            }],
        yAxes: [{
            gridLines: {
            display:false,
            color: "#fff",
            zeroLineColor: "#fff",
            zeroLineWidth: 0
            },
            ticks: {
                fontFamily: "'Open Sans Bold', sans-serif",
                fontSize:11
            },
            stacked: true
            }],
            legend:{
                display:false
            },
        }
    });
        $(document).ready(
```

```
function ()
{
        var canvas = document.getElementById(chartEl);
        canvas.onclick = function (evt)
        {
        var activePoints =
        myChart.getElementsAtEvent(evt);
        var chartData = activePoints[0]
        ['_chart'].config.data;
        var idx = activePoints[0]['_index'];
        var url = links[idx];
        window.location.href = url;
        return false;
        };
    });
},
```

All that remains is to call this function for each student. In Eclipse, open `/overview.php`. Firstly, we need to load the `Chart.js` library which, recall, needs to be loaded before calling `drawbar()`:

```
65  );
66  $PAGE->set_context($context);
67  $title = get_string('overview', 'block_completion_progress');
68  $PAGE->set_title($title);
69  $PAGE->set_heading($title);
70  $PAGE->navbar->add($title);
71  $PAGE->set_pagelayout('report');
72
73  // Check user is logged in and capable of accessing the Overview.
74  require_login($course, false);
75  require_capability('block/completion_progress:overview', $blockcontext);
76  confirm_sesskey();
77
78  // load the chart using Chart.js - needs to be loaded calling js_call_amd()
79  $PAGE->requires->js('/blocks/completion_progress/thirdparty/Chart.js', true);
80
81  // Start page output.
82  echo $OUTPUT->header();
83  echo $OUTPUT->heading($title, 2);
84  echo $OUTPUT->container_start('block_completion_progress');
85
86  // Check if activities/resources have been selected in config.
```

Problems   Console   Browser Output   Debug Output   Search   Debug   Progress

And now, for each user we need to construct a table of charts. Here is the fragment of code that obtains the JSON data and calls, via `js_call_amd()`, the JavaScript `drawbar()` function:

```
// Build array of user information.
$rows = array();
for ($i = $startuser; $i < $enduser; $i++)
{
        if ($CFG->enablenotes || $CFG->messaging)
        {
                $selectattributes = array('type' => 'checkbox', 'class' =>
                'usercheckbox', 'name' => 'user'.$users[$i]->id);
                $select = html_writer::empty_tag('input',
                $selectattributes);
        }
        $picture = $OUTPUT->user_picture($users[$i], array('course' =>
        $course->id));
        $namelink = html_writer::link($CFG->wwwroot.'/user/view.php?
        id='.$users[$i]->id.'&course='.$course->id,
        fullname($users[$i]));
        if (empty($users[$i]->lastonlinetime))
        {
                $lastonline = get_string('never');
        }
        else
        {
                $lastonline = userdate($users[$i]->lastonlinetime);
        }
        $useractivities =
        block_completion_progress_filter_visibility($activities,
        $users[$i]->id, $course->id);
        if (!empty($useractivities))
        {
                $completions =
                block_completion_progress_completions($useractivities,
                $users[$i]->id, $course, $users[$i]->submissions);
                $json = block_completion_progress_json(
                $useractivities,
                $completions,
                $config,
                $users[$i]->id,
                $course->id,
                $block->id);
                // decode the data to obtain the progress
                $data = json_decode($json);
                $chartid = 'progressChart' . $users[$i]->id;
                $progressbar = html_writer::tag('canvas', '',
                array('id'=>$chartid));
```

```
            $progressvalue = $data->percentage;
            $progress = $progressvalue . '%';
            $js_params = array($chartid, $json);
            $PAGE->requires->
            js_call_amd('block_completion_progress/chart_renderer',
            'drawBar', $js_params);
    }
    else
    {
            $progressbar = get_string('no_visible_events_message',
            'block_completion_progress');
            $progressvalue = 0;
            $progress = '?';
    }
    $rows[$i] = array(
    'firstname' => strtoupper($users[$i]->firstname),
    'lastname' => strtoupper($users[$i]->lastname),
    'select' => $select,
    'picture' => $picture,
    'fullname' => $namelink,
    'lastonlinetime' => $users[$i]->lastonlinetime,
    'lastonline' => $lastonline,
    'progressbar' => $progressbar,
    'progressvalue' => $progressvalue,
    'progress' => $progress
    );
}
```

Taking things further

Polar area charts are similar to pie charts except that it is the radius of the segment that varies depending on the value. You will find an example of a polar chart in the Chart.js documentation at http://www.chartjs.org/docs/#polar-area-chart. What's great about polar charts is that you can see at a glance, an overview of a student's progress. Can you rewrite the drawbar() function so that it renders a polar chart instead?

Encouraging learners to start a course

Our client also wants to show learners a simple list of courses, together with a short description and a launch button on the dashboard. The block should give the learner an indication of courses available to them, those they have started, and courses they have completed (this is to complement the progress block we developed in the previous section). The following is the user story:

The user interface consists of a block to display a list of courses and, where appropriate, a button which displays a course overview page. The following are the wireframes that have been agreed with the client. Firstly, the block as they are wanting it to be displayed on the learner dashboard:

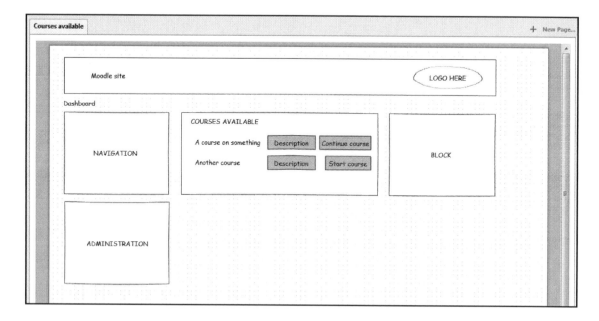

When the learner clicks on the **Description** button, the client wants a **Course information** page to be displayed:

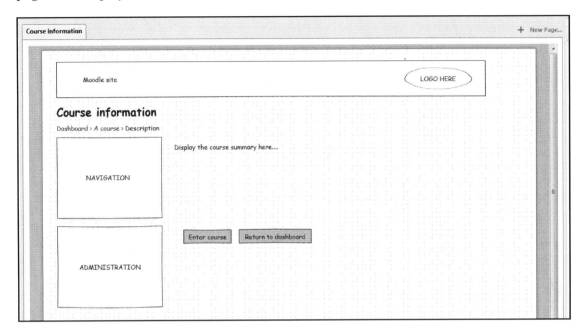

Again, this will also be implemented as a new block - and the version of this block we will be working together to develop is available at
`https://github.com/iandavidwild/moodle-block_courses_available`. Let us go ahead and develop this new block now.

Implementing a new course availability block

Let us start by making a copy of the course progress block we developed in the previous section and, using Eclipse, refactoring this to `course_availability`:

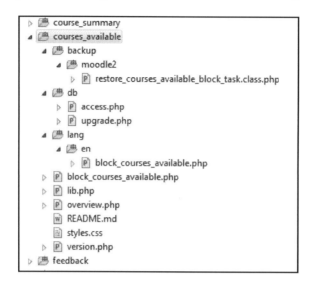

Determining progress

When it came to deciding which courses to display on the dashboard, we checked which courses included course progress blocks. However, this time around we need to display all courses a learner is enrolled on and attempt to determine their progress. Luckily, we can reuse the code from the completion progress block to determine the learner's progress through a course (but more on that later).

First, we need to obtain a list of courses the current user is enrolled on:

```
$courses = enrol_get_my_courses();
// Show a message when the user is not enrolled in any courses.
if (($this->page->user_is_editing() || is_siteadmin()) && empty($courses))
{
    $this->content->text = get_string('nocourses',
    'block_courses_available');
    return $this->content;
}
```

Once that is done, we need to obtain a list of activities from each course. Note the use of the *Activity completion API* in this process (see `https://docs.moodle.org/dev/Activity_completion_API` for details):

```
$courseinstances = array();
foreach ($courses as $courseid => $course)
{
        // Get specific course completion data
        $completion = new completion_info($course);
        if ($course->visible && $completion->is_enabled())
        {
                $context = CONTEXT_COURSE::instance($course->id);
                $params = array('contextid' => $context->id, 'pagetype' =>
                'course-view-%');
                $courseinstance = new stdClass();
                $courseinstance->course = $course;
                $courseinstance->activities =
                block_courses_available_get_activities($course->id);
                $courseinstance->activities =
                block_courses_available_filter_visibility($courseinstance-
                >activities, $USER->id, $course->id);
                $courseinstances[] = $courseinstance;
        }
}
```

Having obtained an array of course instances, together with the activities in each course, we can determine the current user's submissions and completions and create a JSON data string. The following is the fragment of code from the `get_content()` function that does this:

```
foreach ($courseinstances as $courseinstance)
{
        $course = get_course($courseinstance->course->id);
        $row = array();
        $row [] = $course->fullname;
        if (isset($course->summary))
        {
                $link = new moodle_url($CFG-
                >wwwroot.'/blocks/courses_available/overview.php?
                id='.$course->id);
                $buttonString = get_string('description', '
                block_courses_available');
                $button = new single_button($link, $buttonString, 'get');
                $button->class = 'tablebutton';
                $row[] = $OUTPUT->render($button);
        }
        else
```

```
{
        $row[] = '-';
}
$submissions =
block_courses_available_student_submissions($course->id, $USER-
>id);
$completions =
block_courses_available_completions($courseinstance->activities,
$USER->id, $course, $submissions);
$json = block_courses_available_json(
        $courseinstance->activities,
        $completions,
        $this->config,
        $USER->id,
        $courseid,
        $this->instance->id);
```

Finally, we need to construct an HTML table containing course details. Luckily, we have a set of helper functions to support us--see
https://docs.moodle.org/dev/Output_Components#table for details. The following is the second part of the `for` loop introduced in the previous code fragment:

```
$completion_data = json_decode($json);
$url = new moodle_url($CFG->wwwroot.'/course/view.php',
array('id'=>$course->id));
$progress = intval($completion_data->percentage);
if ($progress == 100)
{
        $buttonString = get_string('retakecourse',
        'block_courses_available');
}
elseif ($progress == 0)
{
        $buttonString = get_string('startcourse',
        'block_courses_available');
}
else
{
        $buttonString = get_string('continuecourse',
        'block_courses_available');
}
$button = new single_button($url, $buttonString, 'get');
$button->class = 'tablebutton';
$row[] = $OUTPUT->render($button);
if ($progress == 100)
{
        $completedTable[] = $row;
}
```

```
elseif ($progress == 0)
{
        $toStartTable[] = $row;
}
else
{
        $inProgressTable[] = $row;
}
}// foreach
```

Now the tables have been constructed, we need to return the HTML so that it can be rendered:

```
$table->data = array_merge($inProgressTable, $toStartTable,
$completedTable);
$this->content->text = html_writer::table($table);
```

We only want the block to be displayed once--and there aren't currently any configuration options--so make sure you update the instance_allow_multiple(), instance_allow_config(), and has_config()block_courses_available class member functions accordingly:

```
/**
*   we have global config/settings data
*
* @return bool
*/
public function has_config()
{
        return false;
}
/**
* Controls whether the block is configurable
*
* @return bool
*/
public function instance_allow_config() {
return false;
}
/**
* Controls whether multiple instances of the block are allowed on a page
*
* @return bool
*/
public function instance_allow_multiple()
{
        return false;
}
```

The following is the finished courses available block in action:

Creating the Description page

According to the specification, when the user clicks on the **Description** button they should be taken to an overview of the course:

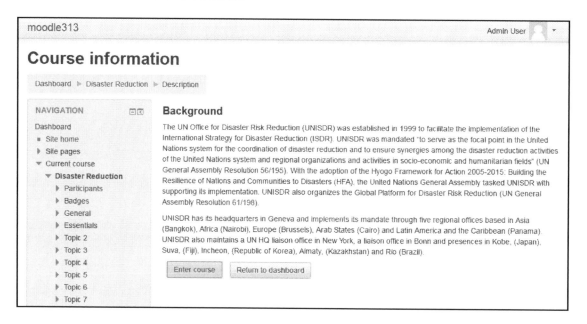

A relatively short fragment of code is needed to achieve this. Here is the `overview.php` script in its entirety:

```php
<?php
// This file is part of Moodle - http://moodle.org/
//
// Moodle is free software: you can redistribute it and/or modify
// it under the terms of the GNU General Public License as published by
// the Free Software Foundation, either version 3 of the License, or
```

```
// (at your option) any later version.
//
// Moodle is distributed in the hope that it will be useful,
// but WITHOUT ANY WARRANTY; without even the implied warranty of
// MERCHANTABILITY or FITNESS FOR A PARTICULAR PURPOSE.  See the
// GNU General Public License for more details.
//
// You should have received a copy of the GNU General Public License
// along with Moodle.  If not, see <http://www.gnu.org/licenses/>.

/**
 * Completion Progress block overview page
 *
 * @package    block_completion_progress
 * @copyright  2017 Ian Wild
 * @license    http://www.gnu.org/copyleft/gpl.html GNU GPL v3 or later
 */
/// Displays external information about a course
require_once("../../config.php");
$id   = optional_param('id', false, PARAM_INT); // Course id
$name = optional_param('name', false, PARAM_RAW); // Course short name
if (!$id and !$name)
{
     print_error("unspecifycourseid");
}
if ($name)
{
     if (!$course = $DB->get_record("course",
         array("shortname"=>$name)))
     {
          print_error("invalidshortname");
     }
}
else
{
     if (!$course = $DB->get_record("course", array("id"=>$id)))
     {
          print_error("invalidcourseid");
     }
}
$site = get_site();
if ($CFG->forcelogin)
{
     require_login();
}
$context = context_course::instance($course->id);
if (!$course->visible and
!has_capability('moodle/course:viewhiddencourses', $context))
```

```
{
    print_error('coursehidden', '', $CFG->wwwroot .'/');
}

$PAGE->set_context($context);
$PAGE->set_pagelayout('standard');
$PAGE->set_url('/blocks/courses_available/overview.php', array('id' =>
        $course->id));
$PAGE->set_title(get_string("summaryof", "", $course->fullname));
$PAGE->set_heading(get_string('courseinfoheading',
        'block_courses_available'));
$PAGE->set_course($course);
$PAGE->navbar->add(get_string('description',
            'block_courses_available'));
echo $OUTPUT->header();
echo $OUTPUT->box_start('generalbox summaryinfo');
echo format_text($course->summary, $course->summaryformat,
array('overflowdiv'=>true), $course->id);
if (!empty($CFG->coursecontact))
{
        $coursecontactroles = explode(',', $CFG->coursecontact);
        foreach ($coursecontactroles as $roleid) {
        $role = $DB->get_record('role', array('id'=>$roleid));
        $roleid = (int) $roleid;
        if ($users = get_role_users($roleid, $context, true))
        {
                foreach ($users as $teacher)
                {
                        $fullname = fullname($teacher,
                        has_capability('moodle/site:viewfullnames',
                        $context));
                        $namesarray[] = format_string(role_get_name($role,
                        $context)).': <a href="'.$CFG-
                        >wwwroot.'/user/view.php?id='.
                        $teacher->
                        id.'&amp;course='.SITEID.'">'.$fullname.'</a>';
                }
        }
}
if (!empty($namesarray))
{
        echo "<ul class=\"teachers\">\n<li>";
        echo implode('</li><li>', $namesarray);
        echo "</li></ul>";
}
}
echo $OUTPUT->box_end();
/*
```

```
* button box
*/
$buttonBox = $OUTPUT->box_start('generalbox icons');
$cancel = new single_button(new moodle_url($CFG->wwwroot.'/my'),
get_string('homepage', 'block_courses_available'), 'get');
$url = new moodle_url($CFG->wwwroot.'/course/view.php',
array('id'=>$course->id));
$continue = new single_button($url, get_string('coursepage',
'block_courses_available'), 'get');
$attr = array('id'=>'summarybuttons','class' => 'buttons');
$buttonBox .= html_writer::tag('div',
$OUTPUT->render($continue).$OUTPUT->render($cancel), $attr);
$buttonBox .= $OUTPUT->box_end();
echo $buttonBox;
echo $OUTPUT->footer();
```

Taking things further

Note that we are re-using the `block_courses_available_json()` function to obtain course completion data, which means there is no reason why we shouldn't display a completion chart on the Course information page. Can you re-code `overview.php` to display a doughnut chart using `Chart.js`?

Can you think of a way of adding other information to the **Course information** page that would encourage a learner to start or continue a course? For example, *badges* are a great way of showing progress--see `https://docs.moodle.org/31/en/Badges`. It might be worth taking a little time to explore displaying course badges on the **Course information** page.

Summary

In this chapter, we learned how gamification can be used to encourage learners to participate in a course, specifically by creating a learner dashboard. We saw how a completion progress block can be developed using `Chart.js` such that learner progress is displayed in an immediate, as well as engaging, way. Along the way, we explored how jQuery can be employed in a Moodle plugin (in an AMD JavaScript module), as well as encountering the Activity Completion API, JSON encoding, and more.

Having spent this chapter developing the learner dashboard, it is time to explore how the look and feel of Moodle can be tailored to suit our learner (and network) requirements, which is the subject of the next chapter.

8
Creating a New Skin

In previous chapters, we have concerned ourselves with functionality. Now it is time to focus on the user experience and how this is affected by aesthetics. The look of a learning platform and "the effectiveness, efficiency, and satisfaction with which users can achieve specified learning (or learning related) goals in a particular environment" are "intrinsically linked", according to *Cooper, Colwell*, and *Jelfs* in their paper, *Embedding accessibility and usability*. Fortunately, the Moodle framework provides us with great flexibility--not only in how the look of a Moodle page can be changed but also in the mechanisms through which a page can be altered. The look-and-feel of a Moodle installation is managed through a specific plugin type called *theme*. Note that this chapter only covers the essentials of theme development, specifically in the context of plugin development. Specifically, we will be showing you how to ensure your plugins are structured ready for theming. This is simply because the full details of theme development are comprehensively covered elsewhere-- particularly in the book *Moodle Theme Development*, also from Packt--`https://www.packtpub.com/web-development/moodle-theme-development`.

We start this chapter with an investigation of basic theme structure. Then we investigate how to ensure that plugins are structured (using *renderers*) such that their look and feel can be manipulated more easily by a Moodle theme (we further develop the *Courses available* block, which we developed together in `Chapter 7`, *Creating a Dashboard - Developing a Learner Homepage*, as we do so).

Finally, we begin to create a brand new theme for our Organizational Resilience website based on the Essential theme (`https://moodle.org/plugins/theme_essential`). Our client has highlighted that the Moodle we are developing needs to work seamlessly on mobile and tablet devices - as well as desktops and laptops. This will require our theme to be *responsive*. We will learn what a responsive theme is and how to ensure your work is responsive later in this chapter.

In this chapter, we will be:

- Learning how to code plugins such that they can be more easily themed
- Building a plugin renderer and overriding this in a theme
- How page templates can be constructed, based on the templating technology, *Mustache*

Let us start with investigating the general structure of a theme, and how different elements of a Moodle page can be manipulated.

Theme plugin structure

Our work in this section is based on the *Clean* theme--see `https://docs.moodle.org/dev/Clean_theme` for details. The Clean theme provides the ideal starting point for learning about Moodle themes: as the name suggests, metaphorically speaking it provides the "scaffolding" (the framework)--and it is then up to us to cover the scaffolding with the "skin" (the look-and-feel). The Clean theme is itself based on a theme called *bootstrapbase*, with Bootstrap being the technology used to provide *responsiveness*. See `https://docs.moodle.org/dev/Bootstrap` for details on responsiveness (which is, basically, the ability of a web page to modify itself through CSS, depending on the size and type of device on which it is rendering).

In Eclipse, open the **theme/clean** folder:

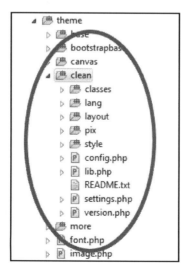

Every theme will have a configuration file, `config.php`. This is arguably the most important script in a theme so we start our investigation with this. But before we do, let us go back to Eclipse and make a copy of the *clean* theme and call it **resilience**:

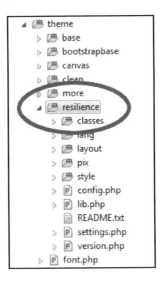

Now open `config.php` and let us update this file for our new theme. First, we need to understand what theme property each variable refers to:

Property	Details
name	Self-explanatory. Change the name to "resilience"
parents	Themes can be children of other themes, and so inherit the attributes and behaviors of their parents. Being a child of the *bootstrapbase* theme means we inherit basic responsive behaviors.
sheets	A list of one of more CSS style sheets. These are listed in the order in which they are loaded (by which styles can be overridden).
rendererfactory	This tells Moodle that our theme will override renderers, and specifies the function which will be called to do so. We will be investigating renderers in the next section.
csspostprocess	Specifies a function which will process any CSS before it is cached.

We need to update the `resilience/classes/core_renderer.php` script. This requires a simple change: rename the class declared in this script to `theme_resilience_core_renderer`.

Page layout

Each Moodle page can have its own corresponding layout script, and these are specified in the theme's /layout folder:

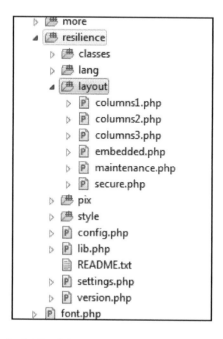

How does this work in practice? The "three column" course layout that the Clean theme renders by default is formatted via the columns3.php script. Each script echoes to the browser the basic HTML structure of a page - minus the content provided (later on in the process) by individual plugins (provided by blocks, for example). Each one of these layout files will need to be updated, so go ahead and do that now.

Theme library functions

Now let us update the new theme's `lib.php` script. Replace any occurrences of the word `clean` with the word `resilience`. Check out the `rendererfactory` and `csspostprocess` functions which we specified in `config.php`.

Next, we need to rename `lang/en/clean.php` to `resilience.php` and update the contents accordingly--specifically the `pluginnam'` string:

Changes in the script

To make our new `resilience` theme operational, we need to update `/version.php`. Let us go ahead and do so now:

```
P version.php ⊠
   6  // the Free Software Foundation, either version 3 of the License, or
   7  // (at your option) any later version.
   8  //
   9  // Moodle is distributed in the hope that it will be useful,
  10  // but WITHOUT ANY WARRANTY; without even the implied warranty of
  11  // MERCHANTABILITY or FITNESS FOR A PARTICULAR PURPOSE.  See the
  12  // GNU General Public License for more details.
  13  //
  14  // You should have received a copy of the GNU General Public License
  15  // along with Moodle.  If not, see <http://www.gnu.org/licenses/>.
  16
  17  /**
  18   * Moodle's Clean theme, an example of how to make a Bootstrap theme
  19   *
  20   * DO NOT MODIFY THIS THEME!
  21   * COPY IT FIRST, THEN RENAME THE COPY AND MODIFY IT INSTEAD.
  22   *
  23   * For full information about creating Moodle themes, see:
  24   * http://docs.moodle.org/dev/Themes_2.0
  25   *
  26   * @package    theme_resilence
  27   * @copyright  2017 Moodle, moodle.org
  28   * @license    http://www.gnu.org/copyleft/gpl.html GNU GPL v3 or later
  29   */
  30
  31  defined('MOODLE_INTERNAL') || die;
  32
  33  $plugin->version    = 2017050200;
  34  $plugin->requires   = 2016051900;
  35  $plugin->component = 'theme_resilience';
  36  $plugin->dependencies = array(
  37      'theme_bootstrapbase'  => 2016051900,
  38  );
  39
```

```
Problems  Console ⊠   Browser Output   Debug Output   Search   Debug   Progr
```

See that we also specify the `bootstrapbase` theme as a dependency in `version.php`.

We can now install our new theme. From the **Administration** block, click on **Notifications** in the **Site administration** menu. Once installed, click on **Site administration**, then **Appearance**, **Themes** and then, finally, **Theme selector**. The **Select device** configuration page is displayed:

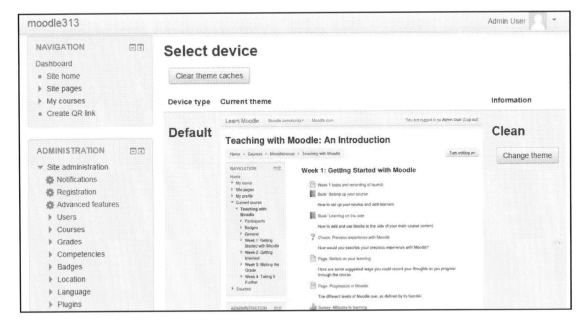

Select device configuration page

For the **Default** device, press the **Change theme** button. The **Select theme for default device** page is displayed. Our new theme will be listed:

The 'Resilience' theme

Press the **Use theme** button to start using the new theme. Obviously at this stage, Moodle will look exactly the same--which is fine as this gives us a great place from which to start further development.

Taking things further - updating the theme screen grab

The theme screen grab displayed on the **Select theme...** pages is found at `/pix/screenshot.jpg`. Try updating the screenshot now.

Renderers

In previous chapters, we have encountered renderers (for example the three-dimensional model viewer we developed in `Chapter 5`, *Creative Teaching - Developing Custom Resources and Activities*) without delving into too much detail regarding why they exist and how they can be used. In fact, renderers aren't obligatory at all: in the previous chapter, we created dashboard blocks that didn't include renderers. Let us use the *Courses available* block as an example. This block outputs its HTML straight from the `get_content()` function. That's fine as far as it goes, but if we were wanting to alter the form and layout of the *Courses available* block in any meaningful way, we would need to alter the block itself. This is especially true if we were going to be installing the block in different Moodle installations, where each installation had its own distinctive look-and-feel. It's certainly true that we could change the look of the block using CSS but, again, that will only take us so far. Implementing a render means that the theme can take over complete control of a plugin's user interface and, through this, the overall user experience.

For more detail on plugin renderers, check out the Moodle developer documentation at `htt ps://docs.moodle.org/dev/Overriding_a_renderer#An_overview_of_renderers`.

Let's make a start by learning how we can use renderers to enhance our *Courses available* block. The first stage is to implement a new renderer, which is the subject of the next section.

Creating a plugin renderer

In Eclipse, open the **courses_available** folder and add a new PHP script called `renderer.php`:

```
3  //
4  // Moodle is free software: you can redistribute it and/or modify
5  // it under the terms of the GNU General Public License as published by
6  // the Free Software Foundation, either version 3 of the License, or
7  // (at your option) any later version.
8  //
9  // Moodle is distributed in the hope that it will be useful,
10 // but WITHOUT ANY WARRANTY; without even the implied warranty of
11 // MERCHANTABILITY or FITNESS FOR A PARTICULAR PURPOSE.  See the
12 // GNU General Public License for more details.
13 //
14 // You should have received a copy of the GNU General Public License
15 // along with Moodle.  If not, see <http://www.gnu.org/licenses/>.
16
17 /**
18  * courses_available block renderer
19  *
20  * @package    block_courses_available
21  * @copyright  2017 Ian Wild
22  * @license    http://www.gnu.org/copyleft/gpl.html GNU GPL v3 or later
23  */
24 defined('MOODLE_INTERNAL') || die;
25
26 /**
27  * Courses_available block renderer
28  *
29  * @copyright  2017 Ian Wild
30  * @license    http://www.gnu.org/copyleft/gpl.html GNU GPL v3 or later
31  */
32 class block_courses_available_renderer extends plugin_renderer_base {
33
34
35 }
36
```

The renderer needs to extend `plugin_renderer_base`, and contain whatever code is necessary to output the block's HTML. When creating a new renderer, it is important to implement separate functions for each of the elements we need to display onscreen. That way it is easy for a theme to extend/enhance/replace any individual element. The following is a screen grab of the block:

There are three basic elements we should implement separate rendering functions for:

- The course title
- A link to the description page
- A link to the course itself

The following are the relevant renderer functions:

```
/**
 * Courses_available block renderer
 *
 * @copyright  2017 Ian Wild
 * @license    http://www.gnu.org/copyleft/gpl.html GNU GPL v3 or later
 */
class block_courses_available_renderer extends plugin_renderer_base
{
    /**
     * Returns the HTML for the course title. For now just return the
     * title as-is.
     *
     * @param unknown $title
     * @return unknown
     */
    public function get_course_title($title)
    {
        return $title;
    }
    /**
     * Returns the HTML for a button that links to the
     * block_courses_available overview page
     *
     * @param unknown $course
     * @return string
     */
    public function get_summary($course)
    {
        $html = '-';
        if(isset($course->summary))
        {
            global $CFG;
            $link = new moodle_url($CFG->
                wwwroot.'/blocks/courses_available
                /overview.php?
                id='.$course->id);
            $buttonString = get_string('description',
                        'block_courses_available');
                        $button = new
```

```
                                               single_button($link,
                                               $buttonString, 'get');
                                               $button->class =
                                               'tablebutton';
                              $html = $this->output->render($button);
                     }
          return $html;
}
/**
* Returns the HTML for a button that navigates to the course. The button
text reflects the user's completion progress.
*
* @param unknown $course
* @param unknown $completion_data
* @return string
*/
public function get_course_link($course, $completion_data)
{
          global $CFG;
          $html = '';
          $url = new moodle_url($CFG->wwwroot.'/course/view.php',
          array('id'=>$course->id));
          $progress = intval($completion_data->percentage);
          if ($progress == 100)
          {
                $buttonString = get_string('retakecourse',
                'block_courses_available');
          }
          elseif ($progress == 0)
          {
                $buttonString = get_string('startcourse',
                'block_courses_available');
          }
          else
          {
                $buttonString = get_string('continuecourse',
                'block_courses_available');
          }
          $button = new single_button($url, $buttonString, 'get');
          $button->class = 'tablebutton';
          $html = $this->output->render($button);
          return $html;
}
```

Next we need to modify `get_content()`. First, we need to instantiate the block's renderer:

```
$renderer = $this->page->get_renderer('block_courses_available');
```

Then, rather than creating fragments of HTML in `get_content()`, we call the relevant renderer function. For example, for the course title and summary:

```
$row[] = $renderer->get_course_title($course->fullname);
$row[] = $renderer->get_summary($course);
```

Then there is the overview page (currently displayed when a user clicks the **Description** button). This too should use a renderer function to display the contents (the complete code is available in GitHub).

Having ensured that the block's output is built using a renderer, let us now investigate how it can be overridden in a theme.

Overriding a component renderer

To override a component renderer, we first need to create a new `/renderers` folder in the root of our theme. In that, create a new PHP script called `block_courses_available_renderer.php`:

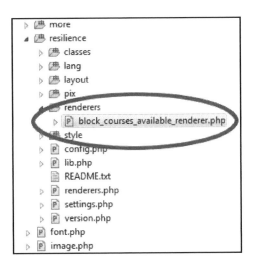

The file `block_courses_available_renderer.php` is where our new component renderer will be declared. To promote maintainability, it is always better to implement separate scripts for each overridden renderer.

Our new renderer needs to extend the course's available block renderer:

```
class theme_resilience_block_courses_available_renderer extends
block_courses_available_renderer {
...
```

Ensure you follow the correct naming convention for renderers overridden in a theme. The name consists of three parts:

- Renderers overridden in a theme always begin with `'theme_'`
- The name of our theme, `'resilience'`
- Finally, `block_courses_available_renderer` is the name of the renderer we are extending

The block's renderer implements four functions that we can, potentially, override:

- `get_course_title($title)`
- `get_summary($course)`
- `get_course_link($course, $completion_data)`
- `get_overview($course)`

By way of example, let us begin by overriding `get_course_link()`. This currently returns a button that, when clicked, takes the learner to the course page. From a technical point of view, this isn't strictly the best way of implementing a link to a course: a button is for submitting data and an *a* tag is for providing a link to a course. Here is the overridden `get_course_link()` function that provides a link:

```
public function get_course_link($course, $completion_data)
{
        global $CFG;
        $html = '';
        $url = new moodle_url($CFG->wwwroot.'/course/view.php',
                array('id'=>$course->id));
        $progress = intval($completion_data->percentage);
        if ($progress == 100)
        {
                $linkString = get_string('retakecourse',
                                'block_courses_available');
        }
        elseif ($progress == 0)
        {
                $linkString = get_string('startcourse',
                                'block_courses_available');
        }
```

```
    else
    {
            $linkString = get_string('continuecourse',
                            'block_courses_available');
    }
    $html = html_writer::link($url, $linkString, array('class' =>
    'button course_link'));
    return $html;
}
```

Return to the Moodle dashboard and you will now see that the buttons linking to courses have been replaced with "proper" links:

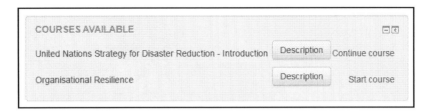

Now let's override the `get_summary()` function, again to provide a link instead of a button:

```
public function get_summary($course)
{
        $html = '-';
        if(isset($course->summary))
        {
                global $CFG;
                $url = new moodle_url($CFG->
                        wwwroot.'/blocks/courses_available
                        /overview.php?id='.$course->id);
                $linkString = get_string('description',
                                'block_courses_available');
                $html = html_writer::link($url, $linkString, array('class'
                        =>'button course_overview'));
        }
        return $html;
}
```

Thanks to our new theme's renderer, the **COURSES AVAILABLE** block now displays links rather than buttons:

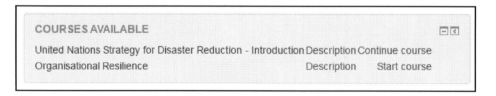

Custom styling

The Description and Course links now rendered in the COURSES AVAILABLE block will need restyling using CSS. In Eclipse, create a new CSS file in the `/style` folder called `block_courses_available.css`:

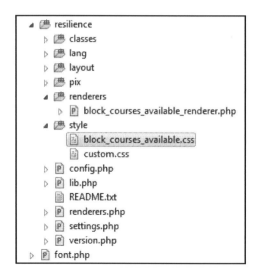

Using the classes we have applied to the links (button and `course_overview`, for example), we can style the links to simulate buttons.

The following is the complete CSS:

```
@CHARSET "ISO-8859-1";
a.button
{
    text-align: left;
    color: #6e6e6e;
```

```css
    font: bold 12px Helvetica, Arial, sans-serif;
    text-decoration: none;
    padding: 7px 12px;
    position: relative;
    display: block;
    text-shadow: 0 1px 0 #fff;
    -webkit-transition: border-color .218s;
    -moz-transition: border .218s;
    -o-transition: border-color .218s;
    transition: border-color .218s;
    background: #f3f3f3;
    background: -webkit-gradient(linear,0% 40%,0%
    70%,from(#F5F5F5),to(#F1F1F1));
    background: -moz-linear-gradient(linear,0% 40%,0%
    70%,from(#F5F5F5),to(#F1F1F1));
    border: solid 1px #dcdcdc;
    border-radius: 2px;
    -webkit-border-radius: 2px;
    -moz-border-radius: 2px;
    margin-right: 10px;
}
a.button:hover
{
    color: #333;
    border-color: #999;
    -moz-box-shadow: 0 2px 0 rgba(0, 0, 0, 0.2);
    -webkit-box-shadow:0 2px 5px rgba(0, 0, 0, 0.2);
    box-shadow: 0 1px 2px rgba(0, 0, 0, 0.15);
}
a.button:active
{
      color: #000;
      border-color: #444;
}
a.course_overview
{
    background: url([[pix:theme|overview]]) 10px 7px no-repeat
    #f3f3f3;
    padding-left: 30px;
}
a.course_link
{
    background: url([[pix:theme|courselink]])  3px 2px no-repeat
    #f3f3f3;
    padding-left: 30px;
}
```

Here is the re-rendered **COURSES AVAILABLE** block:

Including images in CSS

The preceding CSS includes specifying two background images (icons) for our new buttons. There is a magnifying glass icon on the Description button and the Moodle icon on the course link button. The image files need to be copied into the /pix directory:

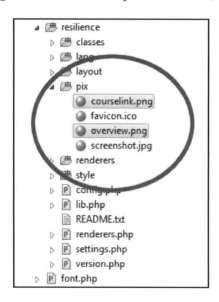

It is important to realize that Moodle preprocesses CSS files before they are served to the browser. This is why we don't specify an image URL but rather use the Moodle-specific image reference. For example, the magnifying glass icon on the **Description** button:

```
background: url([[pix:theme|overview]]) 10px 7px no-repeat #f3f3f3;
```

See https://docs.moodle.org/dev/Using_images_in_a_theme for more information on handling images.

Taking things further - styling button icons

The course link button can currently display one of three status messages: *start*, *continue*, and *retake*. Can you display three different icons depending on the status?

Page layouts

Your theme `config.php` file can be used to specify page-specific layouts. As discussed in `Chapter 6`, *Managing Users - Letting in the Crowds*, our client requires that learners log in via WordPress, rather than directly into Moodle, although we will still need Moodle admins to be able to log into Moodle. To this end, some refactoring of the Moodle login page is required. The following is the wireframe agreed by the client:

This is a simple login page with most page decoration (headers and footers, for example) stripped away.

To implement a new login page layout, we first need to add a new layout script to the theme's /layout folder:

Add the following code fragment to the end of config.php:

```
$THEME->layouts = array(
                  'login' => array(
                  'file' => 'login.php',
                  'regions' => array('side-post'),
                  'defaultregion' => 'side-post',
                  ),
                  );
```

The next step is to add the relevant image files to the /pix directory. In accordance with the wireframe, we will add the refugee camp image and a copy of the standard Moodle logo (all Moodle-related artwork is available from https://moodle.org):

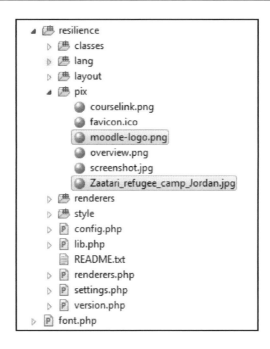

Essentially, we require a stripped down login page. Here is the code from `layout/login.php`:

```php
<?php $OUTPUT->doctype(); ?>
<html>
<head>
    <title><?php get_string('configtitle', 'theme_resilience') ?></title>
    <link rel="shortcut icon" href="<?php echo $OUTPUT->pix_url('favicon',
'theme')?>" />
    <?php echo $OUTPUT->standard_head_html() ?>
</head>
<body id="<?php p($PAGE->bodyid) ?>" >
  <div class="image-container">
        <div id="page" class="container-fluid">
        <!-- Start Main Regions -->
        <div id="page-content" class="row-fluid">
            <section id="region-main" class="span12">
                <?php
                echo $OUTPUT->course_content_header();
                echo $OUTPUT->main_content();
                echo $OUTPUT->course_content_footer();
                ?>
            </section>
        </div>
        <!-- End Main Regions -->
```

```
        </div>
      </div>
  </div>
  <div id="page-footer" class="clearfix">
      <?php
      echo $OUTPUT->standard_footer_html();
      ?>
  </div>
  <?php echo $OUTPUT->standard_end_of_body_html() ?>
  </body>
  </html>
```

We also need to ensure the login page is styled correctly. Here is the relevant styling, which we can add to `style/custom.css`:

```css
/* Login page
------------------------*/
div.image-container
{
    background: url([[pix:theme|Zaatari_refugee_camp_Jordan]]) no-
    repeat 0 0;
    background-size: cover;
}
body#page-login-index
{
    padding-top: 0px;
}
#page-login-index div#page-footer
{
    margin-top: 0em;
}
div.loginpanel
{
    background: url([[pix:theme|moodle-logo]]) no-repeat 70px 10px;
    padding-top: 70px;
}
div.loginbox
{
    background-color: rgba(255,255,255,0.8);
    width: 400px;
    margin: 5% auto 20% auto;
    -moz-box-shadow: 0 0 30px 5px #999;
    -webkit-box-shadow: 0 0 30px 5px #999;
}
```

Here is the finished login page:

The background image (taken in the Zaatari refugee camp, Jordan, in 2013) has been released by the UK government under its Open Government License, meaning not only do we have to acknowledge copyright in this book but we also need to do the same on the Moodle login page we just developed. We are also required to provide a link to a copy of the license (https://www.nationalarchives.gov.uk/doc/open-government-licence/version/1/). Let us finally add the following code fragment to layout/login.php:

```
$description = get_string('backgrounddesc', 'theme_resilience');
$copyright = get_string('ogl1', 'theme_resilience');
$url = new
moodle_url('https://www.nationalarchives.gov.uk/doc/open-government-licence
/version/1/');
$html = html_writer::start_div('image_copyright');
$html .= $description . ' - ';
$html .= html_writer::link($url, $copyright,
array('class'=>'background_copyright', 'target'=>'_blank'));
$html .= html_writer::end_div();
echo $html;
```

With the relevant strings added to `/lang/en/theme_resilience.php`, here's how the bottom of our login page looks:

Zaatari refugee camp, Jordan, 2013. UK Foreign and Commonwealth Office - Open Government License Version 1

Taking things further - doing more with page layouts

Can you apply some more subtle styling to the background image copyright notice in the login page footer?

In the next section, we learn how to format Moodle pages using templates.

Templates

So far, we have been building HTML in renderer functions. Generating pages in this way is great for the developer but it can make life harder for the theme designer. Renderers can contain lots of logic that the theme designer wouldn't necessarily be interested in and this can make developing new formats much more difficult. Templates provide much better separation between the presentation layer and the *business* layer, which we shall see in this section.

Let us revisit the **Courses information** block description page. Recall that this displays an overview of the course:

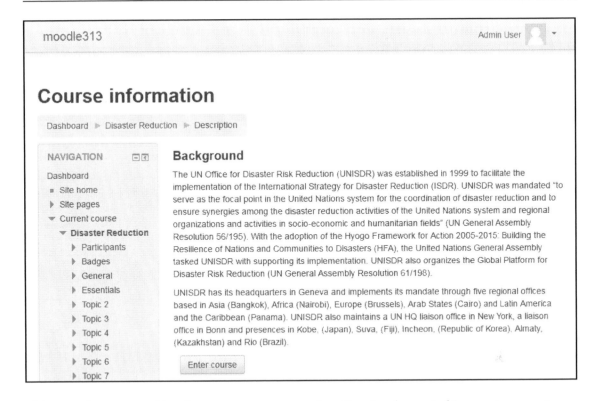

This page is generated by the `get_overview()` function implemented in `renderer.php`. Let us re-implement this page so that it uses a Mustache template.

Mustache

This section only gives a very brief overview of Moodle templates. The templating technology employed is called Mustache (pronounced *moo-stash* not *moo-starsh*... and definitely not *moo-stosh*). For more details on Moodle's use of Mustache, check out the Moodle developer documentation at `https://docs.moodle.org/dev/Templates`.

To start, we need to create a new course overview template. In Eclipse, create a new folder called `templates` and, in that, a new file called `course_overview.mustache`:

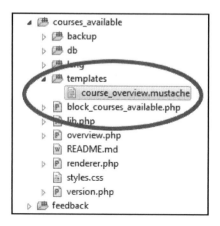

As described in the documentation, a Mustache template is, essentially, an HTML script containing embedded variables. Here is the template used to create the overview page contents:

```
<div class="block_courses_available_overview">
<div class="box generalbox summaryinfo">
            <div class="no-overflow">
            {{{summary}}}
        </div>
</div>
<ul class="teachers">
        {{#names}}
        <li>{{{.}}}</li>
        {{/names}}
</ul>
{{{buttons}}}
</div>
```

Firstly, notice that the entire template is bracketed by a suitably named DIV. Then see that there are three variables we need to pass into the template; each one will be a fragment of HTML: the course summary, an array of role names, and the navigation buttons. See that the three variables are represented by tags that are bracketed by triple braces: {{{ }}}. It is the use of these braces--which, if you tilt your head to one side, look like a gentleman's moustache--that gives this technology its name. To learn more about the different types of tags a Mustache template supports, check out the documentation at `https://docs.moodle.org/dev/Templates#How_do_I_write_a_template.3F`.

Next, the `get_overview()` function needs to be modified to generate the data needed by the template and then load it:

```
public function get_overview($course)
{
        global $CFG, $DB;
        $data = new stdClass();
        $data->summary = format_text($course->summary, $course->
        summaryformat, array('overflowdiv'=>true), $course->id);
        $data->names = array();
        if (!empty($CFG->coursecontact))
        {
                $context = context_course::instance($course->id);
                $coursecontactroles = explode(',', $CFG->coursecontact);
                foreach ($coursecontactroles as $roleid)
                {
                        $role = $DB->get_record('role',
                        array('id'=>$roleid));
                        $roleid = (int) $roleid;
                        if ($users = get_role_users($roleid, $context, true))
                        {
                                foreach ($users as $teacher)
                                {
                                        $fullname = fullname($teacher,
                                        has_capability('moodle/site:
                                        viewfullnames', $context));
                                        $data->names[] =
                                        format_string(role_get_name($role,
                                        $context)).': <a href="'.$CFG->
                                        wwwroot.'/user/view.php?id='.
                                        $teacher>id.'&amp;
                                        course='.SITEID.'">'.$fullname.'</a>';
                                }
                        }
                }
        }
        /*
        * button box
        */
        $buttonBox = $this->output->box_start('generalbox icons');
        $cancel = new single_button(new moodle_url($CFG->wwwroot.'/my'),
        get_string('homepage', 'block_courses_available'), 'get');
        $url = new moodle_url($CFG->wwwroot.'/course/view.php',
        array('id'=>$course->id));
        $continue = new single_button($url, get_string('coursepage',
        'block_courses_available'), 'get');
        $attr = array('id'=>'summarybuttons','class' => 'buttons');
        $buttonBox .= html_writer::tag('div', $this->output->
```

```
render($continue).$this->output->render($cancel), $attr);
$buttonBox .= $this->output->box_end();
$data->buttons = $buttonBox;
return $this->
render_from_template('block_courses_available/course_overview',
$data);
}
```

See that the template is loaded via a call to `render_from_template()`, which is passed two parameters:

- The name of the template (not including the 'mustache' filename extension)
- The required data, as an object

Having now built the template, let us see how templates can be overridden in a theme.

Overriding templates in a theme

Earlier in this chapter, we saw how a theme can override a plugin renderer. Overriding a template is simple. Firstly, create a new folder in our theme called `templates` and, within that, a folder called `block_courses_available`. Simply create a new template of the same name with the required styling in the theme:

Next, implement a new template. In the following example, we are enhancing the course summary with an icon:

```
<div class="block_courses_available_overview_resilience">
    <div class="box generalbox summaryinfo">
        <div class="summarycontainer">
            <div class="overviewicon">
                {{# pix }} f/text-72, core, course summary icon {{/ pix }}
            </div>
            {{{summary}}}
        </div>
    </div>
    <ul class="teachers">
        {{#names}}
        <li>{{{.}}}</li>
        {{/names}}
    </ul>
    {{{buttons}}}
</div>
```

We use the `{{pix}}` tag to load the image (in this example, one of the Moodle core images):

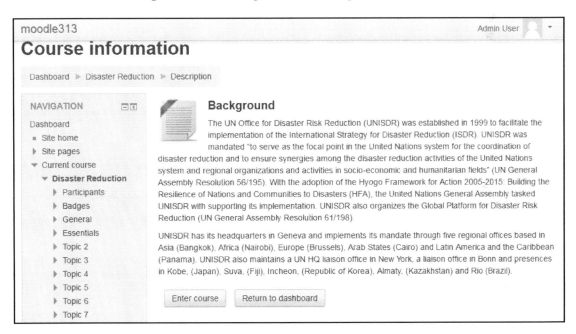

Theme responsiveness

We end this chapter with a short note on building a responsive, mobile-ready theme. Luckily, this is an easy task in Moodle: simply start with a basic responsive theme such as *clean* as we did just now--or one from the community such as *Essential* (`https://moodle.org/plugins/theme_essential`) - and adapt accordingly. It is always easier to find a theme you like and adapt that. In order to be mobile ready, Moodle uses Bootstrap (originally version 2 but latterly version 4; see `https://docs.moodle.org/dev/Bootstrap_2` for details). As there are plenty of good examples in the Moodle developer documentation of how to develop responsive themes, the reader is directed to `https://docs.moodle.org/dev/Themes_overview` for help on getting started.

Summary

In this chapter, we learned how the look-and-feel of Moodle pages can be enhanced with the development of a new Moodle theme. We investigated how plugins should be developed to support easy styling and layout enhancements (through renderers and templates). We saw how ensuring page responsiveness--that is, the ability for a page to render in a manner appropriate to the client device on which it finds itself--is already part of the Moodle theming framework.

The most effective way to develop a new theme in Moodle is to check out the Moodle plugins directory at `https://moodle.org/plugins/browse.php?list=category&id=3` and find a theme that presents a look similar to the one you require and tailor that to your needs. To help you develop your new theme, remember to check out *Moodle Theme Development*, also from Packt.

Having gained a good grasp of user management, course development and, in this chapter, user experience, now it is time to move on to reporting and data intelligence--which is the subject of the next chapter.

9
Moodle Analytics

We have created novel teaching interactions, introduced learners onto the platform, and enrolled them onto courses. Finally, we will arrive at the question, "How do we judge the success of the platform?" This can be answered in a variety of ways, for instance, "How many users have successfully completed which courses?"and "how many users start a course but never finish?" Moodle provides a simple interface to generate reports, and this will be explored in this final chapter.

As you work through this chapter, you will be spending a good deal of your time selecting data out of a MySQL database. Of course, other database types are available (and Moodle will happily run on them), but we focus on MySQL as that is the typical installation stack. If your Moodle is running on a different database, the techniques covered here might be different but the underlying principles will be the same.

In this chapter, we will cover the following:

- How to generate reports that can be used, with metrics, to assess the quality of your learning platform
- Using the Ad-hoc database query plugin to investigate selecting data from the database
- Understanding how queries should be optimized to prevent database stress
- How to generate Excel reports from selected data
- Creating a novel bubble chart report block to better visualize learner engagement

We will also be creating a new external API to allow other applications (for example, a business intelligence server) to extract data securely from Moodle. As part of this work, we will be investigating some basic end-to-end (known as *in transit*) encryption techniques.

Let's start our investigation by understanding the structure of the Moodle database; this is best done by interrogating it for some relevant data.

Reporting

A great place to begin learning how data reports can be developed is with the Open University's *Ad-hoc database queries* plugin, available from the Moodle plugin directory at `https://moodle.org/plugins/report_customsql`. As this plugin essentially lets us query the Moodle database in any way we choose, along with providing the functionality to schedule report generation (including saving reports as a CSV file and emailing them out to a chosen recipient), it makes sense to use this plugin as the foundation for any reporting plugin we develop. To that end, rather than downloading the code from the plugin directory, we can fork it in GitHub. Go to `https://github.com/moodleou/moodle-report_customsql` and click on the **Fork** button:

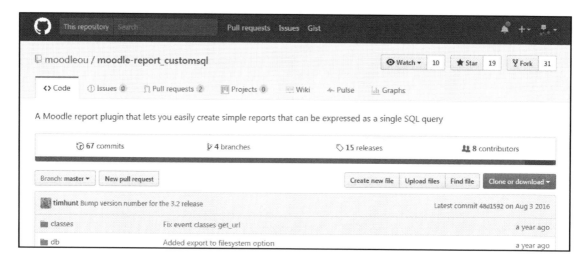

You can now clone your fork to your development machine. Moodle reports are copied into the /report folder:

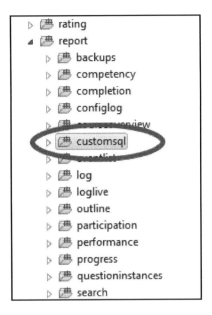

Report plugin structure

Expand the /customsql folder, and you will notice that a report plugin follows the general Moodle plugin structure:

The full details are given in the developer documentation at https://docs.moodle.org/dev/Reports. The /settings.php script adds a link to the report to the site administration menu:

```
$ADMIN->add('reports', new admin_externalpage('report_customsql',
get_string('pluginname', 'report_customsql'),
new moodle_url('/report/customsql/index.php'),
'report/customsql:view'));
```

The /index.php script is the report itself. As this is a more complex report, the report is displayed to the user via the /view.php script. All other scripts are standard (such as language support, supporting PHP classes, and versioning information).

Grabbing data

The ad-hoc database query plugin is supported by a great many reports (essentially, SQL queries) contributed by the Moodle community and freely available from https://docs.moodle.org/31/en/ad-hoc_contributed_reports. As an example, let's pull out a report of the number of enrollments of each course on our Moodle site (https://docs.moodle.org/31/en/ad-hoc_contributed_reports#Enrolment_count_in_ea ch_Course). Here's the complete query:

```
SELECT c.fullname, COUNT(ue.id) AS Enroled
FROM prefix_course AS c
JOIN prefix_enrol AS en ON en.courseid = c.id
JOIN prefix_user_enrolments AS ue ON ue.enrolid = en.id
GROUP BY c.id
ORDER BY c.fullname
```

As we are querying the database directly, we do need to pay attention to the efficiency of the database we are querying. Although databases are specifically designed for the efficient extraction of data, as more data is added, and as datasets are updated (and data is always being added and updated on a busy Moodle site), databases can very quickly become inefficient. Of course, the Moodle database is specifically designed to support the efficient day-to-day operation of a Moodle site. However, if we are extracting and collating data from across the database, we may well inadvertently impair the overall performance of our site as we do so, or in a worse case, bring the entire site down completely. Different types of databases have their own quirks when it comes to ensuring efficient data extraction but, again, in this chapter, we will be focusing on MySQL databases.

Reporting learner success

An important part of the resilience project (refer to Chapter 1, *Getting to Grips with the Moodle 3 Architecture*, for more details on the project) we have been helping to develop throughout this book is user engagement. The project sponsors want to measure the success of the platform, and its associated teaching, by being able to report on the number of learners who have worked through a particular course. Each course will award a certificate of achievement.

The project sponsors would like to be able to report on the number of certificates issued within a given time frame. In order to issue certificates, we will install the *Custom certificate* (also called Ad-hoc database queries) plugin. This can be downloaded from `https://moodl e.org/plugins/mod_customcert`.

Determining certificates issued

We won't be delving deep into the development of SQL queries in this chapter (there is plenty of good advice freely available on the internet). The following is a basic query that, given a user's email and a time frame, selects a list of courses for which certificates have been issued:

```
SELECT
user.email AS email,
course.fullname AS coursename,
certissues.timecreated AS timecreated
FROM mdl_user AS user
INNER JOIN mdl_customcert_issues AS certissues ON user.id =
certissues.userid
INNER JOIN mdl_customcert AS customcert ON certissues.customcertid =
customcert.id
INNER JOIN mdl_course AS course ON customcert.course = course.id
WHERE user.email = "ian@example.com"
AND certissues.timecreated>=0 AND certissues.timecreated<=1495781129
```

As described, we need to ensure the efficient selection of data, but how can we do this? In the following section, we will learn how.

EXPLAIN a query

A MySQL database has a built-in *query optimizer* which, when you issue a SELECT query, will attempt to extract and present the required data as efficiently as possible. We can investigate the optimizer's query plan by prefixing the query with EXPLAIN. This function is easily accessible from the phpMyAdmin tools. For example, here's the query to determine the number of certificates issued, which has been explained by prefixing it with the EXPLAIN keyword:

Your SQL query has been executed successfully.

EXPLAIN SELECT user.email AS email, course.fullname AS coursename, certissues.timecreated AS timecreated FROM mdl_user AS user INNER JOIN mdl_customcert_issues AS certissues ON user.id = certissues.userid INNER JOIN mdl_customcert AS customcert ON certissues.customcertid = customcert.id INNER JOIN mdl_course AS course ON customcert.course = course.id WHERE user.email = "ian@example.com" AND certissues.timecreated>0 AND certissues.timecreated<=1495781129

[Edit inline] [Edit] [Skip Explain SQL] [Analyze Explain at mariadb.org] [Create PHP code]

+ Options

id	select_type	table	partitions	type	possible_keys	key	key_len	ref	rows	filtered	Extra
1	SIMPLE	certissues	NULL	ALL	mdl_custissu_cus_ix	NULL	NULL	NULL	1	100.00	Using where
1	SIMPLE	user	NULL	eq_ref	PRIMARY,mdl_user_ema_ix	PRIMARY	8	moodle316.certissues.userid	1	25.00	Using where
1	SIMPLE	customcert	NULL	eq_ref	PRIMARY	PRIMARY	8	moodle316.certissues.customcertid	1	100.00	NULL
1	SIMPLE	course	NULL	eq_ref	PRIMARY	PRIMARY	8	moodle316.customcert.course	1	100.00	NULL

In order to speed up the extraction of data from a table, a *key* is used. If the data is spread across a number of tables, or needs to be sorted in some way, MySQL may as well create a *temporary table*; this can impair database performance as MySQL writes out to, and reads from, yet another table. Clearly, having access to this information means that we can construct more effective queries. Again, delving into detail is beyond the scope of this book. However, there is plenty of information on the internet to help you produce more effective queries.

For more information on table configuration and management, check out *MySQL Admin Cookbook*, also from Packt (visit
`https://www.packtpub.com/big-data-and-business-intelligence/mysql-admin-cookbook`).

Having extracted data, the next problem is what to do with it. An obvious solution is to save it to a file, the options for which we will explore in the following sections.

Saving data

A new Ad-hoc database query has been configured to allow the currently logged in user to see which courses they have completed:

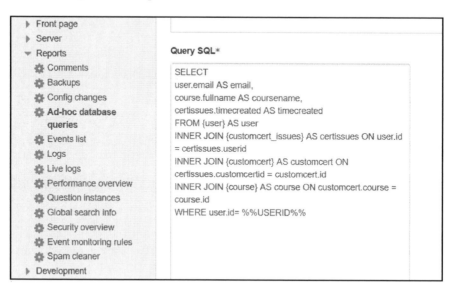

The Ad-hoc database queries plugin provides an option to output selected data to a **Comma Separated Variable (CSV)** file:

The CSV file is output directly to the browser from the `/customsql/download.php` script. Moodle does, however, possess its own internal API for generating standard-format data output files, including CSV files, based on the PHPExcel library. Let's investigate this library now.

Creating spreadsheets

If we are wanting to output Excel, ODS, or CSV spreadsheet-based reports, the PHPExcel library is the most straightforward way to create them. The library is accessed via an internal API called PHPExcel. Let's update the Ad-hoc database queries plugin to allow the user to download Excel files as well as CSV files:

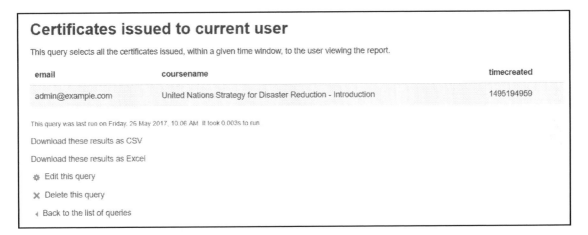

The fully implemented code is available at `https://github.com/iandavidwild/moodle-report_customsql`. This is a forked copy of the original Ad-hoc database query code at `https://github.com/moodleou/moodle-report_c ustomsql`. The modifications described in this section are in the *master* branch.

When the Ad-hoc database query plugin runs a report, the data generated is written to a temporary CSV file. We can direct the PHPExcel library to load this file:

```
list($csvfilename) = report_customsql_csv_filename($report, $csvtimestamp);
if (!is_readable($csvfilename))
{
        print_error('unknowndownloadfile', 'report_customsql',
        report_customsql_url('view.php?id=' . $id));
}
$objReader = PHPExcel_IOFactory::createReader('CSV');
$objPHPExcel = $objReader->load($csvfilename);
```

Then, we can write an excel file straight back out to the browser:

```
$filename = 'results';
header("Pragma: public");
header("Expires: 0");
header("Cache-Control: must-revalidate, post-check=0, pre-check=0");
header("Content-Type: application/force-download");
header("Content-Type: application/octet-stream");
header("Content-Type: application/download");;
header("Content-Disposition: attachment;filename=$filename.xlsx");
header("Content-Transfer-Encoding: binary ");
$objWriter = new PHPExcel_Writer_Excel2007($objPHPExcel);
$objWriter->setOffice2003Compatibility(true);
$objWriter->save('php://output');
```

Taking things further

The PHPExcel library provides a comprehensive set of methods to allow us to manipulate the output file. For example, we can give spreadsheets appropriate names, or automatically set column widths. Take a look at the PHPExcel documentation at `https://github.com/PHPOffice/PHPExcel/wiki/User-documentation` to see how this can be achieved and try it yourself (example code is provided at `https://github.com/iandavidwild/moodle-report_customsql`).

Displaying activity data - a bubble chart example

As a way of gauging the success of the online resources, our resilience project sponsors are wanting to report on the number of interactions users have with particular resources and activities. They want to be able to see, at a glance, which resources have been the most popular. To this end, a number of chart types were suggested, but the one that appealed the most is the *bubble chart*.

The more popular the resource or activity, the bigger the bubble, which means you can gauge the popularity (or otherwise) of resources and activities a course includes at a glance. A wireframe has been produced, which shows a course with a block (which is only visible to teachers) listing different report types:

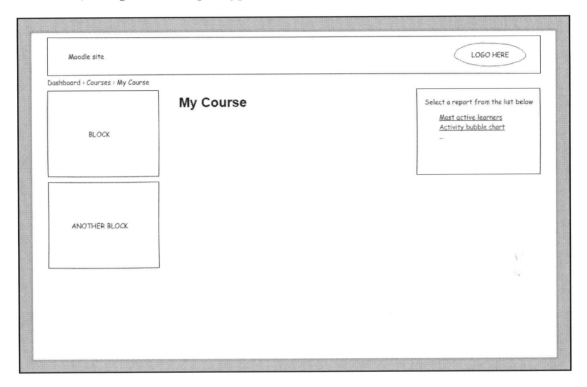

Each report will open a full-page graphic. For example, here's the report showing a bubble chart, as described earlier:

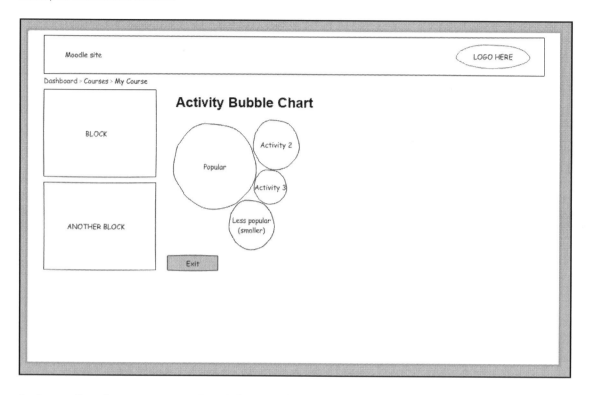

In the earlier chapters, we explored the use of JavaScript graphics libraries to visualize data. Check out `Chapter 7`, *Creating a Dashboard - Developing a Learner Homepage,* for more information. In this section, we will build on that work and take our data visualizations much further. In `Chapter 7`, *Creating a Dashboard - Developing a Learner Homepage* we used `Chart.js` to create pie and doughnut charts. `Chart.js` is certainly a great tool, but the number of charts and graphs it supports is limited. In this section, we will use `D3.js`--visit `https://github.com/d3` for details--to create a bubble chart report.

Accessing the report

This client has requested that the report has the following properties:

- Easy access from a course page
- Only available to users with the correct permissions

The completed block is available from GitHub at `https://github.com/iandavidwild/moodle-block_course_report`. Having agreed to the minimum functionality and having confirmed the user interface with the client, let's start creating our new block.

Building the block

By now, you should be familiar with the structure of a Moodle plugin generally, and Moodle blocks in particular from the earlier chapters. We start by refactoring the HTML block. Copy the HTML block into a new folder called `/course_report`, and then refactor each script accordingly. Remember that using an integrated development environment such as Eclipse makes this task straightforward:

Having updated all the relevant scripts, your new block will be ready to install.

Extracting the data

The code to determine the number of times a user has interacted with a resource or activity, we will take from the *Heatmap* block plugin by *Michael de Raadt* (visit `https://moodle.org/plugins/pluginversions.php?plugin=block_heatmap` for details). We will create a new script called `/locallib.php` and add a new function to return the number of interactions with each resource or activity.

This code can be taken from the *Heatmap* block code:

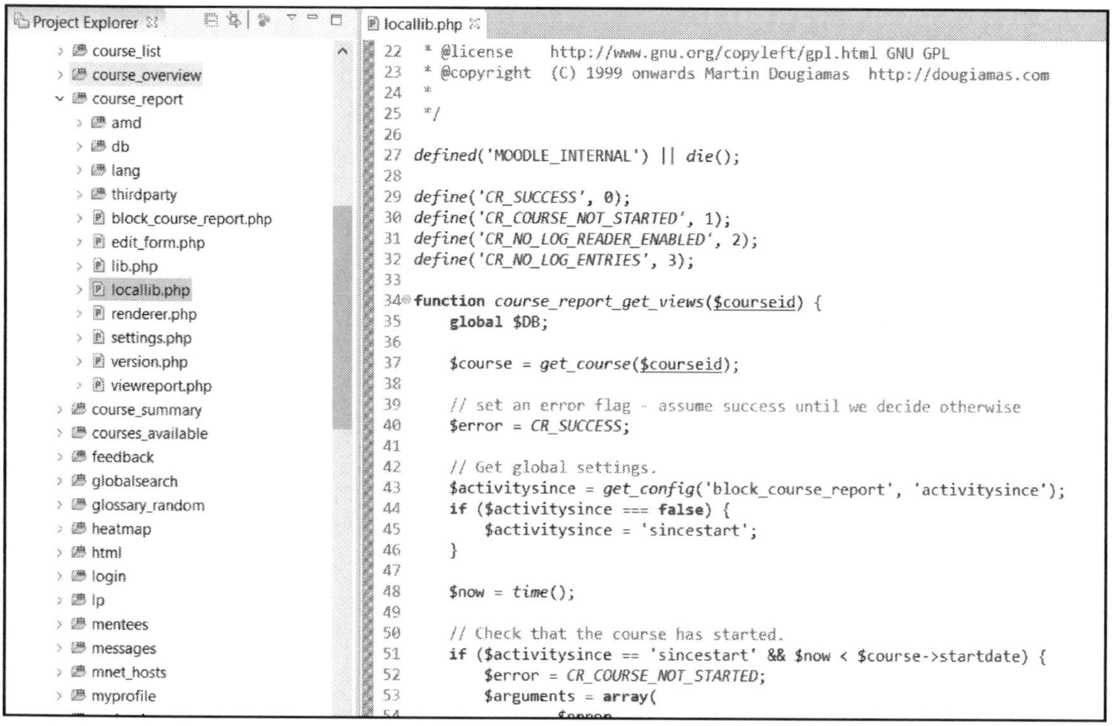

Let's work through this function step by step to see how it operates. The function is passed the ID number of the course for which we need user interaction data:

```
function course_report_get_views($courseid)
{
    global $DB;
    $course = get_course($courseid);
```

Then, we set an error flag, assuming success at the outset:

```
// set an error flag - assume success until we decide otherwise
$error = CR_SUCCESS;
```

Next, we retrieve some block global settings. This includes specifying a time window within which to grab interaction data (either all data or data from when the course started):

```
// Get global settings.
$activitysince = get_config('block_course_report', 'activitysince');
if ($activitysince === false)
{
     $activitysince = 'sincestart';
}
     $now = time();
// Check that the course has started.
if ($activitysince == 'sincestart' && $now < $course->startdate)
{
          $error = CR_COURSE_NOT_STARTED;
          $arguments = array(
                    $error,
          );
          return $arguments;
     }
```

Remember that we are checking whether the course has actually started. If not, an error is returned. Note that we need to ensure that all data the function returns is consistent (hence, we return the error code in an array).

Activity interaction data can be read in two ways:

```
$useinternalreader = false; // Flag to determine if we should use the
internal reader.
$uselegacyreader = false; // Flag to determine if we should use the legacy
reader.
// Get list of readers.
$logmanager = get_log_manager();
$readers = $logmanager->get_readers();
// Get preferred reader.
if (!empty($readers))
{
     foreach ($readers as $readerpluginname => $reader)
     {
     // If sql_internal_table_reader is preferred reader.
     if ($reader instanceof \core\log\sql_internal_table_reader)
     {
          $useinternalreader = true;
          $logtable = $reader->get_internal_log_table_name();
     }
     // If legacy reader is preferred reader.
     if ($readerpluginname == 'logstore_legacy')
     {
          $uselegacyreader = true;
```

```
        }
      }
  }
  // If no legacy and no internal log then don't proceed.
  if (!$uselegacyreader && !$useinternalreader)
  {
        $error = CR_NO_LOG_READER_ENABLED;
        $arguments = array($error, );
        return $arguments;
  }
```

Having decided on how to obtain it, we need to extract the relevant data from the Moodle log:

```
  // Get record from sql_internal_table_reader
  if ($useinternalreader)
  {
        $timesince = ($activitysince == 'sincestart') ? 'AND timecreated
        >= :coursestart' : '';
        $sql = "SELECT contextinstanceid as cmid, COUNT('x') AS numviews,
        COUNT(DISTINCT userid) AS distinctusers
        FROM {" . $logtable . "} l
        WHERE courseid = :courseid
        $timesince
        AND anonymous = 0
        AND crud = 'r'
        AND contextlevel = :contextmodule
        GROUP BY contextinstanceid";
        $params = array('courseid' => $course->id, 'contextmodule' =>
        CONTEXT_MODULE, 'coursestart' => $course->startdate);
        $views = $DB->get_records_sql($sql, $params);
  }
  else if ($uselegacyreader)
  {
        // If using legacy log then get activity usage from old table.
        $logactionlike = $DB->sql_like('l.action', ':action');
        $timesince = ($activitysince == 'sincestart') ? 'AND l.time >=
        :coursestart' : '';
        $sql = "SELECT cm.id, COUNT('x') AS numviews, COUNT(DISTINCT
        userid) AS distinctusers
        FROM {course_modules} cm
        JOIN {modules} m
        ON m.id = cm.module
        JOIN {log} l
        ON l.cmid = cm.id
        WHERE cm.course = :courseid
        $timesince
        AND $logactionlike
```

```
            AND m.visible = 1
            GROUP BY cm.id";
        $params = array('courseid' => $course->id, 'action' => 'view%',
        'coursestart' => $course->startdate);
        if (!empty($minloginternalreader)) {
        $params['timeto'] = $minloginternalreader;
    }
    $views = $DB->get_records_sql($sql, $params);
    }
```

Finally, having extracted some data, we need to cleanse it into a form to be used later:

```
// Get the min, max and totals.
$firstactivity = array_shift($views);
$totalviews = $firstactivity->numviews;
$totalusers = $firstactivity->distinctusers;
$minviews = $firstactivity->numviews;
$maxviews = $firstactivity->numviews;
foreach ($views as $key => $activity)
{
        $totalviews += $activity->numviews;
        if ($activity->numviews < $minviews)
        {
                $minviews = $activity->numviews;
        }
        if ($activity->numviews > $maxviews)
        {
                $maxviews = $activity->numviews;
        }
                $totalusers += $activity->distinctusers;
}
array_unshift($views, $firstactivity);
foreach ($views as $key => $activity)
{
        if($cm = $DB->get_record('course_modules', array('id' =>
        $activity->cmid)))
        {
                $modname = $DB->get_field('modules', 'name', array('id' =>
                $cm->module));
                if ($name = $DB->get_field("$modname", 'name', array('id'
                => $cm->instance)))
                {
                        $activity->name = $name;
                }
        }
        else
        {
                $activity->name = get_string('unknownmod',
```

```
                    \'block_course_report');
            }
    }
    $arguments = array(
                    $error,
                    json_encode($views),
                    $minviews,
                    $maxviews);
      return $arguments;
    }
```

Having obtained the data, we now need to display it. In the next section, we investigate including the D3.js charting library in our new reporting block.

Including D3.js libraries

The D3.js libraries are available directly from https://d3js.org/. Create a new folder called /thirdparty and copy the relevant files into it:

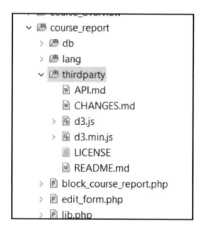

We require a new page to display the chart. In Eclipse, create a new script called `/viewreport.php`:

```
Project Explorer                              viewreport.php
  > course_list                          48  $PAGE->set_title($reportname);
  > course_overview                      49  $PAGE->set_heading($reportname);
  v course_report                        50  $PAGE->set_cacheable( true);
    > amd                                51
    > db                                 52  $PAGE->requires->js('/blocks/course_report/thirdparty/d3.js', true);
    > lang                               53
    > thirdparty                         54  echo $OUTPUT->header();
    > block_course_report.php            55
    > edit_form.php                      56  // get the relevant interaction data
    > lib.php                            57  $data = course_report_get_views($course->id);
    > locallib.php                       58
    > renderer.php                       59  if(isset($data[0])) {
    > settings.php                       60      if($data[0] != CR_SUCCESS) {
    > version.php                         61          // TODO: output a suitable message
    > viewreport.php                      62      } else {
  > course_summary                        63          if(isset($data[1])) {
  > courses_available                     64
  > feedback                              65              $renderer = $PAGE->get_renderer('block_course_report');
  > globalsearch                          66
  > glossary_random                       67              // echo 'return to course' button above and below the chart
  > heatmap                               68              echo $renderer->get_report_exit_btn($course->id);
  > html                                  69
  > login                                 70              // load third party charting code
  > lp                                    71              echo HTML_WRITER::tag('section', '', array('id'=>'graph'));
  > mentees                               72
  > messages                              73              echo $renderer->get_report_exit_btn($course->id);
  > mnet hosts                            74
                                          75
                                          76              $activities = json_decode($data[1]);
                                          77
                                          78              $dataset = array();
```

The `/viewreport.php` script will render the report page. The code is straightforward:

1. Obtain activity data by calling `course_report_get_views()`.
2. Load the `D3.js` library.
3. Call on a JavaScript function to display the bubble chart by passing this function the relevant activity data.

Here's the fragment of code that calls on JavaScript to display the chart:

```
$json_data = json_encode($paramdata);
$js_params = array('graph', $json_data);
$PAGE->requires->js_call_amd('block_course_report/chart_renderer',
'drawChart', $js_params);
```

Rendering a bubble chart

D3.js being a JavaScript library, we need to implement a JavaScript function to load when the page is loaded to create the chart. The function can be loaded via an AMD module (refer to Chapter 5, *Creative Teaching - Developing Custom Resources and Activities*, for more details). Recall that the new module needs to reside in the /amd/src folder:

This is the JavaScript code (an AMD module) to display the chart:

```javascript
define(['jquery'], function($)
{
    var t = {
    drawChart: function(chartEl, dataset)
    {
        var dataset = $.parseJSON(dataset);
        var diameter = 600;
        var color = d3.scaleOrdinal(d3.schemeCategory20);
        var bubble = d3.pack(dataset)
        .size([diameter, diameter])
        .padding(1.5);
        var svg = d3.select("#graph")
        .append("svg")
        .attr("width", diameter)
        .attr("height", diameter)
        .attr("class", "bubble");
        var nodes = d3.hierarchy(dataset)
        .sum(function(d) { return d.interactions; });
```

```
            var node = svg.selectAll(".node")
            .data(bubble(nodes).descendants())
            .enter()
            .filter(function(d){
            return  !d.children
    })
    .append("g")
    .attr("class", "node")
    .attr("transform", function(d)
    {
            return "translate(" + d.x + "," + d.y + ")";
    })
    node.append("circle")
    .attr("r", function(d)
    {
    return d.r;
    })
    .style("fill", function(d)
    {
            return color(d.activity);
    });
    d3.select(self.frameElement)
    .style("height", diameter + "px");
    }
    };
    return t;
});
```

Now, let's include mouse hover text and a title for each bubble:

```
node.append("title").text(function(d)
{
        return d.data.activity + ' : ' + d.data.interactions + '
        interaction/s';
});

node.append("text")
.attr("dy", ".3em")
.style("text-anchor", "middle")
.text(function(d) {
return d.data.activity.substring(0, d.r/3);
});
```

That done, the following is a screen grab of the report in action:

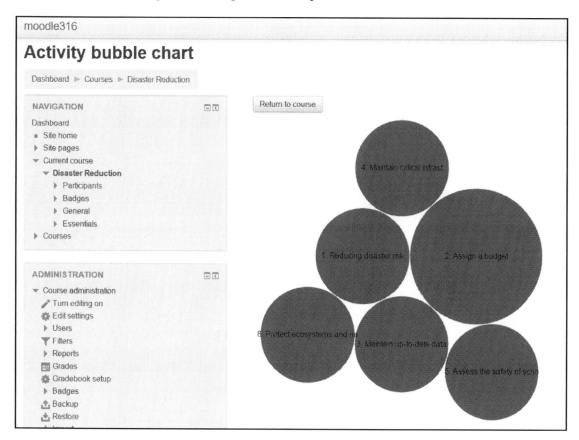

Further improvements

The color of each bubble is currently fixed. Take a look at the `drawChart()` function and see whether you can work out how to change the bubble colors.

Following on from `Chapter 8`, *Creating a New Skin*, we have seen how important it is that we ensure that visual elements are implemented through a renderer. A simple example has been included in the source for this plugin. Can you think of any way in which this can be improved?

Web Services

All through this book, we have been dealing with *internal* interfaces, such as the Page API or the Access API. We end the book by considering *external* interfaces. Integrating applications into a larger product landscape is often how large-scale implementations fail (that is, the failure of one system to properly talk to another). The solution that allows web applications to talk to each other is called a **Web Service**; for more details, visit `https://en.wikipedia.org/wiki/Web_service`.

In this section, we will be investigating methods to export data out of Moodle using the Web Services API. For details on Moodle's Web Services support, refer to the Moodle documentation at `https://docs.moodle.org/dev/Web_services`. Moodle's Web Services API is disabled by default; so, you will need to follow the instructions at `https://docs.moodle.org/31/en/Using_web_services#Enabling_web_services`to enable it. By default, Moodle supports the REST, SOAP, and XML-RPC protocols, and there are advantages and disadvantages to each. As we are simply exporting out data via an external API, SOAP and XML-RPC are more suitable. For the resilience project, because the networks over which we will operate tend to be slow and less robust, it makes sense to utilize the XML-RPC protocol (communicating via SOAP can involve a lot of network traffic). Ensure that you enable the XML-RPC protocol.

We will develop a new Web Services API that will report the number of certificates issued via the *Custom certificate* plugin.

Developing a new external API

Each new external API added to Moodle is wrapped in a Web Services plugin. Luckily, Moodle HQ have provided a sample Web Services plugin at `https://github.com/moodlehq/moodle-local_wstemplate`. Let's use this to develop our new API. Download this now, and let's study the structure.

A hello world API

The "hello world" Web Services example is a *local* plugin, that is, it adds functionality to Moodle *internally*, although at the same time this particular *local* plugin will provide an external API. Copy the plugin to the `/local` folder and click on **Notifications** from the **Site administration** menu to install it. Once installed, navigate to **Plugins|Web services|External services** from the Site administration menu. The new template service will be listed, as shown:

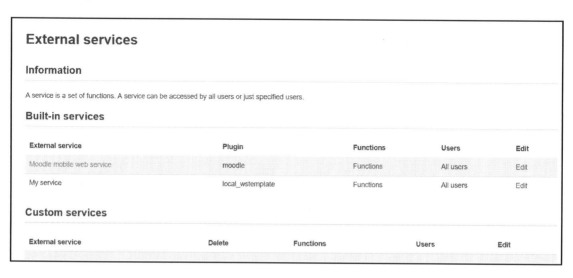

Clicking on the **Function** link will display a list of functions that the API will expose to the outside world:

Add functions to the service "My service"

Function	Description	Required capabilities
local_wstemplate_hello_world	Return Hello World FIRSTNAME. Can change the text (Hello World) sending a new text as parameter	

External API functions are implemented in the plugin's `externallib.php` script. The entire API itself is implemented as a class that extends *external_api*--visit `https://docs.moodle.org/dev/External_functions_API` for details. Each API function is supported by three methods:

- Specify and receive any function parameters; for example, `hello_world_parameters()` in the template
- Actually implement the required functionality; for example, `hello_world()`
- Specify the format of the data provided; for example, `hello_world_returns()`

All API functions and service definitions are declared in `/db/services.php`.

Recall that we need to return certificates issued within a given time window. Let's now implement the required functionality.

Building a new API

The finished API is available to download from GitHub at `https://github.com/iandavidw ild/moodle-local_certificateapi`. There are two external functions implemented in `/externallib.php`:

- `get_certificates_by_email()`
- `get_certificates_by_username()`

As described earlier in the chapter, when interrogating the database, we need to take care that we don't, in any way, overload the database when extracting data. Let's study the `get_certificates_by_email()` function. This is the complete function:

```
public static function get_certificates_by_email($hostid = '',
$learneremail = '', $starttime='01/01/1970', $endtime='01/01/1970')
{
    global $USER, $DB;
    if(DEBUG_TRACE){error_log('get_certificates_by_email(): function
    called $hostid=' . $hostid . ' $learneremail=' . $learneremail .
    ' $starttime=' . $starttime . ' $endtime='. $endtime);}
    if(DEBUG_TRACE){error_log('validating parameters');}
    //Parameter validation
    //REQUIRED
    $params =
    self::validate_parameters(self::get_certificates_
    by_email_parameters(),
    array('hostid' => $hostid, 'learneremail' => $learneremail,
    'starttime' => $starttime, 'endtime' => $endtime));
    if (trim($hostid) == '')
    {
        throw new invalid_parameter_exception('Invalid peer ID');
    }
    if (trim($learneremail) == '')
```

```
{
    throw new invalid_parameter_exception('Invalid learner
    email');
}
if (trim($starttime) == '')
{
    throw new invalid_parameter_exception('Invalid start
    time');
}
if (trim($endtime) == '')
{
    throw new invalid_parameter_exception('Invalid end time');
}
if(DEBUG_TRACE){error_log('context validation');
}
    //Context validation
    //OPTIONAL but in most web service it should present
    $context = get_context_instance(CONTEXT_USER, $USER->id);
    self::validate_context($context);

    if(DEBUG_TRACE){error_log('checking user capabilities');}
    //Capability checking
    //OPTIONAL but in most web service it should present
    if (!has_capability('moodle/user:viewdetails', $context)) {
        throw new moodle_exception('cannotviewprofile');
    }
    $starttime = str_replace('/', '-', $starttime);
    $starttime = strtotime($starttime);
    $endtime = str_replace('/', '-', $endtime);
    $endtime = strtotime($endtime);
    $completions = array();
    $sql = 'SELECT
    user.email AS email,
    course.fullname AS coursename,
    certissues.timecreated AS issuedate
    FROM {user} AS user
    INNER JOIN {customcert_issues} AS certissues ON user.id =
    certissues.userid
    INNER JOIN {customcert} AS customcert ON
    certissues.customcertid = customcert.id
    INNER JOIN {course} AS course ON customcert.course = course.id
    WHERE user.email = :learneremail
    AND certissues.timecreated>=:starttime AND
    certissues.timecreated<=:endtime';
    $params = array('learneremail'=>$learneremail,
    'starttime'=>$starttime, 'endtime'=>$endtime);
    if(DEBUG_QUERIES){error_log($sql);}
    if(DEBUG_QUERIES){error_log('learneremail: ' .
```

```
          $params['learneremail'] . ' starttime: ' .
          $params['starttime'] . ' endtime: ' . $params['endtime'] );}
$completion_data = $DB->get_records_sql($sql, $params);
if($completion_data)
{
          if(DEBUG_TRACE){error_log('completion_data contains ' .
          count($completion_data) . ' entries.');
}
// add field names so we know what they are the other end
$fieldnames = new stdClass();
$fieldnames->coursename = 'coursename';
$fieldnames->learneremail = 'learnerid';
$fieldnames->completiondate = 'completiondate';
$completions[] = (array)$fieldnames;
foreach ($completion_data as $data)
{
          $completion = new stdClass();
          $completion->coursename = $data->coursename;
          $completion->learneremail = $data->email;
          $completion->completiondate = $data->issuedate;
          $completions[] = (array)$completion;
}
}
// implode completions into a tab+newline separated string...
if(DEBUG_TRACE){error_log('Imploding data');}
$callback = function($value) {
return implode("\t", $value);
};
$data = implode("\n", array_map($callback, $completions));
// compress using gzip compression - employ maximum
compression
if(DEBUG_TRACE){error_log('Compressing data');}
$gzdata = gzencode($data, 9);
// encrypt the data
if(DEBUG_TRACE){error_log('Encrypting data');}
$encrypted = certificateapi_encrypt($hostid, $gzdata);
return $encrypted;
}
```

First, we validate the data we are provided. We tidy any text and call the
validate_parameters() function, passing it a reference to the
get_certificates_by_email_parameters() method. Then, we query the database
itself. Note that we pass the text parameters into get_records_sql() separately, rather
than constructing our own query by directly including the parameters. This is because we
are being provided with text parameters from an unknown source, and we need to ensure
that our query is protected from SQL injection hacks.

Having obtained the required information, we then build an array of data, looping through each record. This provides an extra opportunity to further process the data (in our case, making sure that the column names are consistent between API functions).

Recall that we are expecting our data to be transferred over a poor quality network. Rather than hogging bandwidth with, potentially, a good deal of completion data, we compress the data using `gzencode()`. Finally, we encrypt the data. Let's learn more about that process now.

Encrypting data

Our client has insisted that the completion data be protected from unauthorized access in some way as it is being sent across the network (that is, data in transit); It will fall within the remit of the European **General Data Protection Requirements (GPDR)**. In this section, we investigate implementing public key cryptography. Our client provides us with a public key with which to encrypt the data. They then can decrypt the data with a private key which only they possess (visit https://en.wikipedia.org/wiki/Public-key_cryptography for an overview of the process). PHP contains a built-in API that can be used to create a public-private key pair. It is the *OpenSSL extension library* (visit http://php.net/manual/en/book.openssl.php), which is already employed by Moodle to encrypt MNet messages. As with MNet encryption, we will be working with x509 certificates.

It is usual for whoever connects to the API to provide us with a public key. However, our client has suggested that if we can provide a method for creating keys, it would be an advantage. You will notice that we have two scripts to manage the creation of a new key pair in the sample code, `/key_pair.php` and `/key_pair_form.php`. To create an x509 key, there are certain properties required; these will have to be provided by the administrator when they create the keys. The following is the function we use to create the key pair:

```
function certificateapi_generate_keypair($dn = null, $days=28)
{
    global $CFG, $USER, $DB;
    $keypair = array();
    if (is_null($dn))
    {
    return false;
    }
    $dnlimits = array(
            'countryName'           => 2,
            'stateOrProvinceName'   => 128,
            'localityName'          => 128,
            'organizationName'      => 64,
```

```
                    'organizationalUnitName' => 64,
                    'commonName'             => 64,
                    'emailAddress'           => 128
                    );
foreach ($dnlimits as $key => $length)
{
        $dn[$key] = substr($dn[$key], 0, $length);
}
// ensure we remove trailing slashes
$dn["commonName"] = preg_replace(':/$:', '', $dn["commonName"]);
if (!empty($CFG->opensslcnf)) { //allow specification of
openssl.cnf especially for Windows installs
$new_key = openssl_pkey_new(array("config" => $CFG->opensslcnf));
}
else
{
        $new_key = openssl_pkey_new();
}
if ($new_key === false)
{
        // can not generate keys - missing openssl.cnf??
        $error = openssl_error_string();
        return null;
}
if (!empty($CFG->opensslcnf))
{
        //allow specification of
        openssl.cnf especially for Windows installs
        $csr_rsc = openssl_csr_new($dn, $new_key, array("config" =>
        $CFG->opensslcnf));
        $selfSignedCert = openssl_csr_sign($csr_rsc, null,
        $new_key,
        $days, array("config" => $CFG->opensslcnf));
}
else
{
        $csr_rsc = openssl_csr_new($dn, $new_key,
        array('private_key_bits',2048));
        $selfSignedCert = openssl_csr_sign($csr_rsc, null,
        $new_key, $days);
}
unset($csr_rsc); // Free up the resource
// We export our self-signed certificate to a string.
openssl_x509_export($selfSignedCert, $keypair['certificate']);
openssl_x509_free($selfSignedCert);
// Export your public/private key pair as a PEM encoded string.
You
// can protect it with an optional passphrase if you wish.
```

```
            if (!empty($CFG->opensslcnf)) { //allow specification of
            openssl.cnf especially for Windows installs
            $export = openssl_pkey_export($new_key, $keypair['keypair_PEM'],
            null, array("config" => $CFG->opensslcnf));
            }
            else
            {
                  $export = openssl_pkey_export($new_key,
                  $keypair['keypair_PEM'] /* , $passphrase */);
            }
            openssl_pkey_free($new_key);
            unset($new_key); // Free up the resource
            return $keypair;
      }
```

Note that once the private key is created, we only display it on screen; we keep the public key but not the private key, for obvious security reasons.

Here's the function we use to encrypt:

```
function certificateapi_encrypt($clientid, $message)
{
      global $CFG;
      $output = false;
      $host = certificateapi_get_host($clientid);
      if($host != false)
      {
            // Is time window for host valid?
        if(time() < $host->public_key_validfrom)
        {
                  $output = array();
                  $output['data'] = get_string('keynotyetvalid',
                  'local_certificateapi');
                  $output['envelope'] = '';
        }
        elseif (time() > $host->public_key_expires)
        {
                  $output['data'] = get_string('keynolongervalid',
                  'local_certificateapi');
                  $output['envelope'] = '';
        }
        elseif (get_config('local_certificateapi', 'enabled') == false)
        {
                  $output['data'] = get_string('certificateapinotenabled',
                  'local_certificateapi');
                  $output['envelope'] = '';
        }
        else
```

```
        {
                // Generate a key resource from the remote_certificate
                text string
                $publickey = openssl_get_publickey($host->public_key);
                if ( gettype($publickey) != 'resource' )
                {
                        // Remote certificate is faulty.
                        $output = get_string('certfault',
                        'local_certificateapi');
                }
                else
                {
                        // Initialize vars
                        $encryptedstring = '';
                        $symmetric_keys = array();
                        //          passed by ref ->       &$encryptedstring
                        &$symmetric_keys
                        $bool = openssl_seal($message, $encryptedstring,
                        $symmetric_keys, array($publickey));
                        $message = $encryptedstring;
                        $symmetrickey = array_pop($symmetric_keys);
                        $output = array();
                        $output['data'] = base64_encode($message);
                        $output['envelope'] = base64_encode($symmetrickey);
                }
        }
        // update the last connect time, regardless of permissions or
        time window.
        $host->touch();
        }
        else
        {
                $output = get_string('invalidhost',
                'local_certificateapi');
        }

    return $output;
    }
```

Again, both of these functions are based on code used by MNet. Note that they use standard API functions to manage both keys and encryption. In fact, we are reusing code where we can.

Decrypting data in PHP

The sample code at `https://github.com/iandavidwild/moodle-local_certificateapi`
includes an example PHP client (check out the `/client` folder). This will require a means to
connect to our new external API (using curl) and also a method to decrypt the data. Again,
we can use the PHP OpenSSL extension for decryption:

```php
function decrypt($response)
{
    $output = false;
    if(count($response) == 2)
    {
        // response should have 'data' and an 'envelope'
        if(isset($response['data']) &&
        isset($response['envelope'])) {
        $data = base64_decode($response['data']);
        $envelope = base64_decode($response['envelope']);
        // load private key from file
        static $certificateapi_key= null;
        if ($certificateapi_key === null)
        {
            $certificateapi_key=
            file_get_contents(dirname(__FILE__).'/key.txt',
            false);
        }
        // Initialize payload var
        $decryptedenvelope = '';
        $isOpen = openssl_open($data, $decryptedenvelope,
        $envelope, $certificateapi_key);
        if ($isOpen)
        {
            $output = $decryptedenvelope;
        }
        }
    }
    return $output;
}
```

See how the private key is loaded from a separate text file. Remember that it is critical to
keep the private key safe.

Decrypting data in C#

It is always relatively straightforward to encrypt and decrypt data in the same programming language. It can get a little more tricky when encrypting in one language and decrypting in another. To understand the complexities, check out the sample C# Web Services client in GitHub at
`https://github.com/iandavidwild/moodle-local_certificateapi/tree/develop/client s/csharp`. This simple example employs two third-party libraries: one to connect to the Certificate API and obtain the data (`CookComputing.XmlRpc`, `http://xml-rpc.net/`) and one to decrypt the data (*Bouncy Castle*, `https://www.bouncycastle.org/`). Programming encryption and decryption methods are often quite difficult because of the lack of documentation (which, in some ways, is understandable). More details on the development of this client are given in Appendix B.

Summary

In this final chapter, we learned how data can be extracted from the Moodle database and reported directly to the screen via a downloadable file (CSV or Excel) or via a secure external API. We saw that we need to exercise care when selecting data from the database in order to prevent an inefficient query from impairing database performance. We saw that facilities are provided by MySQL to help us; for example, using EXPLAIN to show a query execution plan. We also learned how to export data from Moodle via an external API, and we saw how that data can be protected while it is in transit using end-to-end encryption.

In this book, we explored how the Moodle 3 platform can provide a framework that allows developers to create a fully customized and tailored e-learning solution.

We investigated the different types of plugins available for Moodle, placing particular emphasis on explaining which plugin is the best solution for which particular problem.

In the second part, we continued with an investigation of how new courses can be created and managed by custom plugins. We also saw how custom resource and activity modules can be developed to provide custom e-learning interactions. Along with this, we learned how users can be assigned to courses and granted the necessary permissions, all through the development of new authentication and enrollment plugins. Not only did we investigate user management, we also touched on learning management, specifically how competency frameworks can be managed with custom plugins.

In the third part, we developed a custom user home page using the Dashboard feature along with the skills learned in part two (specifically, the creation of custom blocks). Then, we saw how custom reports can be created and made available to different types of users (such as management reports and compliance reports).

We finished with a discussion on the Web Services API. Web services will allow us to provide custom external APIs that we can use to (potentially) fully automate Moodle 3 in real time.

As a final thought, do remember that the "M" in Moodle stands for *modular*; if a feature that you need is missing from Moodle, there is every opportunity to develop it.

Happy Moodling!

Appendix

Testing

Testing is vital to the development of any new feature (in any software application), so it is important to outline the two main testing tools used by Moodle developers. They are as follows:

- PHPUnit
- Behat

PHPUnit can be considered *technical* testing, that is, does the feature do what it should? Behat is *behavioral* testing , that is, can a user achieve what they need given a particular intention? They sound similar, but the approaches are very different (hence the support of both types of testing).

In this appendix, we provide a basic outline of the features of each--enough to get you up and running. Luckily, there is plenty of support and advice available for both tools online. Check out the developer documentation at `https://docs.moodle.org/dev/Testing` for more details.

PHPUnit

A good description of PHPUnit--together with detailed examples of how write unit tests--is provided in the Moodle developer documentation at `https://docs.moodle.org/dev/PHPUnit`. Check out the sample plugin test case at `https://docs.moodle.org/dev/Writing_PHPUnit_tests#Sample_plugin_testcase`.

Behat

In this book, we have been following an Agile approach to development, where a *minimum viable product* is developed based on *user stories*. For example, in Chapter 9, *Moodle Analytics*, we developed a reporting block which, as a minimum, provided access to a bubble chart of user activity, the basic user story upon which this functionality was developed was as follows:

> As a teacher, I can access a report showing the number of learner interactions with each activity.

This is the minimum that a teacher needed to assess the relative popularity of each activity included in the course for which they were responsible. That the final report was shown as a bubble chart came out of ongoing conversations with both teachers and managers.

In fact, what we are describing here is an example of **behavior-driven development** (BDD). What's great about Moodle Behat integration is that test cases are described as human-readable stories (much like the user story above), which can then be automatically tested.

Check out the *Courses available* block we developed for the learner dashboard in Chapter 7, *Creating a Dashboard - Developing a Learner Homepage*. How would we go about testing this? Firstly, we need to write a test script.

Describing a scenario

Scenarios are described in a human-readable language called *Gherkin*. Gherkin, like Python or CoffeeScript, uses indentation to define structure. Line endings terminate statements (called *steps* in Gherkin), and either spaces or tabs may be used for indentation. Finally, most lines in Gherkin start with a special keyword; consider the following example:

- *Given* a particular set of conditions, multiple conditions are specified with "And"
- *When* a user carries out some action
- *Then* a result should be obtained, which needs to be specific and measurable

Here is a script we can use to (potentially) test the courses available block:

```
@block @block_courses_available
Feature: Courses available block on a dashboard
In order to know which courses I am enrolled on
And to know my progress on each course
```

```
I see a block listing my courses (with links) and my progress
Scenario: Adding HTML block in a course
Given the following "users" exist:
      | username | firstname | lastname | email |
      | student1 | Sam1      | Student1 | student1@example.com |
And the following "courses" exist:
      | fullname | shortname |
      | Course 1 | C1 |
And the following "course enrolments" exist:
      | user     | course | role |
      | student1 | C1     | student |
When I log in as "student1"
Then I should see "courses available " in the "block"
And I should see "course progress" in the "block"
```

The script is introduced by a description of the feature, which reads much like a user story would, followed by a sequence of logical steps. For more information on the Gherkin language, refer to `http://docs.behat.org/en/v2.5/guides/1.gherkin.html`.

This new scenario needs to be added to the `courses_available` block plugin:

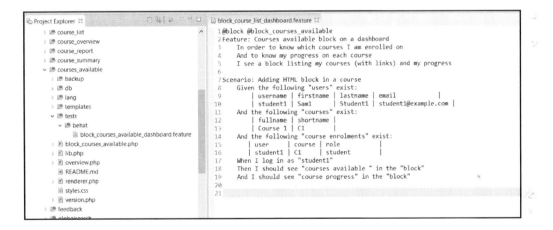

Step definitions

Each step requires a corresponding callback function called a *step definition*. A step definition is written in PHP and consists of a keyword, a regular expression, and a callback. You may need to add your own step definitions (Behat will throw an error if a step definition is missing). There are examples of custom step definitions in Moodle core, for example, in the **learning plan (lp)** admin tool. Use Eclipse to search the code for `behat_base`, the class on which all custom step definitions are based.

This section is intended only to give an overview of Moodle testing with Behat. For more details, log in to your development Moodle, and from the **Site administration** menu, click on **Development** and select **Acceptance testing**:

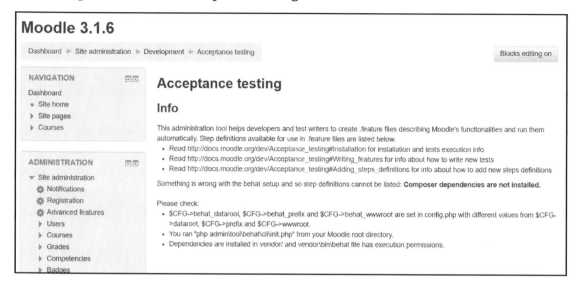

It is likely that Behat won't be installed on your development system (as shown in the preceding screenshot). However, follow the links provided, and you will find lots of good guidance and advice to help you get set up.

Moodle guidelines

When we write code, it is absolutely vital that we can understand what we have written and have a very good idea of why we have written it. That sounds like a statement of the obvious, but I'm sure that, like me, you have encountered one too many developers who take a look at their own code and can't understand why they have written a section of code in a particular way. If a developer can't understand their own code, then what hope is there for the rest of us?

Every project should have its own coding style, supported by fully documented coding guidelines, and Moodle is no exception. Full details of the Moodle guidelines are given in the developer documentation at `https://docs.moodle.org/dev/Coding_style`. In this section, we provide an overview of these guidelines to get you started. We also investigate a code checking tool that will help ensure that your code follows the required standard. Let's begin by getting an overview of Moodle's coding conventions.

General guidelines

Every PHP script you create should immediately open with a full GPL copyright statement. This is followed by a separate docblock statement that needs to contain the following:

- A short one-line description of the file
- A longer description of the file
- `@package` tag (required)
- `@copyright` (required)
- `@license` (required)

```php
<?php
// This file is part of Moodle - http://moodle.org/
//
// Moodle is free software: you can redistribute it and/or modify
// it under the terms of the GNU General Public License as published by
// the Free Software Foundation, either version 3 of the License, or
// (at your option) any later version.
//
// Moodle is distributed in the hope that it will be useful,
// but WITHOUT ANY WARRANTY; without even the implied warranty of
// MERCHANTABILITY or FITNESS FOR A PARTICULAR PURPOSE.  See the
// GNU General Public License for more details.
//
// You should have received a copy of the GNU General Public License
// along with Moodle.  If not, see <http://www.gnu.org/licenses/>.
/**
 * This is a one-line short description of the file.
 *
 * You can have a rather longer description of the file as well,
 * if you like, and it can span multiple lines.
 *
 * @package    mod_mymodule
 * @copyright  2017 Ian Wild
 * @license    http://www.gnu.org/copyleft/gpl.html GNU GPL v3 or later
 */
```

Describing functions and methods

All functions should be commented with a docblock, even if it is immediately obvious what the function does (what might be obvious to you might not necessarily be obvious to the next person).

All functions and methods should have a complete docblock like this:

```
/**
 * Give a description of the function - clearly stating what the purpose
 * of the function is, even if you think it is obvious. To refer to another
 * function use @see. To link to documentation on the web
 * use a @link below. Also, remember to add descriptions
 * for parameters and the return value. Make variable names obvious, too.
 *
 * @see clean_param()
 * @param int    $courseid The PHP type is followed by the variable name
 * @param array $users The PHP type is followed by the variable name
 * @return bool A status indicating success or failure
 */
```

Note, that if you override a method but don't alter the purpose of the method you are overriding--including keeping the same arguments and return types--then omit the comment completely.

Don't worry if this seems like a lot of work; you might even find that your docblock is bigger than your function. Why this is so important is that Eclipse (in fact, most IDEs, both free and paid for) will use your docblocks to provide context help when you are developing your code:

Whitespaces and indentation

Unlike some programming languages (for example, Python), PHP does not use indentation to mark blocks of code. To indent your PHP code, use four leading spaces, not a TAB character. For example, in the following screenshot (taken from Eclipse), you can see that there is no overall indentation and that a line is indented by four spaces:

```
68     * @return int The id of the newly inserted newmodule record
69     */
70  function wavefront_add_instance($wavefront) {
71      global $DB;
72
73      $wavefront->timemodified = time();
74
75      wavefront_set_sizing($wavefront);
76
77      return $DB->insert_record('wavefront', $wavefront);
78  }
79
80  /**
```

Also, ensure that trailing whitespaces are stripped from the end of lines.

Configuring Eclipse indentation

In order to ensure that you indent lines with spaces rather than TAB characters, select **Window** from the Eclipse main menu, then slide down to **Preferences**. In the Preferences dialog, open the **General** tree, click on **Editors**, then **Text Editors**. Make sure that **Insert spaces for tabs** is checked.

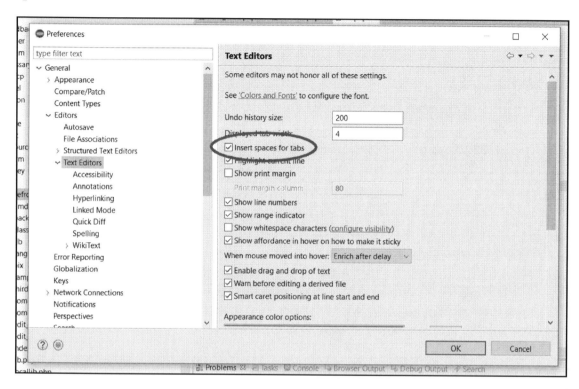

SQL query coding style

Note that there is a separate coding style guideline for SQL queries, described in the Moodle developer documentation at `https://docs.moodle.org/dev/SQL_coding_style`.

Here is an example query, included in a PHP script:

```
105                    $params = array('courseid' => $course->id, 'contextmodule' => CONTEXT_MODULE, 'coursesta
106                    $views = $DB->get_records_sql($sql, $params);
107
108        } else if ($uselegacyreader) {
109            // If using legacy log then get activity usage from old table.
110            $logactionlike = $DB->sql_like('l.action', ':action');
111            $timesince = ($activitysince == 'sincestart') ? 'AND l.time >= :coursestart' : '';
112            $sql = "SELECT cm.id, COUNT('x') AS numviews, COUNT(DISTINCT userid) AS distinctusers
113                      FROM {course_modules} cm
114                      JOIN {modules} m ON m.id = cm.module
115                      JOIN {log} l ON l.cmid = cm.id
116                     WHERE cm.course = :courseid
117                           AND $timesince
118                           AND $logactionlike
119                           AND m.visible = 1
120                  GROUP BY cm.id";
121
122            $params = array('courseid' => $course->id, 'action' => 'view%', 'coursestart' => $course->startdate);
123
124            if (!empty($minloginternalreader)) {
125                $params['timeto'] = $minloginternalreader;
126            }
```

When it comes to SQL queries, remember the following things:

- Use parameter placeholders; if at all possible, avoid creating queries by embedding strings
- All SQL keywords are in uppercase
- SQL queries and fragments should be enclosed in double quotes, not single quotes
- Complex SQL queries should be on multiple lines and indented according to the Moodle convention
- Multiline SQL queries should be right aligned on SELECT, FROM, JOIN, WHERE, and GROUPY BY (refer to the preceding screenshot)
- Always use the AS keyword for column aliases, even though the SQL language doesn't strictly enforce this

The code checking tool

To ensure that you are following Moodle's coding conventions, download and install the code-checker plugin from the Moodle plugins directory at
`https://moodle.org/plugins/view.php?plugin=local_codechecker`. Once installed, the code checker tool is available under **Development** in the **Site administration** menu:

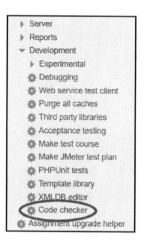

Click on **Code checker** to open the checker configuration page. Specify the path to the plugin you want to check:

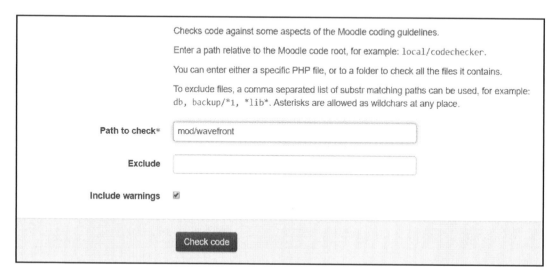

Press the **Check code** button to begin the checking process. Once complete, a report is displayed listing all the files checked, together with a count of errors and warnings:

Clicking on a link will display further details. For example, here is the detailed report for an error in mod\wavefront\comment.php:

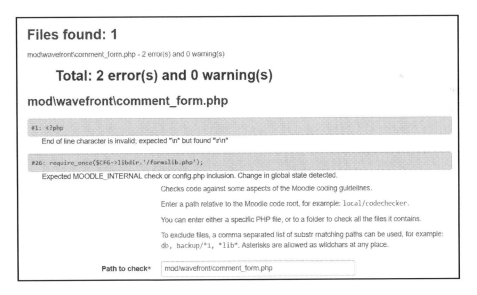

C# client

In this section, you will learn how to develop a desktop Moodle Web Services client in C# using the Microsoft Visual Studio **Integrated Development Environment (IDE)**. Microsoft provides a free version of Visual Studio called *Visual Studio Community*. In Chapter 9, *Moodle Analytics*, you learned how to develop an external Web Services API, which provided details of learners who had been awarded a certificate within a given time window. For reasons of security, *in transit* data is encrypted. We saw that decrypting data in PHP that has been encrypted in PHP is straightforward. However, decrypting data in another programming language, such as C#, is more complicated.

Let's start by installing the tools we need.

Installing Visual Studio

To begin, you will need to download and install a copy of Visual Studio Community from https://www.visualstudio.com/vs/community/. Simply follow the instructions there. Note that you will need to create a new user account with Microsoft in order to use Visual Studio; you will need to sign in to Visual Studio in order to use it (you will need to create a free Visual Studio Online account). Note that a Visual Studio Community free license is issued only if you meet certain criteria:

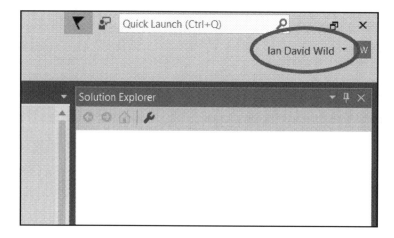

Creating a new project

Once installed, open Visual Studio, and from the **File** menu, slide the mouse pointer to **New** and then click on **Project...**. The New Project dialog is displayed as follows:

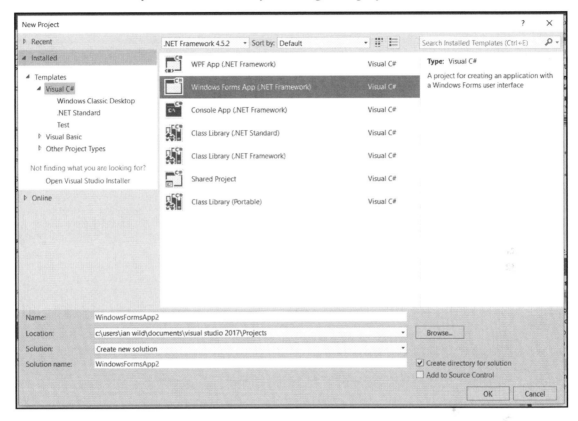

In the **New Project** dialog, specify a suitable application name and solution name (I'm going to call mine `interop_client`), then press the **OK** button.

Creating a test harness

The first step is to create a new form with which we can test the Moodle API. From the **Solution Explorer,** click on Form1.cs and rename it harness.cs. This will also rename the associated solution files:

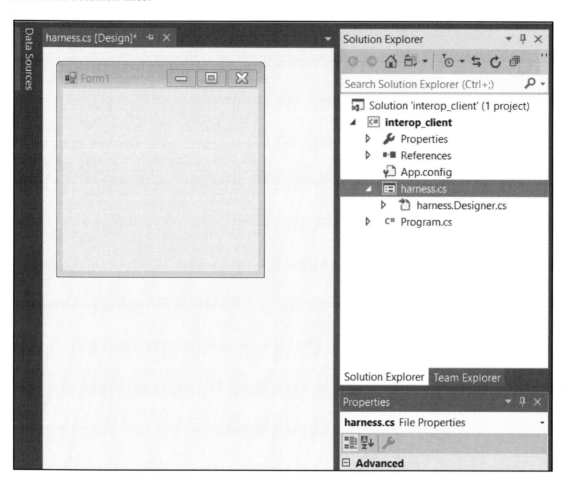

Next, we can add the relevant controls to the form. We will require three text boxes--two to specify the start and end dates for the time window within which we require completion certificates and one to allow us to specify the learner's email address (which we use to identify them):

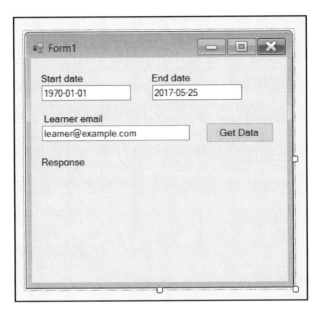

We have also included Response text, which we will update with the response we get back from our Web Services API and a **Get Data** button. Now, we are ready to connect our test client to the Moodle API.

Connecting to an XML-RPC API

As with PHP, the C# language provides a huge number of libraries--both proprietary and third-party--that provide everything from basic string handling to image manipulation. To connect to the XML-RPC API in Moodle, we will use the XML-RPC library developed by *Charles Cook*--check out `http://cookcomputing.com/blog/index.html` for details. The component we need is `CookComputing.XmlRpcV2.dll`. To install this component, download the relevant DLL, and in the **Solution Explorer**, right-click on **References** and select the **Add Reference...** option:

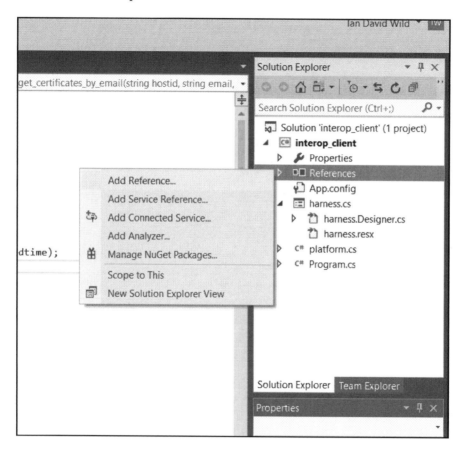

Browse to locate the DLL and follow the instructions to import it. A new reference to `CookComputing.XmlRpcV2` will be added to the project:

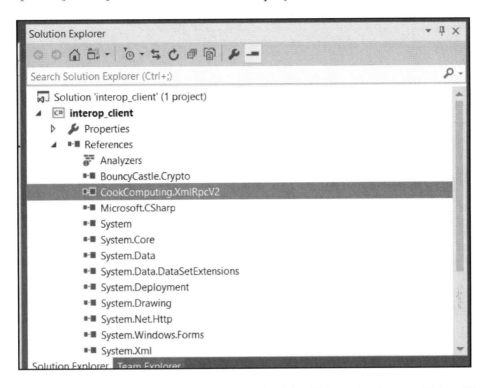

Go back to the application's Windows form and double-click on the button. This will add a new method to `harness.cs` to support the button click event. This is where we will need to add our event handler code, including taking the time window and learner email information from the form and then calling the relevant Moodle API function. Firstly, we need to declare the `XmlRpcV2` interface function:

```
[XmlRpcUrl("http://moodle316.localhost/webservice/xmlrpc/server.php?wstoken
=bb34847d964227b44c4700cbca40d5e0")]
public interface IGetLearnerCompletionsByEmail : IXmlRpcProxy
{
    [XmlRpcMethod("local_certificateapi_get_certificates_by_email")]

    System.Object local_certificateapi_get_certificates_by_email(string
hostid, string email, string starttime, string endtime);
}
```

Note that the `XmlRpcUrl` includes the Web Services token used to call on any API functions; update this URL as appropriate.

We need to call on this function when the **Get Data** button is pressed:

```
IGetLearnerCompletionsByEmail proxy =
XmlRpcProxyGen.Create<IGetLearnerCompletionsByEmail>();

System.Object myResults =
proxy.local_certificateapi_get_certificates_by_email("testing",
emailTxt.Text, startTxt.Text, endTxt.Text);
```

The function returns both the encrypted data and an *envelope,* which is used to decrypt the data:

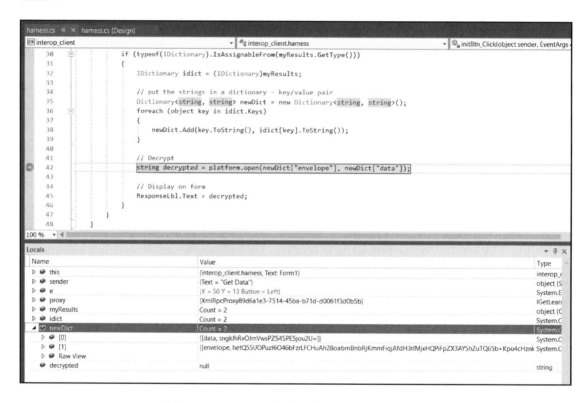

This, we can parse out of the response ready for decrypting, which we will cover in the next section.

Decrypting data

We will use the *Bouncy Castle* extension to decrypt the data passed over from Moodle by the API--refer to `https://www.bouncycastle.org/` for details. This extension needs to be added to the project in the same manner as the XML-RPC library.

Let's create a new class to handle the data. From the **Solution Explorer**, right-click on the project name, slide down to **Add** and then select the **Class...** option:

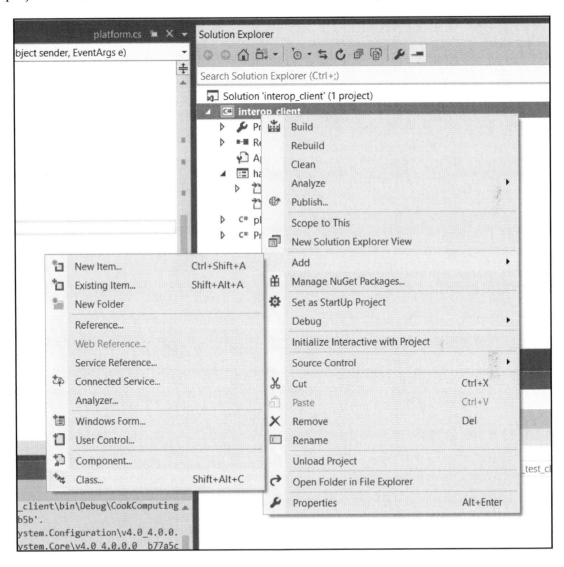

We used two methods to decode the data. The first, to extract the private key details (recall that Moodle will use our public key to encrypt the data and only we can decrypt it because we should be the only ones in possession of the private key), GetPrivateKey() has been called. It is passed a string that references a path to the private key file:

```
public static RsaPrivateCrtKeyParameters GetPrivateKey(String pemFile)
{
    if (string.IsNullOrEmpty(pemFile))
    throw new ArgumentNullException("pemFile");
    string privateKey = File.Exists(pemFile)  ?
    File.ReadAllText(pemFile)  :  pemFile;
    var reader = new PemReader(new StringReader(privateKey));
    RsaPrivateCrtKeyParameters privkey =
    (RsaPrivateCrtKeyParameters)reader.ReadObject();
    return privkey;
}
```

The second *opens* the data envelope and decrypts it:

```
public static string open(string envelope, string data)
{
    var privateKeyParameters = GetPrivateKey(@"C:\path_to\key.pem");
    var rsaCipher = CipherUtilities.GetCipher("RSA//PKCS1PADDING");
    rsaCipher.Init(false, privateKeyParameters);
    var keyBytes =
    rsaCipher.DoFinal(Convert.FromBase64String(envelope));
    /* decrypt key using RSA */
    var rc4CipherDecrypt = CipherUtilities.GetCipher("RC4");
    var decryptParameter = new KeyParameter(keyBytes);
    rc4CipherDecrypt.Init(false, decryptParameter);
    var rc4DataBytesDecrypt =
    rc4CipherDecrypt.DoFinal(Convert.FromBase64String(data)); /*
    decrypt data using RC4 */
    var dataString = Encoding.ASCII.GetString(rc4DataBytesDecrypt);
    return dataString;
}
```

Decrypting the data is a two-step process:

1. Extract the cipher from the private key.
2. Decrypt the data.

Both of these steps use the Bouncy Castle library. The technique we employ here is taken from Alex Mirzaynov's blog post at http://geekswithblogs.net/Strenium/archive /2013/01/27/converting-phprsquos-ldquoopenssl_sealrdquo-and-ldquoopenssl_open rdquo-into-.net.aspx.

Decompressing data

Recall that the data is GZIP compressed before being sent over the network, as bandwidth was identified as an issue. Alter the end of the open() function to this:

```
...
var decompressed = _gzipDecompress(rc4DataBytesDecrypt);
return decompressed;
}
```

Final testing

When all is working, you will be able to step through the code to see how it functions. The returned data--decrypted and decompressed--will be displayed on the form, as follows:

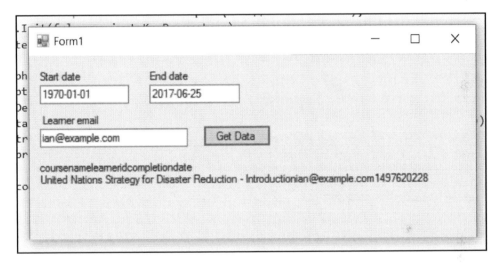

Source control with GitHub

In this section, you learn how to manage source code--specifically using GitHub and Git Bash. This appendix is intended purely as an overview to using GitHub and Git Bash. For more details, refer to *GitHub Fundamentals [Video]*, also from Packt Publishing (`https://www.packtpub.com/application-development/github-fundamentals-video`).

Version control is vital to any project, and this applies to any collection of information and not just computer source code. For example, certainly for our resilience project, the second page of each written document has a version history:

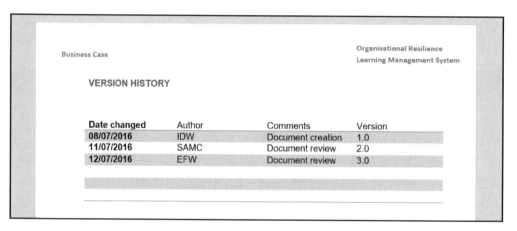

Each change in the document is commented on--together with who changed the document. It's the same with the code for our plugins, except the tool we use to manage the version control is the online tool, GitHub at `https://github.com/`. GitHub is more than a version control system--among other tools, GitHub also provides an issue/bug tracker and a project Wiki. As an example, let's take a look at the Moodle WordPress authentication plugin repository we developed in `Chapter 6`, *Managing Users - Letting in the Crowds*.

The GitHub repository for this plugin is at `https://github.com/iandavidwild/moodle-au th_wordpress`. You will see that there is an issue tracker:

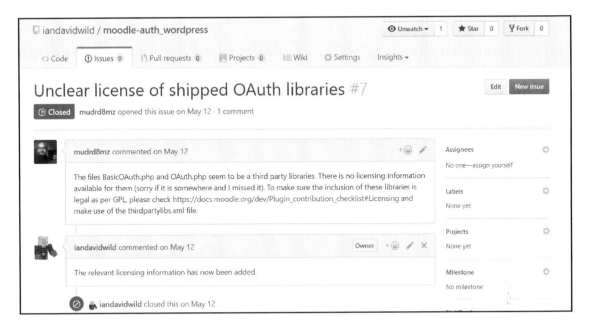

There is also a **Wiki**, which provides an overview for the WordPress plugin:

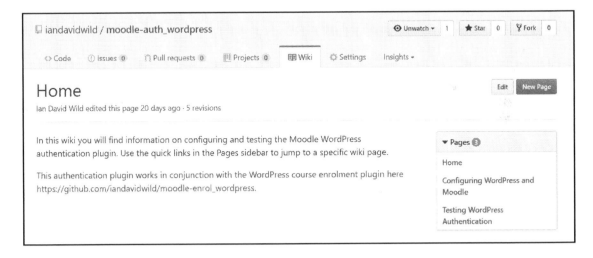

The Moodle source code--and distributed development--is managed in GitHub, so it makes sense to use Git and GitHub to manage the source code for our plugins too. In this appendix, you learn how.

Installing Git

To begin, you will need to download and install Git on your development machine. Visit `https://git-scm.com/downloads` for more information. The installation instructions are easy to follow.

Configuring SSH

Rather than having to authenticate with GitHub every time you connect to it, you can configure your development machine to connect with SSH using automatic authentication. Follow the instructions at `https://help.github.com/articles/connecting-to-github-with-ssh/` for details. Again, the configuration instructions are easy to follow.

Once installed, two new menu options will be added to your mouse (right-click) context
menu:

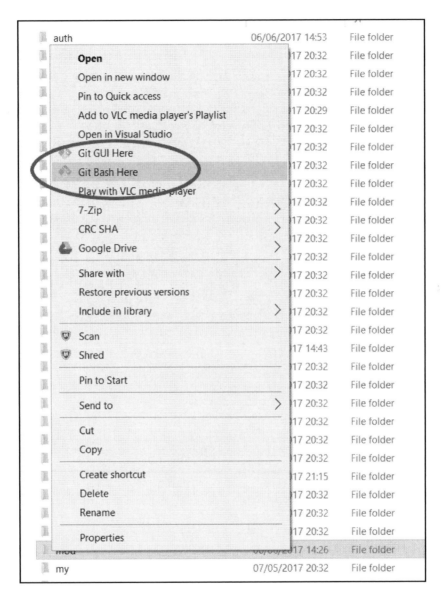

In the preceding screenshot, the **mod** folder is selected. Now, choose the **Git Bash Here** option from the menu. The Git Bash window will be displayed, as follows:

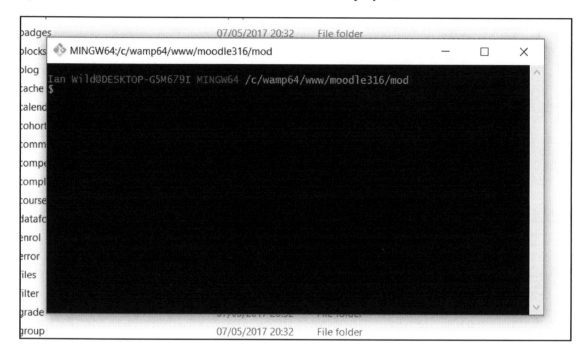

Now, you can clone a repository from GitHub to your development machine. Visit `https://github.com/iandavidwild/moodle-mod_wavefront` and then look for the **Clone or download** button:

Click on the **Clone or download** button and copy the SSH link:

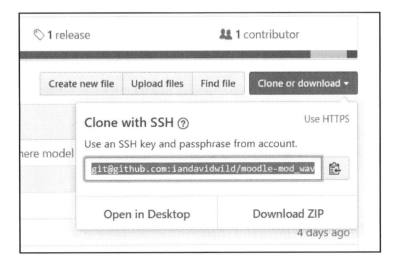

Type `git clone` into the Git Bash window, followed by a space, right-click and paste the SSH link you just copied from GitHub, then specify the directory into which you want to make the repository clone:

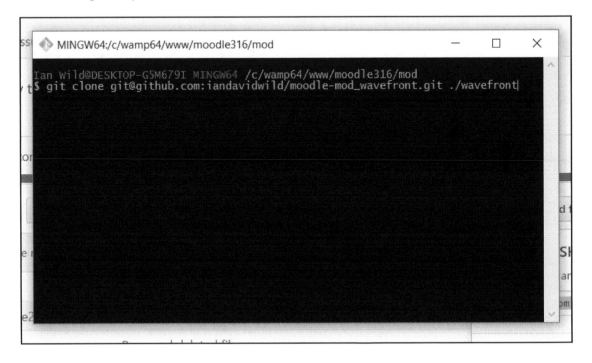

Press *Enter* to clone the repository from GitHub to your development machine:

Note, that we now have a separate clone of the GitHub repository on our local development machine.

Committing changes

Once a change to the code is made, we will need to commit them both into our local repository and to GitHub. Ensure that Git Bash is set to the correct working directory. Once the directory is correct, type `git status` to check what changes have been made locally in Git Bash:

Determine the changes that have been implemented in each file using the `git diff` command:

```
MINGW64:/c/wamp64/www/moodle316/mod/wavefront                    —    □    ×

Ian Wild@DESKTOP-G5M679I MINGW64 /c/wamp64/www/moodle316/mod/wavefront (develop)
$ git diff edit_model_form.php
diff --git a/edit_model_form.php b/edit_model_form.php
index c447d19..e722559 100644
--- a/edit_model_form.php
+++ b/edit_model_form.php
@@ -1,4 +1,25 @@
 <?php
+// This file is part of Moodle - http://moodle.org/
+//
+// Moodle is free software: you can redistribute it and/or modify
+// it under the terms of the GNU General Public License as published by
+// the Free Software Foundation, either version 3 of the License, or
+// (at your option) any later version.
+//
+// Moodle is distributed in the hope that it will be useful,
+// but WITHOUT ANY WARRANTY; without even the implied warranty of
+// MERCHANTABILITY or FITNESS FOR A PARTICULAR PURPOSE.  See the
+// GNU General Public License for more details.
+//
+// You should have received a copy of the GNU General Public License
+// along with Moodle.  If not, see <http://www.gnu.org/licenses/>.
+
+/**
+ * @package    mod_wavefront
+ * @copyright 2017 Ian Wild
+ * @license    http://www.gnu.org/copyleft/gpl.html GNU GPL v3 or later
+ */
+
 if (!defined('MOODLE_INTERNAL')) {
     die('Direct access to this script is forbidden.');    ///  It must be inclu
ded from a Moodle page
 }

Ian Wild@DESKTOP-G5M679I MINGW64 /c/wamp64/www/moodle316/mod/wavefront (develop)
$
```

Lines that have been added are shown in green and prefixed with a "+". Those lines which have been removed are shown in red and prefixed with a "-".

To commit a change, use the `git commit` command:

```
orm +//
orm +// You should have received a copy of the GNU General Public License
orm +// along with Moodle.  If not, see <http://www.gnu.org/licenses/>.
    +
    +/**
---+ * @package    mod_wavefront
is-+ * @copyright 2017 Ian Wild
   + * @license    http://www.gnu.org/copyleft/gpl.html GNU GPL v3 or later
   + */
---+
is- if (!defined('MOODLE_INTERNAL')) {
        die('Direct access to this script is forbidden.');    ///  It must be inclu
   ded from a Moodle page
   }

n v Ian Wild@DESKTOP-G5M679I MINGW64 /c/wamp64/www/moodle316/mod/wavefront (develop)
bal $ git commit edit_model_form.php -m"Added missing copyright Moodle copyright not
ror ice."
    [develop f25be65] Added missing copyright Moodle copyright notice.
     1 file changed, 21 insertions(+)
urn
    Ian Wild@DESKTOP-G5M679I MINGW64 /c/wamp64/www/moodle316/mod/wavefront (develop)
    $
```

Remember to include a comment using the `-m` switch.

Once all of your changes have been committed to your local repository, you need to push them up to GitHub using the `git push` command:

```
orm
orm Ian Wild@DESKTOP-G5M679I MINGW64 /c/wamp64/www/moodle316/mod/wavefront (develop)
    $ git status
    On branch develop
---Your branch is ahead of 'origin/develop' by 7 commits.
      (use "git push" to publish your local commits)
is-nothing to commit, working tree clean

---Ian Wild@DESKTOP-G5M679I MINGW64 /c/wamp64/www/moodle316/mod/wavefront (develop)
is-$ git push
    Enter passphrase for key '/c/Users/Ian Wild/.ssh/id_rsa':
    Counting objects: 27, done.
    Delta compression using up to 4 threads.
n v Compressing objects: 100% (24/24), done.
    Writing objects: 100% (27/27), 4.71 KiB | 0 bytes/s, done.
bal Total 27 (delta 16), reused 0 (delta 0)
ror remote: Resolving deltas: 100% (16/16), completed with 8 local objects.
    To github.com:iandavidwild/moodle-mod_wavefront.git
       4364245..de76f8a  develop -> develop
urn
    Ian Wild@DESKTOP-G5M679I MINGW64 /c/wamp64/www/moodle316/mod/wavefront (develop)
    $
```

Your latest changes will be visible in GitHub, as follows:

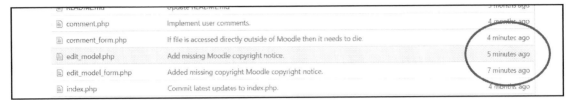

Atomised commits

Rather than committing a number of different changes to a repository in one commit, it is far better to apply one commit per change. This technique ensures that it is easy to roll back if a bug is introduced during changes.

Index